THE BOUNDS OF SENSE

by the same author

INTRODUCTION TO LOGICAL THEORY

INDIVIDUALS

THE BOUNDS OF SENSE

An Essay on Kant's *Critique of Pure Reason*

P. F. STRAWSON

METHUEN & CO LTD
11 New Fetter Lane, London EC4

First published in 1966 by
Methuen & Co. Ltd, London
© 1966 by P. F. Strawson
Printed and bound in Great Britain by
Richard Clay (The Chaucer Press), Ltd,
Bungay, Suffolk

CONTENTS

Part Three: Transcendent Metaphysics

IV. GOD

Part Four: The Metaphysics of Transcendental Idealism

Part Five: Kant's Theory of Geometry

PREFACE

This book originated in lectures on Kant's *Critique of Pure Reason* given in alternate years from 1959 onwards in the University of Oxford. As any Kantian scholar who may read it will quickly detect, it is by no means a work of historical-philosophical scholarship. I have not been assiduous in studying the writings of Kant's lesser predecessors, his own minor works or the very numerous commentaries which two succeeding centuries have produced. I have written for those students of the *Critique* who, like myself, have read and re-read the work with a commingled sense of great insights and great mystification. I have tried to present a clear, uncluttered and unified interpretation, at least strongly supported by the text as it stands, of the system of thought which the *Critique* contains; I have tried to show how certain great parts of the structure can be held apart from each other, while showing also how, within the system itself, they are conceived of as related; I have tried to give decisive reasons for rejecting some parts altogether; and I have tried to indicate, though no more than indicate, how the arguments and conclusions of other parts might be so modified or reconstructed as to be made more acceptable. In pursuit of these aims I have relegated some features of the work to a very subordinate place, notably much architectonic detail and much of the theory of "transcendental psychology". It is not that I think that nothing can be made of the latter. The attempt to reconstruct it would be, at least, a profitable exercise in the philosophy of mind. But I have thought that some loss of balance and of clarity of line would certainly result if I made such an attempt in the present book.

I have given the book its title not only in partial echo of a title Kant himself considered but also because it alludes compendiously to the three main strands in his thought. In two ways he draws the bounds of sense, and in a third he traverses them. He argues, on the one hand, that a certain minimum structure is essential to any conception of experience which we can make truly intelligible to ourselves; on the other, that the attempt to extend beyond the limits of experience the use of structural concepts, or of any other concepts, leads only to claims empty of meaning. Dogmatic rationalism exceeds the upper bound of sense, as classical empiricism falls short of the lower. But Kant's arguments for these limiting conclusions are developed within the framework of a set of doctrines which themselves appear to violate his own critical principles. He seeks to draw the bounds of sense from a point outside them, a point which, if they are rightly drawn, cannot exist.

In the General Review, with which this book opens, I have distinguished these three main strands of thought under the headings "The Metaphysics of Experience", "Transcendent Metaphysics" and "The Metaphysics of Transcendental Idealism", each of which forms the title of one of the three major succeeding Parts. But these parts are not, and cannot be, wholly independent of each other. Only when the picture is complete can the significance of any part of it be fully grasped.

I wish to acknowledge my great indebtedness to Professor H. L. A. Hart, who read the entire book in manuscript and for whose help and encouragement I am very grateful; to the governing body of my College, which gave me leave of absence from my duties from January to June of 1965, during which time, and the ensuing long vacation, the greater part of the book, in its present form, was written; and to Miss Ruby Meager, who read the proofs and made many valuable suggestions for improvements, most of which I have adopted.

All quotations from the *Critique* are taken, with very few modifications, from Kemp Smith's translation. References are given with the usual "A" and "B" numbering, both numbers being given for passages common to the first and second editions.

P. F. S.

Oxford
June, 1966

PART ONE

General Review

GENERAL REVIEW

It is possible to imagine kinds of world very different from the world as we know it. It is possible to describe types of experience very different from the experience we actually have. But not any purported and grammatically permissible description of a possible kind of experience would be a truly intelligible description. There are limits to what we can conceive of, or make intelligible to ourselves, as a possible general structure of experience. The investigation of these limits, the investigation of the set of ideas which forms the limiting framework of all our thought about the world and experience of the world, is, evidently, an important and interesting philosophical undertaking. No philosopher has made a more strenuous attempt on it than Kant.

A central difficulty in understanding his attempt lies in the fact that he himself thought of it in terms of a certain misleading analogy. It is a commonplace of casual, and of scientific, observation, that the character of our experience, the way things appear to us, is partly determined by our human constitution, by the nature of our sense organs and nervous system. The workings of the human perceptual mechanism, the ways in which our experience is causally dependent on those workings, are matters for empirical, or scientific, not philosophical, investigation. Kant was well aware of this; he knew very well that such an empirical inquiry was of a quite different kind from the investigation he proposed into the fundamental structure of ideas in terms of which alone we can make intelligible to ourselves the idea of experience of the world. Yet, in spite of this awareness, he conceived the latter investigation on a kind of strained analogy with the former. Wherever he found limiting or necessary general features of experience, he declared their source to lie in our own cognitive constitution; and this doctrine he considered indispensable as an explanation of the possibility of knowledge of the necessary structure of experience. Yet there is no doubt that this doctrine is incoherent in itself and masks, rather than explains, the real character of his inquiry; so that a central problem in understanding the *Critique* is precisely that of disentangling all that hangs on this doctrine from the analytical argument which is in fact independent of it.

The separation of these two strands in the *Critique*, however, is only part of a wider task of division between what remains fruitful and interesting and what no longer appears acceptable, or even promising, in its doctrines. Accordingly, I shall begin this introductory survey by setting out, in rough opposition, the elements of this division. I shall follow this with a slightly fuller but still introductory account of some of the central themes of the work.

Like many of his predecessors and successors, Kant laid stress on the fact that the results hitherto achieved in philosophy contrasted unfavourably with those achieved in mathematics and natural science. If philosophy too was to be set "on the sure path of a science", one requisite was that it should limit its pretensions; and a major instrument of this necessary limitation was a principle repeatedly enunciated and applied by Kant throughout the *Critique*. This is the principle that there can be no legitimate, or even meaningful, employment of ideas or concepts which does not relate them to empirical or experiential conditions of their application. If we wish to use a concept in a certain way, but are unable to specify the kind of experience-situation to which the concept, used in that way, would apply, then we are not really envisaging any legitimate use of that concept at all.[1] In so using it, we shall not merely be saying what we do not know; we shall not really know what we are saying.

This principle, which I shall refer to as Kant's principle of significance, is one with which empiricist philosophers have no difficulty in sympathizing. They sympathize just as readily with the consequence which Kant drew from it: viz. the complete repudiation of transcendent metaphysics. Whole regions of philosophy –

---

[1] "All concepts, and with them all principles, even such as are possible *a priori*, relate to empirical intuitions, that is, to the data for a possible experience. Apart from this relation they have no objective validity" (B 195). Of the most general of concepts, the categories, Kant says that they "allow only of empirical employment and have no meaning whatsoever when not applied to objects of possible experience, that is, to the world of sense" (B 724). These sentences are typical of dozens in the *Critique*.

regions of maximum pretension and minimum agreement – owed their existence, he maintained, to disregard of the principle of significance. Freed from the obligation to specify the empirical conditions of application of the concepts they used, philosophers might seem to be giving information about the nature of Reality as it is in itself, instead of as it appears in the limited and sense-bound experience of creatures such as ourselves; but their seeming knowledge was delusion, and the first task of a critical and scientific philosophy was to ensure that it was recognized as such. The first task of philosophy is to set its own limits.

Kant was not content merely to draw this general negative conclusion about the impossibility of transcendent metaphysics. He thought that the propensity to think in terms of ideas for which no empirical conditions of application could be specified was not merely a philosophers' aberration, but a natural and in-evitable propensity of human reason. It was even, in some ways, a beneficial propensity. Certain ideas which had in themselves no empirical application or significance nevertheless inevitably arose in the course of scientific inquiry, and might even serve a useful function in stimulating the indefinite extension of empirical knowledge.[1] The illusion of *metaphysical* knowledge arose only when it was thought that there must be realities answering to these ideas and that it was possible to obtain knowledge of these realities by pure thought, unmixed with experience. It was in this kind of thinking that the principle of significance was violated. A substantial proportion of the *Critique* is devoted to showing how, in particular celebrated instances, we are tempted to violate the principle and to demonstrating the empty, and sometimes conflicting, character of the metaphysical knowledge-claims which result from our doing so.

Transcendent metaphysics, then, is declared in general, and demonstrated in detail, to be impossible as a form of knowledge, or, as Kant would say, as a science. But this does not mean that no form of scientific metaphysics is possible at all. On the contrary,

---

[1] This was not, in Kant's view, the only function of ideas which lacked empirical significance. He thought that the moral life depended on such ideas; but he sharply distinguished between moral thinking and the sort of thinking which aimed at knowledge. The principle of significance, though to be interpreted strictly as far as theoretical speculations and claims to know-ledge were concerned, had to be understood, it will be seen, with certain reservations.

B

there is a large positive task for a genuinely scientific metaphysics, a task which, according to Kant, can be discharged once for all, and which is at least partially carried out by him in the most original, interesting, and difficult part of the *Critique*. This is the task I have already referred to: the investigation of that limiting framework of ideas and principles the use and application of which are essential to empirical knowledge, and which are implicit in any coherent conception of experience which we can form. It is of course possible to feel and express scepticism, not only about the details of Kant's execution of this programme, but about the programme itself; it may be thought unlikely that such an inquiry could yield any but the slenderest results. But if these doubts are unjustified, and a fruitful inquiry of this kind is possible, then it will fully deserve the title of metaphysics. It will be, as metaphysics was always said to be, the most general and fundamental of studies; and its method will be non-empirical, or *a priori*, not because, like transcendent metaphysics, it claims to be concerned with a realm of objects inaccessible to experience, but because it is concerned with the conceptual structure which is presupposed in all empirical inquiries. This kind of investigation Kant sometimes calls "transcendental", as distinct from "transcendent", though he is by no means consistent in his use of this expression.

In his espousal of the principle of significance and in his consequential repudiation of transcendent metaphysics, Kant is close to the tradition of classical empiricism, the tradition of Berkeley and Hume, which has probably, at least in England, received its clearest modern expression in the writings of A. J. Ayer. But in the elaboration of his positive metaphysics of experience, Kant departs sharply from that tradition. The central problem of classical empiricism was set by the assumption that experience really offers us nothing but separate and fleeting sense-impressions, images and feelings; and the problem was to show how, on this exiguous basis, we could supply a rational justification of our ordinary picture of the world as containing continuously and independently existing and interacting material things and persons. Hume, it is true, rejected the problem in this form, holding that such a justification was impossible, but also unnecessary, since the gaps found, and left, by reason were filled by the helpful fictions of the imagination. Between the views of Hume, the most sophisticated of the classical empiricists, and those of Kant, there is a subtle and interesting parallelism. But there is also a great gap. For Kant rejected the basic empiricist dogma which Hume never questioned. He did not reject it in the spirit of naïve, or refined, common sense which has sometimes, in England, seemed to be the twentieth-century alternative to classical empiricism. His rejection took the form, rather, of a proof that the minimal empiricist conception of experience was incoherent in isolation, that it made sense only within a larger framework which necessarily included the use and application in experience of concepts of an objective world. Thus the execution of Kant's programme for a positive metaphysics is held to entail the rejection of what he calls "problematic" idealism, even if such idealism is only the methodological starting-point, rather than the terminus, of philosophical reflection. Any philosopher who invites, or challenges, us to justify our belief in the objective world by working outwards, as it were, from the private data of individual consciousness thereby demonstrates his failure to have grasped the conditions of the possibility of experience in general. Philosophers as unlike in other respects as Descartes and Hume are held to be alike in this respect, to be alike guilty of this failure.

These themes of the *Critique* which I have so far referred to have an evident harmony. Together they form, one might be tempted to claim, the framework of a truly empiricist philosophy, freed, on the one hand, from the delusions of transcendent metaphysics, on the other, from the classical empiricist obsession with the private contents of consciousness. Together they present the blander, the more acceptable face of the *Critique*. But it would be a very one-sided account of the work which referred to these themes alone. Their exposition and development is throughout interwoven with more questionable doctrines, one of the sources of which I have already indicated. It is true that Kant thought of himself as investigating the general structure of ideas and principles which is presupposed in all our empirical knowledge; but he thought of this investigation as possible only because he conceived of it also, and primarily, as an investigation into the structure and workings of the cognitive capacities of beings such as ourselves. The idiom of the work is throughout a psychological idiom. Whatever necessities Kant found in our conception of experience he ascribed to the nature of our faculties.

He prepares the ground for this ascription by the manner in

which he presents a certain fundamental duality, inescapable in any philosophical thinking about experience or empirical knowledge. This is the duality of general concepts, on the one hand, and particular instances of general concepts, encountered in experience, on the other. If any item is even to enter our conscious experience we must be able to classify it in some way, to recognize it as possessing some general characteristics. To say that we must have general concepts in order for empirical knowledge to be possible is just to say that we must have such recognitional abilities as these. No less evidently, if these abilities are ever to be exercised, we must have material on which to exercise them; particular instances of general concepts must be encountered in experience. The importance of this fundamental duality is fully recognized by Kant. His word for awareness in experience of particular instances of general concepts is "intuition"; and the point epitomized in his famous dictum, that "thoughts without content are empty, intuitions without concepts are blind",[1] is one which he repeatedly emphasizes.

There are many idioms in which this inescapable duality can be expressed. Kant's idiom is psychological, the idiom of departments or faculties of the mind. He distinguishes between the *receptive* faculty of *sensibility*, through which we have intuitions, and the *active* faculty of *understanding*, which is the source of concepts; and thereby prepares the way for ascribing to these faculties, as their source, those limiting features which he finds in the notion of experience in general. Thus it seems that there is no conceivable way in which concepts could be instantiated in our experience except by our being aware of instances of them in space and time – or, at least, in time. Space and time themselves are accordingly declared to be "in us", to be simply the forms of our sensibility, nothing but our ways of being aware of particular things capable of being brought under concepts. Again, it is argued that unless the concepts we employed in application to our experience implicitly involved the application of certain very general notions (the categories), it would be impossible that there should be any such thing as self-conscious awareness of the succession of experience in time. The applicability of these notions is, then, a further necessary condition of the possibility of anything which deserves the name of experience or empirical knowledge.

[1] A 51/B 75.

But this necessity once more is presented as a consequence of our cognitive constitution; only it is assigned, this time, to our faculty of understanding, which is described as acting on our sensibility to bring about the satisfaction of its own requirements.

These allocations contain already the seeds of that disastrous model which, as we shall see, Kant had such powerful motives for prizing. The natural world as we know it, the whole content of our experience, is thoroughly conditioned by the features just referred to: our experience is essentially experience of a spatio-temporal world of law-governed objects conceived of as distinct from our temporally successive experiences of them. But all these limiting features alike simply represent ways in which things must appear in the experience of beings constituted as we are, with such a sensibility and such an understanding as ours. Of things as they are in themselves as opposed to these appearances of them, we have, and can have, no knowledge whatever; for knowledge is possible only of what can be experienced, and nothing can be experienced except as subjected to the forms imposed by our sensibility and our understanding.

This "transcendental idealism", according to which the whole world of Nature is merely appearance, is sharply distinguished by Kant from other forms of idealism. The typical "empirical" idealist, as Kant calls him, takes as certainly real the temporally successive states of consciousness and questions or denies the real existence, or our knowledge of the existence, of bodies in space. The transcendental idealist, on the other hand, is, Kant says, an empirical realist, according no superiority of status, as regards reality or certainty of existence, to states of consciousness over physical objects. When we see how Kant supports this claim, however, we must view it with scepticism. It is true that he grants us as immediate a knowledge of the physical objects of "outer sense", whose form is space, as he does of the psychological states, the objects of "inner sense", whose form is time. It is true, too, that he says that our inner-directed experience no more yields us knowledge of ourselves as we are in ourselves than our outer-directed experience yields us knowledge of other things as they are in themselves. But *these* parities do not really amount to according equal reality to bodies in space ("outer objects") and states of consciousness ("inner determinations"). The doctrine that the material and the mental constituents of the natural world are alike only appearances turns out, in the end, to bear with unequal weight on bodies and states of consciousness. Kant, as transcendental idealist, is closer to Berkeley than he acknowledges.

The doctrines of transcendental idealism, and the associated picture of the receiving and ordering apparatus of the mind producing Nature as we know it out of the unknowable reality of things as they are in themselves, are undoubtedly the chief obstacles to a sympathetic understanding of the *Critique*. We may be tempted by weakened interpretations of these doctrines, representing them as expository devices perhaps not wholly understood by their user. Thus the doctrine that we can have knowledge only of things as objects of possible experience, and not of things as they are in themselves, has a certain ambiguity; and we may be tempted, at times, by its subtler or ironical sense, which Kant himself seems, at times, almost to endorse. Again, we may be tempted to interpret the whole model of mind-made Nature as simply a device for presenting an analytical or conceptual inquiry in a form readily grasped by the picture-loving imagination. All such interpretations would, however, involve reading into much of the *Critique* a tone of at least half-conscious irony quite foreign to its character; and there are other, more decisive reasons for thinking that they would altogether fail to answer to Kant's intentions.

One of them is made clear enough in the Preface. As Kant there says, he is concerned not only to curb the pretensions of dogmatic metaphysics to give us supersensible knowledge; he is concerned also to curb the pretensions of sensibility to be coextensive with the real. The proof of our necessary ignorance of the supersensible safeguards the interests of morality and religion by securing the supersensible realm from our scepticism as well as from our knowledge. There are other indications of a different kind, more important still in the present context, as being more immediately related to the main concerns of this *Critique*. Thus the principle of significance itself, as applied to the categories, is derived by Kant as a *consequence* of the nature of the part played by the faculty of understanding in ordering experience; and the very possibility of knowledge of necessary features of experience is seen by him as dependent upon his transcendental subjectivism, the theory of the mind making Nature. This indeed is the essence of the "Copernican Revolution" which he proudly announced as the key to a reformed and scientific metaphysics. It is only because objects of experience must conform to the constitution of our minds that we can have the sort of *a priori* knowledge of the nature of experience which is demonstrated, in outline, in the *Critique* itself. Finally, Kant's claim to find in the solution of the first Antinomy decisive confirmation of the thesis of the ideality of space and time would be quite extraordinarily misleading if he meant by it no more than that the solution vindicated the application of the principle of significance to the question whether the world is or is not bounded in space and time.

Those interconnected doctrines which centre on the thesis of transcendental idealism are not the only obstacles to sympathetic understanding. Others are attributable in part to the state of scientific knowledge at the time at which Kant wrote. He believed without question in the finality of Euclidean geometry, Newtonian physics, and Aristotelian logic; and on these beliefs he founded others, still more questionable. Thus he believed that Euclidean geometry provided a unique body, not only of truths, but of necessary truths, about the structure of physical space; and in this belief found what seemed to him a further powerful argument for the thesis that space was transcendentally "in us". Kant's theory of geometry, though not defensible as a whole, contains valuable insights; and, being relatively independent of the main structure of the *Critique*, does not succeed in obscuring anything we may wish to preserve of that structure. It is otherwise with his conviction that what he took to be the presuppositions of Newtonian physics embodied conditions of the possibility of empirical knowledge in general; for the anxiety to arrive, by way of conclusion, at supposed *a priori* principles of natural science really does have the effect of obscuring what there is of substance in the arguments of a central, and crucial, section of the book, viz. the Analogies of Experience. As for the effect of Kant's uncritical acceptance, and unconstrained manipulation, of the forms and classifications of traditional logic, this is of a rather different kind. It may be held in part responsible for his boundless faith in a certain structural framework, elaborate and symmetrical, which he adapts freely from formal logic as he understands it and determinedly imposes on the whole range of his material. Over and over again the same pattern of divisions, distinctions, and connexions is reproduced in different departments of the work. The artificial and elaborate symmetry of this imposed structure has a character which, if anything in philosophy deserves the title of baroque, deserves that title. But this is a feature which, though it may cause us unnecessary trouble and give us irrelevant pleasure, we can in the end discount without anxiety.

2. THE METAPHYSICS OF EXPERIENCE

The heart of the *Critique of Pure Reason*, and its most difficult passages, are contained in the Division entitled Transcendental Analytic; for it is there, with some dependence on the earlier section concerned with space and time and called Transcendental Aesthetic, that Kant attempts to show what the limiting features must be of any notion of experience which we can make intelligible to ourselves. I shall try to indicate in outline the nature of this attempt and to estimate the degree of success it achieves.

Among the general theses which Kant assumes or argues for it is possible to distinguish the following:

1. that experience essentially exhibits temporal succession (the temporality thesis);

2. that there must be such unity among the members of some temporally extended series of experiences as is required for the possibility of self-consciousness, or self-ascription of experiences, on the part of a subject of such experiences (the thesis of the necessary unity of consciousness);

3. that experience must include awareness of objects which are distinguishable from experiences of them in the sense that judgements about these objects are judgements about what is the case irrespective of the actual occurrence of particular subjective experiences of them (the thesis of objectivity);

4. that the objects referred to in (3) are essentially spatial (the spatiality thesis);

5. that there must be one unified (spatio-temporal) framework of empirical reality embracing all experience and its objects (the thesis of spatio-temporal unity);

6. that certain principles of permanence and causality must be satisfied in the physical or objective world of things in space (the theses of the Analogies).

Of these theses the first is treated by Kant throughout as an unquestionable datum to which we cannot comprehend the possibility of any alternative; and as such we may be content to regard it. The second is seen by Kant as inseparably linked with the requirement of the conceptualizability of experience, with the requirement that *particular* contents of experience should be recognized as having some *general* character; and, so linked, may reasonably be seen as a standard-setting definition of what is to count as "experience". I doubt if any philosopher, even the most economical of empiricists, has ever in practice worked, or tried to work, with a more limited conception. This thesis, or standard-setting definition, serves as the premise of the Transcendental Deduction of the Categories, that section of the *Critique* which cost Kant, and costs his readers, the greatest labour, being one of the most abstruse passages of argument, as also one of the most impressive and exciting, in the whole of philosophy. The only other of the listed theses which is assumed rather than argued for by Kant is that which I have numbered (4), the spatiality thesis. In fact, this is scarcely distinguished by Kant as a separate thesis at all, though it should be. From the truth that objects of our experience conceived of as existing independently of experience of them are in fact spatial objects, it does not seem to follow immediately that the spatial is the only mode in which we could conceive of such objects. That the spatial is the only conceivable mode of existence of such objects might nevertheless perhaps be allowed if we stripped the concept of spatiality of its usual sensory associations and gave it a mainly formal meaning; and even if we allow the concept to carry its normal visual and tactile associations, it can still be maintained that the spatial mode is at least that *on analogy with which* any alternative mode of existence of independent objects of our experience would have to be conceived by us.

All the remaining listed theses are explicitly or implicitly argued for in the Analytic. The order of Kant's exposition may be misleading on this point. For in the Aesthetic, which precedes the Analytic, it is already affirmed that there is but one Space and Time, and it is at any rate natural to assume that the space there declared to be essentially one is the space of objects conceived of as existing independently of our experiences of awareness of them, since the thesis of spatial unity has no other plausible application. We might by this be misled into supposing that the Analytic starts with the assumption that experience is necessarily of independently existing objects forming a unified spatio-temporal system and seeks on this basis to establish further necessary conditions of the possibility of experience. This would be a false impression. The thesis of objectivity – which might be abbreviated to the statement that experience must include awareness of objects which form the topic of objective judgements – is certainly implicitly argued for in the Analytic, and so is the thesis that these objects must possess the kind of unity of relation provided for by the doctrine that they belong to a unitary spatio-temporal system.

The essential premise of the Analytic is, as I have already remarked, the thesis of the necessary unity of consciousness. This "necessary unity" is called by many other names in the *Critique*. Kant's favourite expression for it is "the transcendental unity of apperception"; and this unity of apperception or consciousness is sometimes also called a unity of "self-consciousness". Sometimes Kant's employment of this last phrase might give the impression that what he has in mind is some special kind of consciousness of self, different from such ordinary or empirical self-awareness as is expressed in the commonplace self-ascription of perceptions, feelings, etc. But this is not really so. He is concerned, as I have remarked, with the general conditions of the employment of concepts, of the recognition of the particular contents of experience as having some general character; and he regards these conditions as being at the same time the fundamental conditions of the possibility of ordinary or empirical self-consciousness. The fulfilment of these conditions sets a minimum standard for what is to count as experience; and the standard-setting requirement, Kant argues, can be satisfied by nothing less than this: that the temporally extended series of experiences which are to form the contents of a possible experience should be so connected among themselves as to yield a picture of a unified objective world, of which these experiences – or some of them – *are* experiences. The argument to this effect is developed in the Transcendental Deduction of the Categories and in certain sections of the Analytic of Principles; and again the order and detail of exposition are not such as to facilitate understanding. In the Deduction we find a repeated insistence that a certain connectedness and unity among our experiences is necessary to constitute them experiences of an objective and law-governed world; that the concepts of the objective which we apply in experience embody the rules of such unity; and that this rule-governed connexion of experiences under concepts of the objective is precisely what is required for the necessary unity of consciousness, i.e. for the possibility of self-consciousness.

The force of these contentions is by no means immediately obvious. It becomes somewhat clearer when we turn to certain sections of the Principles, which are supposed to contain a more detailed working out of the implications of the Deduction; notably, to the argument called the Refutation of Idealism and the arguments of the Analogies. Experiences occur in temporal relation; but for *self*-consciousness to be possible ("consciousness of my own existence as determined in time"), it must at least be possible to distinguish between the order and arrangement of our *experiences* on the one hand and the order and arrangement which *objects* of those experiences independently enjoy. For this, in turn, to be possible, objects of experience must be conceived of as existing within an *abiding* framework within which they can enjoy their own relations of co-existence and succession and within which we can encounter them at different times, these encounters yielding the merely subjective order of our experiences of them. The abiding framework, of course, is spatial, is physical space; and Kant's immediate concern in the Refutation of Idealism is to point out that these necessary distinctions of temporal relation must be drawn *within* experience and hence we must be immediately, or non-inferentially, aware of objects in space. "The consciousness of my existence is at the same time an immediate consciousness of the existence of other things outside me." [1]

The fundamental thoughts which underlie the whole complex argument of these sections might be roughly expressed as follows. First, no one could be conscious of a temporally extended series of experiences as *his* unless he could be aware of them as yielding knowledge of a unified objective world, through which the series of experiences in question forms just one subjective or experiential route. Second, this conception, necessary to the possibility of self-consciousness, must be implicit in the character of the concepts actually employed, and directly applied, in experience. Not any set

[1] B 276.

of concepts would by themselves suffice to yield, i.e. to demand, this conception. (For example, the jejune empiricist array of simple sensory quality concepts would not.) At least the concepts applied must include concepts of persistent and re-identifiable objects in space; and any objects which could fall under such concepts as these must exhibit some degree of "regularity in their operations"[1], i.e. the changes to which they are subject must themselves, at least in general, be subject to causal law.

Kant supposed himself to have established stricter necessities than these. He certainly argued that the necessary distinctions between subjective and objective time-relations implied the necessary applicability within experience of concepts of permanence and causality. But he was not satisfied with the merely relative permanence of re-identifiable bodies in space, though this is in fact the most that the argument establishes; nor with any such weakened corollary about causation as I have suggested. From the argument for permanence in the first Analogy he derives a quantitative conservation principle which does not follow from it and is quite irrelevant to the satisfaction of those conditions which the argument shows must be satisfied; and in the famous argument of the second Analogy he claims to show that the experience of objective change, of succession as occurring in the objective world and not merely in the series of our subjective experiences, is possible only if every event is taken to be causally determined; but the crucial step in this reasoning can seem legitimate only if the critical faculty is numbed by the grossness of the *non sequitur*. In his determination to establish the principles which he regarded as the necessary foundations of physical science, Kant attempts, throughout the Analogies, to force from the argument more than it will yield.

Nevertheless the Transcendental Deduction, the Analogies, and the Refutation together establish important general conclusions. The standard-setting definition of experience (thesis (2)) is surely acceptable. There is, no doubt, reason to think that there are forms of sentience which fall short of this standard. But the fulfilment of the fundamental conditions of the possibility of self-consciousness, of self-ascription of experiences, seems to be necessary to any concept of experience which can be of interest to

[1] The phrase is adapted from Hume. See *Treatise of Human Nature*, Book I, Part IV, Chapter 2.

us, indeed to the very existence of any *concept* of experience at all. Kant's genius nowhere shows itself more clearly than in his identification of the most fundamental of these conditions in its most general form: viz. the possibility of distinguishing between a temporal order of subjective perceptions and an order and arrangement which objects of those perceptions independently possess – a unified and enduring framework of relations between constituents of an objective world. Almost equally important is his recognition that this distinction must be implicit in the concepts under which the contents of experience are brought, since there is no question of perceiving, as it were, the pure framework itself. These are very great and novel gains in epistemology, so great and so novel that, nearly two hundred years after they were made, they have still not been fully absorbed into the philosophical consciousness.

There is, of course, plenty of scope for further discussion of these themes. It may perhaps be held that Kant has not stated the *full* conditions for the possibility of empirical self-consciousness. To this it may be replied that he has stated the most fundamental conditions. Again, it may perhaps be questioned whether the thesis of objectivity really carries with it the thesis of unity in the unqualified form in which Kant asserts it. Even if the unity of consciousness demands the original context of one unified spatial (or quasi-spatial) world, does it not then possess a potentially wider scope? Could it not conceivably serve as a link between, say, spatially independent objective worlds? On fantasies which profess to exploit this potentiality, we may safely make the Kantian comment that readiness to allow our concept of the objective to range over spatially independent worlds would be altogether dependent on the possibility, if it is one, of representing them as systematically integrated in other ways; for Kant was surely right in insisting on the general connexion between objectivity and systematic unity.

The above account of the central argument of the Analytic omits much that is to be found in the course of its development; and on these omissions I must now comment. The Transcendental Deduction of the Categories lies between a section which Kant subsequently refers to as the Metaphysical Deduction and a celebrated passage called the Schematism. To understand this arrangement, it is above all necessary to remember the importance which Kant attaches to the idiom of faculties, and in particular the seriousness with which he takes the duality of understanding and sensibility. Their co-operation is essential to experience, understanding as the source of concepts, sensibility as supplying the forms of intuition. Experience, empirical knowledge, is possible only when intuitions are brought under concepts, when empirical judgements are made. But the general functions of understanding can be investigated in abstraction from the modes of sensibility. In fact, there is already in existence a science which investigates those functions, viz. the science of formal logic. Since this science supplies us with a complete account of those forms into one or another of which all our judgements must fall, whatever their content, we may hope to find in these forms a clue to whatever necessities are imposed by understanding alone on the character of our experience. This investigation is not undertaken in formal logic itself, which simply offers us analytic truths about the logical relations between these forms, rules of formally valid inference; it abstracts altogether from any question about the conditions under which these forms can be *applied* to yield individually true or valid judgements about objects. By raising precisely this question in its most general form, Kant claimed to derive, from what he regarded as twelve fundamental propositional forms, twelve "pure concepts of the understanding" or categories, each of which must have application in experience if true judgements of the corresponding forms were to be made. This is the "Metaphysical Deduction" of the categories.

Now in the Transcendental Deduction, as we have seen, there is a general argument to the effect that the concepts under which we bring the contents of our experience must be such as to confer upon that experience a certain rule-governed connectedness or unity. Kant concludes that the general principles of that unity are precisely such as are secured by the necessary applicability in experience of the already derived categories. But the "pure" categories, as derived in the Metaphysical Deduction, are derived, in complete abstraction from the modes of sensibility, simply from the requirements of understanding, the faculty of concepts. Therefore, to appreciate the actual significance of the categories in application to experience, which requires the co-operation of understanding *and* sensibility, we must interpret the pure categories in terms of the general form of sensible intuition. This is the role of the Schematism, which makes the transition from pure categories to categories-in-use by interpreting the former in terms of time. It is sufficient, in the Schematism, to give the interpretation in terms of time alone, without explicit mention of space; for it is the temporal character of experience that is invoked in the premises of the argument of both the Deduction and the Principles; that the application of the categories requires a framework which we cannot but conceive of as spatial (or on analogy with space) is something that emerges in the course of the argument.

It requires only moderate acquaintance with formal logic to be both critical of the list of forms which is to be the basis of Kant's derivation in the Metaphysical Deduction and sceptical of the whole conception of the derivation itself. It requires none at all to be astonished by most of the transitions from form to category that he actually makes. The list of twelve categories, in four sets of three, remains with us, however, to impose its own artificialities of arrangement at various stages in the book. The elucidation of what the necessary application of the categories is held to involve is contained in the chapter which follows the Schematism and which sets out the "principles of pure understanding". On the parts of that chapter which really do form, together with the Transcendental Deduction, one complex argument about the necessary unity and objectivity of experience (notably the Analogies and the Refutation of Idealism) I have already commented. Of the remaining principles, the Postulates of Empirical Thought contain instructions and warnings about the employment of the concepts of possibility and necessity in senses other than the narrowly logical, but add little that is new. The "mathematical" principles (Axioms of Intuition and Anticipations of Perception) are held to state what are, from the point of view of the understanding, the necessary conditions of the application of mathematics to objects of experience; but their connexion with the general themes of the Analytic is tenuous and is made, as far as it is made at all, through the concept of "synthesis".

Of that concept, though it figures largely in the Transcendental Deduction, especially in the first edition version, I have so far said nothing. I have treated the Deduction as an *argument*, which proceeds by analysis of the concept of experience in general to the conclusion that a certain objectivity and a certain unity are necessary conditions of the possibility of experience. And such an argument it is. But it is also an essay in the imaginary subject of transcendental psychology. Since Kant regards the necessary unity and connectedness of experience as being, like all transcendental necessities, the product of the mind's operations, he feels himself obliged to give some account of those operations. Such an account is obtained by thinking of the necessary unity of experience as produced by our faculties (specifically by memory and imagination controlled by understanding) out of impressions or data of sense themselves unconnected and separate; and this process of producing unity is called by Kant "synthesis". The theory of synthesis, like any essay in transcendental psychology, is exposed to the *ad hominem* objection that we can claim no empirical knowledge of its truth; for this would be to claim empirical knowledge of the occurrence of that which is held to be the antecedent condition of empirical knowledge. Belief in the occurrence of the process of synthesis as an antecedent condition of experience and belief in the antecedent occurrence of disconnected impressions as materials for the process to work on are beliefs which support each other and are necessary to each other. But, by hypothesis, experience can support neither belief; and since neither is necessary to the strictly analytical argument, the entire theory is best regarded as one of the aberrations into which Kant's explanatory model inevitably led him.

The discarding of the story of synthesis might seem to leave us with questions to answer: viz. when we speak of the necessary unity of experiences, what are the items so unified, and in what does their necessary unity consist? To these questions the answers are commonplace enough and, indeed, implicit in what has already been said. First, the unified items are just the experiences reported in our ordinary reports of what we see, feel, hear, etc. No faithful reports of these experiences are in general possible which do not make use of the concepts of the objects which our experiences are experiences of. Second, the unity of these experiences under the rules embodied in the concepts of objects is just what is exemplified in the general coherence and *consistency* of our ordinary descriptions of what we see, hear, feel, etc. The employability of such concepts as these, hence the objectivity of experience in general, is necessarily bound up with the fulfilment of this requirement of consistency or unity. In telling the story of a dream, the requirement of consistency may indeed be waived; but the employment of concepts of objective reality in telling of a dream is a secondary employment, just because those concepts are then liberated from that condition of their use which makes them concepts of an objective reality.

3. TRANSCENDENT METAPHYSICS

After construction, demolition; after the Transcendental Analytic, the Transcendental Dialectic. This lengthy and imposing section of the *Critique* is substantially easier to understand than the Analytic and I shall devote proportionately less space to it.

The primary aim of the Dialectic is the exposure of metaphysical illusion; the primary instrument of exposure is the principle of significance. Kant advances, as I earlier remarked, a secondary thesis to the effect that certain ideas for which no empirical conditions of application can be specified and which are therefore a source of illusion if taken as relating to objects of possible knowledge may nevertheless have a useful, and even a necessary, function in the extension of empirical knowledge, when employed in a different way, which he entitles "regulative". Such ideas are those of God, and of the soul conceived of as a simple immaterial substance. Though it would be illusion to think we can have knowledge, or even form any definite conception, of objects corresponding to either idea, yet advances in psychology and in science in general, Kant holds, are assisted by, even dependent on, thinking of inner states *as if* they were states of an immaterial substance and thinking of the natural world in general *as if* it were the creation of a divine intelligence. So to think is to make a regulative employment of these ideas. Kant's contention that such a use of the ideas is natural, even necessary, to human reason, when it is busy with scientific matters, is evidently quite unplausible. But it becomes clearer why he should have held this view when we consider the general structure of the Dialectic.

For illusion, too, has a systematic structure. Nowhere, indeed, does Kant's passion for system enjoy a more uninhibited indulgence than in the construction of the framework, again based upon formal logic, within which he treats the topics of the Dialectic. The logical framework itself is little more than a

c

philosophical curiosity.[1] But some observation of genuine analogies and connexions goes into its construction. Kant notes that it is typical of systematic rational inquiry to raise questions such that the answer to one such question may itself form the topic of another question of the same general kind. Thus it is typical of the scientific enterprise to seek for ever greater generality of explanation, to try to bring ever wider ranges of phenomena within the scope of a unifying theory; and this search for ever greater comprehensiveness of explanation has parallels in other natural tendencies of both primitive and sophisticated inquiry, such as the tendency to press our investigations farther and farther into remoter regions of space and of past time, and to inquire ever more minutely into the composition of matter in general. We might name this parallelism by saying that all these types of inquiry have a *serial* character, that the items they disclose form a *series*, each item having a typical relation to its predecessor. Kant held that an inevitable concomitant of certain types of serial inquiry was the idea of the *totality* of the series of items disclosed in the course of the inquiry; and this conception seems to force upon us the necessity of a certain alternative. Either the series has an ultimate, limiting term – the absolute beginning of the world in time and its limits in space, the ultimate ground or condition of everything in Nature, the ultimate constituents of matter, etc. – or it has no limiting term, it is an infinite or unlimited series. Where this disjunction does seem forced upon us, Kant thought he could prove that embracing either limb of it led to contradiction; whence he called this division of the Dialectic the Antinomy of Pure Reason. His solution of these "conflicts of pure reason with itself" turns on invoking the principle of significance. In operating with the concept of the series as a whole, we fail to consider whether any possible intuition, or experience, might answer to this concept. But there is, Kant maintains, no way in which experience could decide in favour of either limb of the disjunction. The question of which of the apparently necessary

---

[1] Its basis is a "demonstration" that there are three, and only three, types of inevitable dialectical illusion, each correlated with one of three forms of deductive reasoning, and all springing from a unitary "demand of reason", conceived as the faculty of mediate inference, for completeness in the premises of a given conclusion. Further elaborations are held to be determined by the fourfold division of the categories.

alternatives holds is empirically unsettleable; and hence the concept of absolute totality which seems to force the disjunction upon us has no empirical use. "In its empirical meaning the word 'whole' is always only comparative."[1]

Kant treats his solution as a confirmation of the thesis of transcendental idealism. If space and time, and the world in space and time, existed as things in themselves, the disjunctions in each case would hold as necessary truths. Since the assumption that they do hold leads to contradiction, we have as good a proof as could be desired that space and time and the natural world do not exist as things in themselves, but only as appearances, are only in us, etc. This proof appears to rest on the premise that if things in space and time *were* things in themselves, then the principle of significance would not apply to them; they would be things of such a kind that concepts could be properly used of them without consideration of empirical criteria for their use. The conclusion that things in space and time are not such things as these *might* be construed as an ironically framed repudiation of the whole conception of "things as they are in themselves" and an oblique affirmation of the autonomy of the principle of significance. If this were the correct construction, one could only think that the thesis of transcendental idealism is generally expressed with a misleading excess of irony. But irony, except of a cheerfully obvious kind, is not characteristic of Kant. What really emerges here is that aspect of transcendental idealism which finally denies to the natural world any existence independent of our "representations" or perceptions, an aspect to which I have already referred in remarking that Kant is closer to Berkeley than he acknowledges.

Many other issues will have to be raised in the detailed discussion of the Antinomies. The validity of the arguments Kant uses to derive the contradictions is highly questionable; and it is not so plain as it appeared to him that no empirical resolution of any of these "conflicts of reason" is possible. Thus developments in physical science, unforeseeable at that time, appear to give empirical significance to the notion of physical space, and the world in space, as finite, though unbounded. These issues I now leave aside, to revert to the question of the general structure of the Dialectic.

Its unifying thesis, as I have already remarked, is that human reason is inevitably led, in the search for systematic knowledge, to

[1] A 483/B 511.

entertain certain ideas of an *absolute* character, for which no empirical condition of application can be specified but which may have a useful regulative role in the advancement of knowledge. This thesis is a complex one, with four parts which must be clearly distinguished: (1) that the ideas in question all have the character which Kant expresses by the words *"absolute"* or *"unconditioned"* (e.g. an absolute totality, an absolutely first beginning, an ultimate, unconditioned ground, an absolutely simple constituent of matter, etc.); (2) that we are *inevitably* led, by the nature of systematic inquiry, to entertain such ideas; (3) that all such ideas are essentially *transcendent* of any possible experience; (4) that, in each sphere in which they arise, some such idea has *regulative utility*. Even in the case of the cosmological types of inquiry considered in the Antinomies, this complex doctrine, as I indicated in the preceding paragraph, does not seem to be true in all its parts. But if we set on one side post-Kantian developments in science, some at least of these types of inquiry do seem to offer brilliant examples of the necessary interconnectedness of these four features; and the Kantian suggestion that the appropriate regulative idea for science in these cases is that of the totality conceived as an unlimited series, setting a never completable task for inquiry, seems entirely reasonable.

The success of the general thesis in the case of cosmological inquiries must have encouraged Kant to form an exaggerated notion of its plausibility in what he regarded as the two other spheres of inevitable dialectical illusion: namely, theology and psychology. The history of philosophy certainly suggests that the belief that we can have knowledge of the soul as an absolutely unitary, enduring immaterial thing or substance is a natural, though not an inevitable, *philosophical* illusion. But it is false that this idea is one we are naturally led to entertain by the systematic empirical study of psychology, and equally false that it has any regulative utility in this connexion. Again, the topic of God certainly gives plenty of scope for the notions of the absolute and the ultimate. God is absolutely necessary existence, absolute perfection, the ultimate ground of everything, etc. But it is only in so far as the idea of God rests upon notions treated of in the Antinomies, viz. those of absolute beginnings and original causes, that it is at all plausible to contend that we are inevitably led by reason to entertain such an idea; and even then, as Kant recognizes, this basis is inadequate to sustain the idea of God. There is, on the other hand, no plausibility at all in Kant's suggestion that the entire enterprise of science is necessarily conducted under the aegis of the idea of an intelligent creator, and that we are thus inevitably led to this idea by Reason's characteristic search for general explanations. Ideas of God, or of gods, have many sources, some of them not markedly connected with Reason; and the relating of any such idea to scientific explanation is something that presents an awkward problem to the theologian rather than a necessary inspiration to the scientist.

Kant's exposure, in the Paralogisms, of the metaphysical illusion of knowledge of the soul is of peculiar brilliance in itself, and also of particular interest because of its connexion with the general argument of the Analytic. The target of attack is the doctrine that each of us can know of the existence, in his own case, of one persisting, purely immaterial, non-composite, thinking thing, the thing referred to by each of us as "I". The line of attack is that prescribed by the principle of significance. If we are to make any legitimate employment of the crucial concepts of unity or numerical identity through time, we must apply them, in the light of empirical criteria, to objects encountered in experience. But if we abstract entirely from the body and consider simply our experiences or states of consciousness as such (the contents of inner sense), it is evident not only that we do not, but that we could not, encounter within this field anything which we could identify as the permanent subject of states of consciousness. How, then, does the illusion arise? A slogan-like summary of Kant's answer would be: the unity of experience is confused with the experience of unity. It has already been argued that, for self-consciousness to be possible at all, there must be such unity among the members of a series of experiences as to constitute them experiences of a single objective world. Now while the fulfilment of this condition constitutes the basic ground of the possibility of self-consciousness, further conditions (it may be held) are required for the actual ascription of experiences to oneself. There must exist empirically applicable criteria of identity through time of a subject of experience. Such criteria do exist: as Kant himself seems to recognize, they involve the fact that "the thinking being (as man) is itself . . . an object of outer sense",[1] i.e. a body in space.

[1] B 415.

But we are tempted to overlook the relevance of such criteria by the fact that we do not actually have to employ them when we use the word "I" in ascribing current or remembered experiences to ourselves. (When I am in pain, for example, I do not have to look and see that it is *I* who am in pain.) Thus we are tempted to think that we have knowledge of a continuing, identical subject, as such, knowledge which is independent of any empirical criteria of identity. We try, as it were, to abstract the force of "I" from the background of empirical criteria which give it its power of referring to a continuing subject and yet still view it as possessing that power. But if we do perform this abstraction, there is nothing for the word to express except consciousness in general, or the general conditions of the possibility of experience. Thus we confound the unity of experience with the experience of unity; and thus there arises the illusion of knowledge of the soul as a persisting immaterial thing. But it is only an illusion; and if we succumb to it, we are powerless to defend such a view of the soul against rival and less flattering theories, since no empirical means of decision between them is available. Kant adds that it is essential to his own critical philosophy to demonstrate the emptiness of any such claim to knowledge; for if it were allowable, then our knowledge must have transcended the realm of experience and entered that of things as they are in themselves.

4. THE METAPHYSICS OF TRANSCENDENTAL IDEALISM

Something more must now be said of the doctrines of transcendental idealism. I have mentioned the anodyne interpretations by which we may be tempted and to which some of Kant's own observations give colour; and have said that, with whatever degree of reluctance, we must conclude that they do not answer, or do not steadily answer, to Kant's intentions. The doctrine is not merely that we can have no knowledge of a supersensible reality. The doctrine is that reality is supersensible and that we can have no knowledge of it. There are points in plenty at which the doctrine takes swift plunges into unintelligibility. Consider, for instance, the view that since space and time are nothing but forms of our sensibility, our awareness of all things in space and time, including ourselves, is awareness of things only as they appear and not as they are in themselves. We are aware, then, of ourselves in a temporal guise and hence only as we appear to ourselves and not as we are in ourselves. But what sort of a truth about ourselves is it, that we appear to ourselves in a temporal guise? Do we really so appear to ourselves or only appear to ourselves so to appear to ourselves? It seems that we must either choose the first alternative at once or uselessly delay a uselessly elaborated variant of it. Then is it a temporal fact, a fact about what happens in time, that we really so appear to ourselves? To say this would be to go back on our choice; for all that occurs in time belongs on the side of appearances. So it is not a fact about what happens in time that we really appear to ourselves in a temporal guise. I really do *appear* to myself temporally; but I do not really *temporally* appear to myself. But now what does "really do appear" mean? The question is unanswerable; the bounds of intelligibility have been traversed, on any standard. Kant can scarcely claim that the fact is unalarming, on the ground that it agrees with the standard set by his own principle of significance, which is itself derived from the set of doctrines to which the present doctrine belongs. It is not a defence of an unintelligible doctrine that its unintelligibility is certified by a principle derived from it.[1]

This is but one instance of many incoherences into which these doctrines swiftly lead. But this kind of *ad hominem* criticism is not enough for understanding. We must see what notions are misapplied, what truths perverted, in these doctrines; and how they are misapplied or perverted. Here we must revert to the analogy, or model, mentioned at the beginning of this introduction. We know that to any being who is a member of the natural spatio-temporal world of science and everyday observation the spatio-temporal objects of that world can sensibly *appear* only by *affecting* in some way the constitution of that being. The way in which objects *do* appear, what characteristics they appear as having, depends in part upon the constitution of the being to which they appear. Were that constitution different, the same things would appear differently. These facts have seemed to many philosophers, e.g. Locke and Lord Russell, to be good reasons for denying that we are sensibly or perceptually aware of things as they really are, or are in themselves. For example, objects appear to be coloured, but, it is held, are not really coloured;

---

[1] The incoherence of this doctrine is more fully displayed in Part IV Section 4 below.

what is really the case is that objects have certain physical properties, and we have a certain physical constitution, such that the effect of the former on the latter is to make objects appear to us coloured. This line of reasoning, though not compelling, is perfectly intelligible. We still know what is meant by "objects as they really are". They are objects thought of as endowed with only such properties as are ascribed to them in physical theories, especially the theories which supply explanations of the causal mechanism of perception. They are objects thought of as really possessing those (primary) properties which make them capable of appearing differently to beings differently equipped with sensory and nervous apparatus, but not as possessing those further (secondary) properties their apparent possession of which is explained by the effect of the primary properties on that apparatus.

This conception, though perhaps not attractive, is not unintelligible. The scientifically minded philosopher who embraces it departs, indeed, from some ordinary applications of the contrast between appearance and reality; for there are (as Berkeley complained) *no* circumstances in which things as he says they really are can *appear* as they really are. But he does not cut us off from empirical knowledge of things as they really are. The connexion with sensible experience is still there; only it is less direct.

Kant's conception of the contrast between things as they are in themselves and things as they appear seems to have the same starting-point as the scientifically minded philosopher's conception of the contrast. They hold in common that, because we are aware of objects only in being affected by them and only as they appear as a result of our being so affected, we are not aware of objects as they are in themselves. But the next step is quite different. The scientifically minded philosopher does not deny us empirical knowledge of those things, as they are in themselves, which affect us to produce sensible appearances. He only denies that the properties which, under normal conditions, those things sensibly appear to us to have are included (or are *all* included) among the properties which they have, and which we know them to have, as they are in themselves. But Kant denies the possibility of any empirical knowledge at all of those things, as they are in themselves, which affect us to produce sensible experience. It is evidently consistent with, indeed required by, this denial to deny also that the physical objects of science *are* those things, as they are in themselves, which affect us to produce sensible experience. By assigning the whole spatio-temporal framework of the natural world to the receptive constitution of the subject of experience, by declaring the whole natural world to be mere appearance, Kant is able, in form, to reconcile these denials with the common starting-point, which he shares with the scientifically-minded philosopher, for the application of the contrast between things as they are in themselves and things as they appear. But the price of the formal reconciliation is high. For the resultant transposition of the terminology of objects "affecting" the constitution of subjects takes that terminology altogether out of the range of its intelligible employment, viz. the spatio-temporal range. The doctrine that we are aware of things only as they appear and not as they are in themselves because their appearances to us are the result of our constitution being affected by the objects, is a doctrine that we can understand just so long as the "affecting" is thought of as something that occurs in space and time; but when it is added that we are to understand by space and time themselves nothing but a capacity or liability of ours to be affected in a certain way by objects not themselves in space and time, then we can no longer understand the doctrine, for we no longer know what "affecting" means, or what we are to understand by "ourselves".

Kant indeed offers further information, but not further enlightenment, on the subject of "affecting". Any mode of awareness which is dependent on the existence of the object of awareness is one in which "the subject's faculty of representation is affected by the object". So awareness of things as they are in themselves ("non-sensible or intellectual intuition") would be a *creative* awareness which produced its own object; a kind of awareness which, "so far as we can judge, can belong only to the primordial being".[1] Kant points out that we are unable to comprehend the possibility of such a kind of awareness. He does not point out that whatever obscurity surrounds these notions surrounds also the entire doctrine that things in space and time are appearances.

The doctrines of phenomena and noumena, of transcendental idealism, of the ultimate subjectivity of the natural world, can, then, be understood in this sense: that we can trace the steps by which the original model, the governing analogy, is perverted or

[1] B 72.

transposed into a form in which it violates any acceptable requirement of intelligibility, including Kant's own principle of significance. Further, we can understand the role of the resulting
model or picture as a help to Kant in his wielding of more acceptable ideas: as appearing both to certify the principle of significance
and to explain the possibility of his programme for a "scientific"
metaphysics of experience. We can even, and should, find room
in philosophy for a concept which performs at least some of the
negative functions of the Kantian concept of the noumenal. In
rejecting the senseless dogma that our conceptual scheme corresponds at no point with Reality, we must not embrace the
restrictive dogma that Reality is completely comprehended by
that scheme as it actually is. We admit readily that there are facts
we do not know. We must admit also that there may be *kinds* of
fact of which we have, at present, no more conception than our
human predecessors had of some kinds of fact admitted in our
conceptual schemes but not in theirs. We learn not only how to
answer old questions, but how to ask new ones. The idea of the
aspects of Reality which would be described in the answers to the
questions we do not yet know how to ask is one which, like the
idea of the realm of the noumenal, though not in the same drastic
style, limits the claim of actual human knowledge and experience
to be "co-extensive with the real".

This seems to be the necessary, and not very advanced, limit
of sympathy with the metaphysics of transcendental idealism.
Though it is difficult to disentangle its doctrines from the analytical argument of Kant's positive metaphysics of experience,
yet, when the disentangling operation has been carried out, it is
remarkable how little those doctrines appear to have distorted
that argument.

5. CONCLUSION

Many questions about the *Critique* and its problems are left so far
untouched on in this brief account. I conclude by considering
two, which are not unconnected with each other.

In the course of the *Critique* Kant frequently makes use of a
certain distinction to which I have made no reference, the
distinction between analytic and synthetic *a priori* propositions.
Both types of proposition are said to have this in common, that
they can be known by us to be, not only true, but such that no

experience could possibly disconfirm or provide a counter-instance to them. In this respect, both types of proposition are contrasted with true empirical propositions, which are such that we can know them to be true only because, and in so far as, they are confirmed in experience. Kant holds that whereas the *a priori* character of analytic propositions presents no profound philosophical problem, it is far otherwise with *a priori* synthetic propositions. Indeed he says in the Introduction that the whole problem which the *Critique of Pure Reason* is devoted to solving can be epitomized in the question: How are *a priori* synthetic judgements possible?

It might be felt that more account should be taken of a distinction to which Kant attaches such importance. But it is doubtful whether this would in fact be advantageous. Kant nowhere gives an even moderately satisfactory theoretical account of the dichotomy between analytic and synthetic *a priori* propositions; nor can any be gleaned from his casually scattered examples. Among propositions generally counted as *a priori* there are, of course, many distinguishable subclasses; and in the history of controversy concerning such propositions, many philosophers have followed Kant at least to the extent of wishing to restrict the title "analytic" to the members of one or more of these subclasses. But it is very doubtful indeed whether any clearly presentable general restriction of this kind would release into a contrasted class of synthetic *a priori* propositions just those types of proposition which Kant's epitomizing question was meant to be about. We can enumerate, as belonging to this intended class, truths of geometry and arithmetic and supposed *a priori* presuppositions of empirical science. But we can really form no general conception of the intended class except in terms of Kant's answer to his epitomizing question. What Kant means in general by synthetic *a priori* propositions is really just that class of propositions our knowledge of the necessity of which could, he supposed, be explained only by mobilizing the entire Copernican resources of the *Critique*, by appealing to the model of "objects conforming to our modes of representation", i.e. to our sensibility's constitution and the understanding's rules. Since, as I have already argued, nothing whatever really is, or could be, explained by this model – for it is incoherent – it must be concluded that Kant really has no clear and general conception of the synthetic *a priori* at all.

Still, it might be said, there is a problem here, even if it is not happily stated in the form of Kant's epitomizing question. I have represented as the major positive achievement of the *Critique* the carrying out, or partial carrying out, of a certain programme. The programme was that of determining the fundamental general structure of any conception of experience such as we can make intelligible to ourselves. Whether or not we choose to entitle the propositions descriptive of that structure "synthetic *a priori*", it is clear at least that they have a distinctive character or status; and Kant's Copernican theory was an attempt to explain that status. Is it not, after all, easy to read the very formulation of the programme – "the determination of the fundamental general structure of any conception of experience such as *we* can make intelligible to ourselves" – in such a way as to suggest the Kantian-seeming thought that any necessary limits we find in such a conception are limits imposed by *our* capacities? And if we nevertheless discard, as incoherent in itself and failing in its purpose, the Kantian explanation of the feasibility of the programme, what other are we prepared to offer? To this I can only reply that I see no reason why any high doctrine at all should be necessary here. The set of ideas, or schemes of thought, employed by human beings reflect, of course, their nature, their needs and their situation. They are not static schemes, but allow of that indefinite refinement, correction, and extension which accompany the advance of science and the development of social forms. At the stage of conceptual self-consciousness which is philosophical reflection, people may, among other things, conceive of variations in the character of their own situation and needs and discuss intelligibly the ways in which their schemes of thought might be adapted to such variations. But it is no matter for wonder if conceivable variations are intelligible only as variations within a certain fundamental general framework of ideas, if further developments are conceivable only as developments of, or from, a certain general basis. There is nothing here to demand, or permit, an explanation such as Kant's. In order to set limits to coherent thinking, it is not necessary, as Kant, in spite of his disclaimers, attempted to do, to think both sides of those limits. It is enough to think up to them. No philosopher in any book has come nearer to achieving this strenuous aim than Kant himself in the *Critique of Pure Reason*.

PART TWO

The Metaphysics of Experience

I

SPACE AND TIME

Four great dualities dominate Kant's theory of the nature of human experience: the duality of appearances and of things as they are in themselves; of intuitions and concepts; of the *a priori* and the empirical; of the inner and the outer. All four of them appear in the first major section of the work, the Transcendental Aesthetic. It is by way of the duality of intuitions and concepts that we approach the task of trying to understand how they are there related.

1. SPACE AND TIME AS FORMS OF INTUITION: THE AUSTERE INTERPRETATION

The duality of intuitions and concepts is in fact but one form or aspect of a duality which must be recognized in any philosophy which is seriously concerned with human knowledge, its objects or its expression and communication. These are three different directions of philosophical concern rather than three different concerns. The theory of being, the theory of knowledge, and the theory of statement are not truly separable; and our duality necessarily appears in all three, under different forms. In the first, we cannot avoid the distinction between particular items and the general kinds or characteristics they exemplify; in the second, we must acknowledge the necessity of our both possessing general concepts and becoming aware in experience of things, not themselves concepts, which fall under them; in the third, we must recognize the need for such linguistic or other devices as will enable us both to classify or describe in general terms and to indicate to what particular cases our classifications or descriptions are being applied.

To make the second, or epistemological, aspect of these concerns the dominant one, as Kant does, is no bad thing in itself, even though, as his own example spectacularly shows, it has its perils. These will emerge soon enough. To begin with, we can surely acknowledge that we can form no conception of experience, of empirical knowledge, which does not allow of our becoming aware in experience of particular items which we are able to recognize or classify as instances of general kinds or characteristics. We must have the capacities for such recognitions and classifications, i.e. we must have general concepts; and we must have the occasions for the exercise and development of these capacities, i.e. we must have what Kant calls intuitions.

Kant expresses these necessities in his richer idiom of departments or faculties of the mind, thereby enormously heightening the risks of the epistemological approach. He distinguishes between the sensibility, which is receptive and through which objects are "given" to us and the understanding, which is active and through which objects are "thought". Through the former we have intuitions; the latter is the source of concepts. The co-operation of both is necessary for experience, for empirical knowledge. For the moment we will allow the dangerous potentialities of this idiom to remain latent. For the moment the doctrine of the necessary co-operation of faculties can be read as a vivid re-assertion of the more austerely phrased necessities of the previous paragraph.

Now what of the doctrine that space and time are forms of intuition? This too we can begin by taking in a fairly low key. The duality of intuition and concept is merely the epistemological aspect of the duality of particular instance and general type. It is merely the thought of the particular instance as encountered in experience and there recognized as an instance of some general type. There is no reason why we should not invoke any or all aspects of this duality to help us understand the doctrine about space and time. Clearly the thought, at its most general, is of some peculiarly intimate connexion between space and time, on the one hand, and the idea of the particular item, the particular instance of the general concept, on the other. That this thought has force seems evident. Take any general concept you please, any idea you like of a general type of item – provided only that the items falling under it, if any, are such as conceivably could be encountered in experience and become the objects of empirical awareness – and it will seem evident enough that any particular instances of it which actually occur must actually occur *some-when*, that any particular instances of it which can actually be found must actually be found *somewhere*. To acquire application to a particular instance, a general name must find a local habitation – or, one might more cautiously say, if not also a local, at least a temporal, habitation. Identity, as well as existence, of particular instances of general concepts – that is, again, of those general concepts of which the particular instances, if any, are such as to be empirically encounterable – is bound up with space and time. Spatio-temporal position provides the fundamental ground of distinction between one particular item and another of the same general type, hence the fundamental ground of identity of particular items.[1]

Now let us introduce another of the Kantian dualities, that of the *a priori* and the empirical. For this duality too we may, to begin with, look for a relatively austere interpretation. A variant on "*a priori*" is "pure"[2] while "empirical" goes with "derived from experience" and "belonging to sensation". "*A priori*" and "pure" are regularly connected with "prior to experience" and also with "in us"; but this last connexion of all we shall ignore so long as we are in quest of the austere interpretation of the contrast. In my general review of the *Critique* I suggested that Kant's major positive achievement in metaphysics was to be sought in his attempt to articulate the general structure of any conception of experience which we could make truly intelligible to ourselves. If there is such a structure, if there is a set of ideas which enter

---

[1] The theory of empirical statement is a direction of philosophical concern which Kant does not follow (far) in the *Critique*. But it is worth noting how a modern philosopher reproduces our fundamental duality when he seeks to state the semantic conditions of the possibility of empirical statement in general and how he implicitly connects the "particular" side of the duality with space and time. J. L. Austin says that empirical statement requires the existence of two kinds of *conventions*, which he describes as follows:

"*Descriptive* conventions correlating the words with the *types* of situation, thing, event, etc., to be found in the world;

Demonstrative conventions correlating the words with the *historic situations*, etc., to be found in the world."

Austin's duality of semantic conventions corresponds to Kant's duality of cognitive faculties. By the demonstrative (i.e. particularizing) conventions, correlation is said to be achieved with historic situations. Since "historic" is evidently a time-word and "situations", fundamentally at any rate, a space-word, this balances very happily Kant's doctrine that the forms of intuition are space and time.

[2] Kant draws a distinction between "pure" and "a priori" (see B 3); but no confusion will result from ignoring it here.

D

indispensably into such a structure, then the members of this set will surely have a distinctive status. It will be proper to contrast them with those less general ideas corresponding to features of our experience which we can abstract from without imperilling the entire structure of the conception of experience itself. And as with the concepts, so with the features of which they are concepts.

Suppose we appropriate in this sense the contrast between the *a priori* and the empirical and then, in the sense of this appropriation, confront the Kantian doctrine that space and time are not only forms of intuition, but *a priori* forms of intuition. We are confronted not merely with the thought of an intimate link between the idea of particular items capable of being encountered in experience and the idea of their being temporally and spatially ordered items. We are confronted with the thought of this link being so vital that it cannot be broken without nullifying the whole conception of experience. And our first impulse may be to react in one way to this thought where temporal ordering is concerned and in another way where spatial ordering is concerned. To abstract altogether from the idea of time, of temporal sequence, while preserving that of experience in general we may admit at once to be a task beyond our powers. We refer, in common speech, to moments of experience of a particularly elevated kind as "timeless" moments. But they are moments none the less, having their place in a temporal procession, followed and preceded by others. We could not otherwise conceive them as forming part of anything we could understand by "experience". So the idea of experience in general seems to be truly inseparable from that of a temporal succession of experience. But it may, at least at first, seem otherwise with the idea of spatial ordering. The hearing of a sequence of notes, for example, may seem to be a case of a type of experience which can be coherently considered in isolation from everything else. Is it not conceivable that experience in general should consist exclusively of such sequences of auditory experience? And where then would be any necessary (or even possible) place for the notion of a spatial ordering of particular items encountered in experience?

In the Transcendental Aesthetic Kant does not argue for, or even explicitly assert, the thesis that a spatial ordering of at least some particular items encountered in experience is a necessary element in any conception of experience which we can render intelligible to ourselves. Later on he will assert this view, in its Kantian form, i.e. that intuitions of "outer sense" are a necessary condition of the possibility of experience – most explicitly in the Refutation of Idealism and the General Note on the System of Principles. Having argued that the possibility of empirical self-consciousness and knowledge of objects through the categories are mutually dependent and both necessary to the possibility of experience in general, he will declare, in the Refutation, that the occurrence of intuition of spatial objects is a necessary condition of the former and, in the General Note, that it is a necessary condition of our understanding the possibility of the latter. There remains something not wholly explicit about this process of argument. It would have been clearer, and perhaps more characteristic of the philosopher, to argue that the general conditions of the possibility of experience require the existence of *some* mode of sensible ordering, different from the temporal and at least analogous to the spatial, of particular items encountered in experience; and then to proceed to the declaration that, as things are, we cannot conceive of any alternative to the spatial mode itself. If this last assertion were challenged, as it might be, it would then be possible to retreat to the lesser claim; viz. that any system of relations between particular items such as previous arguments have shown to be necessary to the possibility of experience must be conceived, at least by us, on analogy with space. In the general review I tried to correct this element of unexplicitness in Kant's development of his views by separately listing the thesis of objectivity and the spatiality thesis.

2. SPACE AND TIME AS FORMS OF INTUITION: THE
TRANSCENDENTAL IDEALIST INTERPRETATION

The last paragraph is anticipatory. The point to retain from it is that though Kant does indeed regard space and time as *a priori* forms of intuition in the sense in which I suggested we might appropriate the term, this is not the primary sense the term "*a priori*" has for him or the sense which is uppermost when he advances the doctrine of the Aesthetic. The sense which is uppermost there is that which introduces us ineluctably and immediately to the doctrinal fantasies of transcendental idealism. The model which we are to strive to detach from Kant's analytical account of experience is already present, in almost its full force, in the opening paragraphs of the Aesthetic. We must allow all those connotations of the Kantian terminology which have so far been suppressed or ignored to emerge into the light.

As a preliminary we reconsider the statement that space and time are forms of intuition, leaving out the qualification "*a priori*". This I represented as an epistemologically slanted statement of the intimate connexion between the idea of the particular instance and those of spatial and temporal ordering: space and time are the forms of particularity. But the epistemological slant is by itself sufficient to introduce a perilous ambiguity into the statement. Let it read: the spatial and the temporal are the modes in which we become aware of particular instances of general concepts as ordered in relation to each other. Here the ambiguity shows itself. Are the spatial and the temporal the ways in which particular instances are ordered and *hence* the ways in which *we* become aware of them as ordered? Or are they *our* ways of becoming aware of particular instances as ordered and *hence* the ways in which they are ordered? It is enough to read the statement with the stress on "we" to tip the balance towards subjectivity.

So much we may note as simply something inherent in the epistemological slant. But Kant is far more deliberate. The essential framework of the model is consciously presented in the doctrine that space and time are forms of sensible intuition.

Let us attend first to the doctrine that human intuition is essentially *sensible* intuition. By itself there seems nothing philosophically adventurist in this. It amounts, as Kant explains, to the doctrine that our awareness, or perception, of an object requires that we be *affected* by the object. This in its turn amounts to no more than that the existence of an object perceived is one existence and our perception of it another and distinct existence, which is dependent on the former, therefore, in a non-logical or causal sense, even though the correctness of the description of it as a perception of the object is logically dependent on the existence of the object. Any theory which holds that we are aware of objects whose existence is independent of our awareness of them is committed to so much. If, thinking of Kant as analyst of the conception of experience in general, we are puzzled by so early and unsupported an affirmation of this thesis, it will only be because we think of it as a thesis which, in any conscientious discharge of the analytical enterprise, must be shown by argument to state a necessary feature of experience. For it is not obvious that there could be no possible experience – or none of which we could form a coherent conception – in which the esse of objects of awareness was nothing but their percipi.

Still, the thesis in itself is unremarkable. What utterly transforms the situation is the addition, to the doctrine that our intuition is, in this sense, sensible, of the further doctrine, understood as Kant understands it, that space and time are nothing but forms of our sensibility. The addition need not transform the situation so long as we read the latter doctrine as merely an epistemologically slanted statement of the thesis that the spatial and the temporal are the forms of particularity. So long as we read it thus, we can suppose that the "affecting" objects upon the existence of which – since our intuition is "sensible" – our awareness of particular items non-logically or causally depends are simply those spatially and temporally ordered items themselves to which we apply our general concepts. But beyond any possibility of doubt it is made clear that this is not the intended reading.[1] Spatially and temporally ordered items are not the affecting objects in question, but only, at most, their effects, appearances they present to beings equipped, as we are, with spatial and temporal modes of sensible intuition. Here is the full subjective force of the doctrine that space and time are forms of such intuition. To call them also *a priori* forms is simply to emphasize the subjectivity: space and time are "in us, prior to experience"; it is a feature of our cognitive constitution, and for this reason a condition of the possibility of such experience as we have, that objects affects us in such a way as to produce awareness of items spatially and temporally ordered. Since intuition is essential to knowledge of objects, and we have no modes of intuition but the sensible, we can have no knowledge of the affecting objects as they are in themselves, except the negative knowledge that they are not things in space and time.

It is obvious enough that such a doctrine, in which theses apparently so sober suddenly assume so startling and revolutionary a sense, is likely to prove fertile of paradoxes. These I shall consider more fully later on. But there is one complication, which Kant confronts now, in the Aesthetic, which must be given at

[1] See, e.g. A 42/B 59.

least some preliminary consideration at this stage, and which must be brought into relation with the fourth of those dualities I mentioned at the outset, the duality of the inner and the outer. Space and time are both alike assigned to the subjective constitution of our minds, and all spatially or temporally ordered items occurring in our experience are declared to be merely the outcome of that constitution's being affected by objects as they unknowably are in themselves. But do not our own experiences or states of consciousness, some of them perceptions of spatially related items and others not, essentially occur in temporal order? And do we not at least, in knowing what our own states of consciousness are, know something about ourselves as we really are, or are in ourselves, even if we know nothing about any other objects as they are in themselves? And is not the admission of both these points incompatible with the doctrine that knowledge of temporally ordered items is not knowledge of anything as it is in itself?

Kant clearly felt this as a difficulty, or saw that it would be felt as one. His solution involves denying the second of the two propositions which appear to be jointly incompatible with the doctrine that knowledge of temporally ordered items is not knowledge of anything as it is in itself. That is to say, he denies that in knowing what our (temporally ordered) states of consciousness are, we thereby know something about ourselves, or our minds, as they are in themselves. And he links this denial with the general theory of forms of sensibility, by means of the doctrine that, of the two modes, the spatial and the temporal, in which particular items encountered in experience are ordered, time is specifically that in which particular items appear as ordered as a result of *self-affection* on the part of ourselves as we are in ourselves. Because the affecting objects are ourselves, we may entitle the results of the affection *appearances of ourselves*, and may legitimately speak of empirical self-consciousness, of being conscious of *our own* (temporally ordered) states of mind, so long as we remember that this is not knowledge of ourselves as we really are but only of ourselves as we appear. This is the force, though not yet fully elaborated, of the doctrine that time is the form of *inner* sense. Part of what it means we can readily accept as something to which we cannot really conceive of any alternative: viz. that all particular states of consciousness – including our perceptions of spatially ordered objects – are temporally ordered. The rest of what it means is that the appearance of such states, so ordered, is the outcome of an atemporal self-affection of ourselves as we are in ourselves. Time is *nothing but* the form of inner sense.

Temporally ordered states of consciousness include perceptions of spatially ordered things. (As I have remarked, it has yet to be affirmed, but will be affirmed, that we can form no conception of a possible experience for which this does not hold.) Awareness of particular items as spatially ordered and possessing such spatial characteristics as extension and shape depends upon our possession of a faculty of spatial or "outer" intuition, called *outer sense*. To say that space is just a form of our sensibility (the form of outer sense) carries *some* of the same implications as to say that time is. That is to say, it is simply a feature of our cognitive constitution that the effect of objects as they are in themselves upon that constitution is to yield awareness of items spatially ordered and possessing spatial characteristics. But there are differences between what can be affirmed regarding the two forms of sensible intuition. Thus, regarding those things as they are in themselves which affect our faculty of outer sense to yield awareness of spatial items, we cannot affirm that they are the same as, or of the same nature as, ourselves as we are in ourselves. We cannot affirm this, and we cannot deny it either.[1] It is a point on which we must remain ignorant. But however that may be, there is something else which we can affirm. Whether the objects which affect our faculty of outer sense to produce awareness of spatially ordered particular items are in themselves identical with or distinct from ourselves as we are in ourselves, or whether they are of the same nature or of a different nature, we can be sure that their appearances, i.e. the spatially ordered items to our awareness of which they give rise, must be ordered in time as well as in space, i.e. must exhibit relations of simultaneous or successive existence. For all particular states of consciousness, including our perceptions of spatially ordered items, are necessarily ordered in time, and hence those spatially ordered items are so too. Time "is the immediate condition of inner appearances (of our souls) and thereby the mediate condition of outer appearances. . . . All appearances whatever . . . necessarily stand in time-relations."[2]

[1] This point is not explicitly made in the Aesthetic; but it is made later on in the *Critique*, notably in the Paralogisms.

[2] A 34/B 50–1.

That Kant should thus represent the time-relatedness of all spatially related objects of awareness as a consequence of the necessary time-relatedness of all states of consciousness, though perfectly consistent with what has gone before, is a sufficiently striking fact to deserve further comment. It throws into relief a feature of transcendental idealism which we (and he) may at times be prone to overlook, though at other times it is forced upon our attention by his own readiness, at these times, to invoke it. Kant very often accompanies his own assertions of the transcendental ideality of both time and space with an assertion of the empirical reality of both. This, he claims with evident sincerity, distinguishes his idealism from that of Berkeley who "degrades bodies to mere illusion".[1] But we may wonder whether the distinction is as clear as he thought. He may seem, in claiming equal empirical reality for both space and time, to be saying that particular items in space and time, whatever their character, whether that of bodies in space (and time) or states of consciousness in time alone, are on an equal footing as regards actual existence (have equal empirical reality) though all of them are only appearances of things in themselves, i.e. are dependent for their existence on the affecting of ourselves as we are in ourselves by other (or the same) things as they are in themselves. But this is not really the import of his doctrine. The doctrine is not that, by affecting our cognitive constitution, things (including ourselves) as they are in themselves produce two distinct kinds of existences, viz. bodies in space (and time) on the one hand and temporally ordered states of consciousness, including perceptions of those bodies in space, on the other. Rather, *all* the actual effects of these transactions between things in themselves are temporally ordered states of consciousness; but these include (and, it is later argued, if experience is to be possible, they *must* include) states of consciousness that we rate as perceptions of bodies in space. So space and time, bodies and states of consciousness, are not really on the same footing at all. The point may be obscured for us (and for Kant) by his insistence that all things in space and time are equally appearances; but the doctrine has a quite different force in respect of these two classes of things. States of consciousness, ordered in time, are appearances because they are merely effects of things as they are in themselves and not states of some such

[1] B 71.

things (ourselves) as they (we) really, atemporally, are. But bodies in space are appearances in a much stronger sense. They are not even effects of things as they are in themselves. It is simply that among the effects of things as they are in themselves are some states of consciousness which we are constrained to regard as perceptions of bodies in space; and apart from these perceptions bodies are nothing at all.

This aspect of transcendental idealism comes decisively to the fore at certain points where the doctrine is being worked very hard, as it notably is in the solution to the first and second antinomies. It recedes into the background at just the points where the doctrine itself is playing no very active role. Upon the doctrine as a whole I shall forbear now to comment. We must wait till all its ramifications are displayed before attempting a final assessment. Viewing Kant in the imposed role of analyst of the conception of a possible experience, we shall often be able to ignore it altogether. But we must at least have its initial statement before us.

3. FORM AND MATTER: RELATIONS AND SENSATION

Naturally we must ask by what arguments these remarkable doctrines regarding space and time are supported in the Transcendental Aesthetic. Far and away the most important argument, in the case of space, is derived from Kant's view of the nature of the propositions of geometry, of "the mathematics of space" as he elsewhere calls it. It is paralleled by some rather perfunctory references to propositions relating to time which he conceived of as having the same nature as the axioms and theorems of geometry and our knowledge of which therefore seemed to him to require the same kind of explanation. In general the considerations urged in the case of space are richer in content than those urged in the case of time. The latter are but fainter parallels of the former where such parallels are available. To the former, therefore, I shall mainly direct attention. But since Kant's theory of geometry deserves a prolonged consideration which to give it now would too much interrupt the exposition and reconstruction of his general theory of experience, I postpone examination of it to a later part, saying now only that, for all its great insight, it is no longer tenable as a theory of "the mathematics of space" and has no force to establish the thesis of transcendental idealism as regards space.

What other considerations remain? If we set aside the theory of geometry, we must, I think, be struck by the paucity of actual argument for the thesis of transcendental idealism. In so far as we are concerned with Kant's intellectual history, we can refer to those earlier debates, which much engaged his attention, between upholders of absolute and of relational theories of space (and time); and can remark that he thought of transcendental idealism as reconciling the truth in both without falling into the errors of either. But all this is too sketchily indicated in the text to yield an argument independent of that which leans, once more, on the nature of geometrical truth. There are, on the other hand, in the Metaphysical Exposition of the Concept of Space (and the corresponding section relating to time) four passages presented, and numbered, as arguments. Two of them relate to the singularity – or oneness – of space and time, and I shall refer to them in the next section. The other two, though weak in the extreme, I shall consider now; but only to indicate how unilluminating, taken by themselves, they are.

Kant argues, first, that the idea of space cannot be derived from the experience of objects as spatially related to one another or to ourselves. For such experience presupposes the representation of space.[1] The argument is really too short. It is difficult to extract from it anything remotely to the purpose except the tautology that we could not become aware of objects as spatially related unless we had the capacity to do so. If the "presupposing" of the "representation of space" means more than this, the argument, by itself, sheds no light on what more it means.

The next argument turns on the assertions that (*a*) "we can never represent to ourselves the absence of space" though (*b*) "we can quite well think it as empty of objects".[2] This suggests a kind of thought-experiment which we are invited to undertake. But in spite of Kant's confident announcement of the results, it is far from clear what the experiment is or what its results imply. We can, say, close our eyes and imagine a featureless blackness; or say to ourselves the words "limitless empty space" and seem to be meaning something. Does this verify (*b*)? And, if so, what is shown thereby? Is it held that we could not do such things unless

[1] A 23/B 38.   [2] A 24/B 38-9.

the spatial relatedness of items which we are aware of as so related were entirely due to our cognitive constitution? This seems too large a step. What about (*a*)? Perhaps it means that we cannot really make intelligible to ourselves the conception of a wholly non-spatial experience. Perhaps we cannot indeed. But, if so, the point has still to be argued; and, if successfully argued, would establish that space was an *a priori* feature of experience in the sense of the austere interpretation, rather than in that of the transcendental idealist interpretation, of "*a priori*". To derive a transcendental idealist conclusion, we should need a further argument to show that no feature of experience could be *a priori* in the first sense without being *a priori* in the second.

It is clear that little is to be gained by poring over these small units of argument alone. Rather we must try to pick up, from the general course of the Aesthetic, such clues as we can to any considerations other than the argument from geometry which may have seemed to Kant to constitute grounds for the thesis of ideality.

A pointer is suggested by the way in which, in the third paragraph of the Aesthetic, he draws the distinction between the *form* and the *matter* of appearances, i.e. of what we are aware of when we have experience of particular items falling under general concepts. The form is said to be "that which brings it about that the manifold of appearance [i.e. the complex of elements of appearance] allows of being ordered in certain *relations*". The matter is said to be that in appearances which corresponds to *sensation*. Since form is immediately ascribed to the mind, to our cognitive faculties, and since sensation is said to be that in appearances for which responsibility is to be ascribed, not to our cognitive faculties, but to the object which affects them, the general framework of the idealist thesis is already given with this opposition between form and matter; it remains only to ascribe space and time to the formal rather than the material side of it. Nevertheless it seems that we may extract two clues from this rapid construction. The first resides in the connexion between form and relation; the second in the opposition between form and sensation. Can the point of connexion and the point of opposition both be made good in respect of space and time in such a way as to give any independent ground, or even the appearance of any independent ground, for the thesis of ideality?

On the first point we may quote Kant against himself. He admits that there is no inconsistency in both maintaining a relational view of space and time and denying their transcendental ideality.[1] The objection to such a position, he says, is that it leaves us unable to account for that knowledge of necessary truths regarding things in space and time of which geometry provides a brilliant example. We can free ourselves of the Newtonian encumbrances of space and time considered as independent existences ("two eternal and infinite self-subsistent non-entities")[2] simply by regarding them as systems of relations between particular items such as we encounter in experience. But if we stop at this point, we shall have no adequate theory of our mathematical knowledge of Nature. We shall have to conclude that if the propositions of geometry hold of spatial things, it is merely a contingent truth that they do so. But this conclusion we know to be false. We can avoid this conclusion only by taking the further step of acknowledging that the spatial and temporal systems of relations between particular items encountered in experience have their source in our own minds alone. So Kant argues; and, in so arguing, he makes it clear that there is no independent step from the relational character of space and time (as features of appearances) to their ideality. The argument from geometry cannot thus be dispensed with.

Illusion may be fostered on this point, as I have already hinted, by the epistemological slant of the inquiry. Stressing the connexion between "form" and "relation", and removing the epistemological slant, we could express the doctrine that space and time are the forms of intuition by writing: space and time are the fundamental systems of relations between particular items encountered in experience; or by writing: the spatial and the temporal are the fundamental modes in which particular items encountered in experience are related to one another. Re-introducing the epistemological slant, we re-write the latter formulation as follows: the spatial and the temporal are the fundamental modes in which *we become aware of* particular items encountered in experience as related to one another. The re-writing introduces the ambiguity I have already remarked on.

What of the opposition between space and time, as forms, on the one hand, and "what belongs to sensation" on the other?

---

[1] See A 39–41/B 56–8.   [2] A 39/B 56.

Kant particularizes the nature of the opposition in the case of space, and, in doing so, shows that the point has not so much to do with space as with spatiality, not so much with the idea of a system of spatially related items as with the idea of spatial characteristics and relations in general. After remarking that a pure form of sensibility may also itself be called a pure intuition, he proceeds:

> If I take away from the representation of body . . . what belongs to sensation, impenetrability, hardness, colour, etc., something still remains over from this empirical intuition, namely extension and figure. These belong to pure intuition which, even without any actual object of the senses or of sensation, exists in the mind *a priori*.[1]

We are, it seems, on familiar ground, ground trodden over by Locke and, in a different spirit, by Berkeley. We may be tempted immediately to echo Berkeley's criticisms of Locke. If we really abstract from colour and hardness and all that "belongs to sensation", so far from being left with with "pure" notions of extension and figure, we are left with nothing but words emptied of meaning – emptied at least of all meaning which could plausibly be represented as connected with any kind of intuition, i.e. with anything at all analogous to sensible awareness of particular items. (The words in question might have conferred upon them a purely logical force by their place as uninterpreted signs in a formal system.) But however just the Berkeleian protest may be in itself, it would, to some extent, be misdirected here. Kant's doctrine of pure intuition is not conceived in the same spirit as Locke's doctrine of primary qualities. Of the two sentences I quoted it is the second, not the first, which provides the truer indication of the nature of that doctrine. The doctrine is that "without any *actual* object of the senses, or of sensation" being present, we have the faculty of giving ourselves, in imagination, individual exemplars of figures answering to certain spatial concepts (e.g. that of a triangle) with the help of which we can determine that all things answering to those concepts necessarily possess certain other properties or relations their possession of which does not follow logically from those concepts alone.[2]

The Berkeleian protest, it is true, is muted rather than silenced.

[1] A 20–1/B 35.   [2] Cf. A 713/B 741.

The first of the two quoted sentences must at least be judged misleading. For it may be pointed out that we could not exercise this faculty of imaginative construction without exercising it in some sensory mode, say the visual; and it is hard to understand what could be meant by visualizing a line without visualizing what, in the broadest sense of the expression, can be called a colour-boundary. But we need not press the protest. We can see that the point Kant is really concerned to make – however misleadingly he makes it – in opposing to "what belongs to sensation" a certain class of spatial concepts, including, notably, concepts of spatial figures, is the point that we do not depend upon the results of empirical observation of the characteristics and relations of objects actually encountered in experience in order to determine that certain properties necessarily belong to things falling under concepts belonging to this class. We depend, indeed, for this result, on the exercise of our faculty of sensible intuition: but only on its "pure", not on its "empirical", exercise.

My suggestion is, then, that the most we can find, beyond a mere affirmation of the doctrine of transcendental idealism, in the opposition between space and time and what "belongs to sensation" is a brief and possibly confused presentation of the doctrine of pure intuition which is to be developed to solve the problem of our knowledge of geometrical truths.[1] Once more we find no independent argument for the thesis that space is *a priori* in the sense of transcendental idealism. All the considerations we have so far before us, if they are more than simple affirmations of that doctrine, rest upon the argument from geometry.

4. THE UNITY OF SPACE AND TIME

There are at least three distinguishable, though connected, ways in which Kant couples the expressions "*a priori*" and "intuition" in his discussion of space. At least two of them have parallels in the case of time. First, he declares that *space and time are* a priori

---

[1] The charge of confusion might be variously based. E.g. it might be pointed out that Kant's claim that we have knowledge, not grounded in empirical observation, of propositions relating to geometrical figures could be paralleled by a similar claim regarding propositions about colour-relations. But colour is instanced by Kant as a prime example of "what belongs to sensation".

forms of empirical intuition – a doctrine we have already discussed both in its austere and in its transcendental idealist interpretation. Second, he declares that *we have a faculty or power of* a priori *or non-empirical spatial intuition*, by the exercise of which we have knowledge of geometrical truths – a doctrine we have alluded to. Third, he declares that *space and time are themselves* a priori *intuitions*.

It is the third doctrine, set out in the last two numbered paragraphs of the Metaphysical Expositions, which now concerns us. The central thoughts appear to be that there is but one space and one time and that both are infinite. Let us attend, first, to the former thought. We can best understand its force by considering an objection which might, in the case of space, be raised against it. To say that there is only one space is to say at least that every spatially related object is spatially related to every other such object. It is to say that there is only one system of spatially related things. To this it might be objected that there do in fact exist spatially independent systems of spatially related things. For example, the elements of one person's (X's) visual image may have spatial relations to each other, and so may the elements of another person's (Y's) visual image. But it makes no sense to inquire about the spatial relations between elements in X's visual image and elements in Y's visual image. They have no common space. Further, it makes no sense to inquire about the spatial relations between elements in my visual image and parts of my body or objects in my room. The space which includes the ink-bottle on my table does not include the ink-bottle in my mind's eye. The ink-bottle in my mind's eye does not take up or occupy any part of the space to which my physical ink-bottle belongs.

It is clear that even if what is contended in this objection is true, Kant would regard it as irrelevant. The class of spatially related items of which he asserts that every member is spatially related to every other in a single comprehensive system is the class of public physical bodies, conceived of by us as objects of our perception distinct from our perceptions of them and from states of consciousness in general. It is the space occupied by such bodies that he declares to be unitary and unique.

Now it seems true that we do have such a conception of physical space, and it also seems true that, even without the limitation implied by the word "physical", we have a similar conception of time. Of any actual item that stands in temporal relation to any other we think that it stands in temporal relations to *every* other such item. All actual temporal particulars we think of as related in a single system of temporal relations, just as all material particulars are thought of as related in a single spatial system. We have, that is, the conception of a single spatio-temporal system embracing everything that happens and everything that physically exists.[1]

How is the fact that we conceive of space and time in this way to be related to Kant's assertion that space and time are pure or *a priori* intuitions? As regards the word "intuition", again contrasted with "concept", we may take him, in part at least, to be making the point that the word "space" is used in two different ways, in one of which it is a general-concept word and in the other of which it is not. Thus we may think of a particular space of three cubic feet as an instance of the general concept "space of three cubic feet". Again we may say that the space bounded by the floor, walls, and ceiling of one room is larger than the space bounded by the floor, walls, and ceiling of another; both are particular instances of the concept of "a space". But these particular spaces, though each is an instance of "a space", are not instances of space (or Space) in the sense in which we have just been using the word, i.e. in relation to the comprehensive system of spatially related physical things. Rather, they are *parts* of space. Similarly for "times" and "time".

Let this serve, for the moment, as an elucidation of this use of "intuition" in connexion with space and time. So understood, the employment of the word evidently adds nothing to the doctrine of the uniqueness of space and time. What, then, of the qualification "*a priori*"? Are we to take it that the *singularity* of space and time is itself to be attributed to our faculty of sensibility? Perhaps so. But the convergence of different lines of thought at this point,

[1] It would be incorrect to say that relativity physics has forced us to abandon this conception. It has only forced us to modify it. We still think of every physical particular (event or object) as spatially and temporally related to every other; only we may no longer think that determinations of temporal relations, length, speed of change, etc., are independent of the reference-point from which these determinations are made. The fundamental conception of a single comprehensive system is not imperilled by the non-uniqueness of possible ways of ordering (in space or in time) the items which it comprehends.

and a certain lack of integration of the doctrine of the Aesthetic with that of the Transcendental Analytic makes for some difficulty in interpretation.

Let us turn first to our relatively austere sense of "*a priori*". To hold that the unity of space and time was in this sense *a priori* would be to hold that it was an essential element in any coherent conception of experience that we could form. I have already remarked that the space declared to be "essentially one" can only be understood to be physical space, the space in which there stand, mutually related, public physical bodies conceived of by us as objects distinct from our perceptions of them. To hold that the conception of a single unitary spatio-temporal system is "*a priori*" in the austere sense is, then, already to be involved in a quite complex commitment regarding necessary features of our experience: a commitment, first, to (a form of) the objectivity thesis; second, to the spatiality thesis; and, finally, to the thesis of spatio-temporal unity. There is no doubt that Kant is committed on all these points; and if the *Critique* as a whole has a single governing idea, it is that the existence of *a priori* necessities in the austere sense is explicable only by the thesis that such necessities reflect nothing but features of our cognitive constitution. But to appeal at this point to these necessities to justify the attribution of the singularity of space and time to our faculty of sensibility would seem to lack consonance with the fact that the topics of objectivity and unity are among the central themes of the Analytic, which is supposed to explore the conditions imposed by understanding, rather than sensibility, on the nature of our experience. The point is worth making, not with a view to trying to make Kant's model of faculties work smoothly, but with a view to ascertaining to what extent theses affirmed in the Aesthetic are to be regarded as presupposed in the argument of the Analytic.

If we turn to the actual remarks in the text by which Kant supports the declaration that space and time are not only intuitions (i.e. each essentially one) but pure or *a priori* intuitions, they seem to amount to this: that the notions of a single unlimited or infinite space and a single unlimited or infinite time are in some sense *prior* to any notions we may form of particular or limited spaces or times. We cannot arrive at the idea of an infinite all-embracing space by making it up (composing it), as it were, out of previously given constituent spaces; on the contrary, we only get the idea of

E

particular spaces through limitation introduced into the one infinite and all-embracing space.

How are we to interpret this? We can scarcely take it as a remark about the order in which ideas are explicitly framed in human thinking. So taken, we should have to regard it as unsatisfactory, since the two alternatives mentioned are not exhaustive and neither is so plausible as a third: viz. that, while we do not indeed form the idea of the one all-embracing space merely by a kind of mental addition of different experienced spaces, we do form it subsequently to operation with spatial concepts over limited extents (experience of diverse spaces).

If we take the remark as relating to an order of conceptual presupposition rather than an order of the temporal framing of concepts, it is equally unsatisfactory. It could well be maintained that the idea of the one all-embracing space was really implicit in our ordinary mode of operation with ordinary spatial concepts in application to empirical reality, to what we count as real physical space. But this would not constitute a case for an award of conceptual priority. The idea of particular spaces, determined by particular sets of spatially related physical objects, perhaps involves the idea of the one all-embracing space, comprehending all such objects; but the idea of the one all-embracing space, comprehending all spatially related physical objects, quite certainly involves the idea of particular spaces, determined by particular sets of such things.

I do not think we can understand Kant's thought here without referring once more to the argument from geometry. In Kant's view our knowledge of geometrical truths, though dependent upon intuition, is independent of empirical intuition. It depends in no way upon observation of actual physical objects such as we become aware of through the senses. It depends entirely on the exercise of the faculty of pure spatial intuition. We may, if we like, exercise this faculty with the help of physical lines drawn on physical paper. But we can equally well exercise it in imagination. By its exercise we obtain knowledge not merely of the necessary characteristics of spatial figures (e.g. triangles and circles) which we construct in pure intuition; we obtain knowledge also of the necessary characteristics of the space in which we construct them, e.g. that it is infinite and three-dimensional. We can thus properly describe infinite (Euclidean) space itself as a pure intuition, i.e. as a product of the exercise of the faculty of pure intuition. The thesis of transcendental idealism, as regards space, is the complex thesis that the faculty of spatial intuition, or spatial awareness, which *can* be exercised *purely*, i.e. quite independently of any affecting of our cognitive constitution by things as they are in themselves, is the very same faculty which, in a different role, is, as it were, excited by the effect upon us of things as they are in themselves and which is then responsible for our awareness of spatially ordered and spatially characterized items in empirical intuition. This is the reason why the pure mathematics of space is also the mathematics of physical space, why the propositions of pure geometry necessarily hold of the physical objects of empirical intuition.

This theory of geometry is, as I have said, to be evaluated later. But reference to it now helps to make some things clearer. When Kant claims the status of *a priori* intuition for infinite space, we can understand him to be thinking of the results of the pure or non-empirical exercise of the faculty of spatial intuition. We do not have to suppose him committed to affirming that the idea of particular *empirical* spaces, determined by particular sets of spatially related bodies, involves that of the one all-embracing space, which comprehends all bodies so related, while denying the converse implication. On the contrary – though it is far from obvious that Kant was clear on this point – the way is open for the admission that the thesis of the necessary unity of physical space, comprehending all spatially related bodies, cannot rest on considerations advanced in the Aesthetic alone. Geometry has nothing to say about there being only one comprehensive system of physical bodies.

Even the first two numbered paragraphs of the Metaphysical Exposition, which I dismissed as unhelpful, become clearer in this light. The presupposed "representation of space" of argument 1, the ability to "think it empty of objects" of argument 2, can perhaps both be understood as allusions to the pure or non-empirical exercise of the faculty of spatial intuition. Of course, if we do understand these phrases in this way, we reduce the paragraphs which contain them to mere dependents of the argument from geometry. They lose their status as independent arguments. But that, in their case, is not very much to lose.

Once more, then, we are led to the conclusion that the qualification of space and time as *"a priori"* in the sense or senses of transcendental subjectivism (in any sense which implies that they are "in us prior to experience"), whether it takes the form of declaring that space and time are themselves *a priori* intuitions or that of declaring that they are *a priori* forms of (empirical) intuition, rests on no ground independent of the argument from geometry or its perfunctory parallel in the case of time.

5. "*A PRIORI*" AND "INNATE"

I have referred so far to two senses or interpretations of the expression "*a priori*". In the first, or austere, interpretation a concept or feature (element) could be called *a priori* if it was an essential structural element in any conception of experience which we could make intelligible to ourselves. In the second, or transcendental idealist, interpretation to call an element *a priori* was to claim that its presence as a feature of experience was attributable entirely to the nature of our cognitive constitution and not at all to the nature of those things, as they are in themselves, which affect that constitution to yield experience. It might be urged that in limiting attention to these two interpretations of the expression, I have neglected a third sense which it may bear, one which is familiar in the history of philosophy; and that some of Kant's arguments might be more satisfactorily taken as intended to establish that our *ideas* of space and time (rather than space and time themselves) were *a priori* in this third sense. The third sense is that expressed, in those old and picturesque debates regarding the origin of our ideas, by the word "innate". Perhaps at least some of Kant's arguments should be interpreted as intended to establish that the ideas of space and time had the character which Descartes and Leibniz claimed for at least some of our ideas and which Locke and Hume, in asserting that all our ideas were derived from experience, denied to them all.

There are two good reasons for rejecting this suggestion. In the first place, whatever genuine questions were at issue in these debates, they tended to be hopelessly obscured by the terms in which the debates were conducted. Those terms are rich enough, over-rich, in metaphorical suggestion: ideas as characters written on the tablets of the mind (copied from experienced originals or inscribed by the hand of God); or ideas as furnishings of the mind's house (picked up at that general store, experience, or built-in structural features). Even if a determined effort is made to escape from such pictures, the debate about origins is apt to remain a sterile exchange of points: on the one hand, that all capacities to think, recognize, classify, etc., have to be acquired (for an infant does not think at all), on the other, that the acquisition of such capacities presupposes the capacity to acquire them.

The second reason for rejecting the suggestion is decisive. Whatever the thesis of innateness might be supposed to mean, it would have no interest for Kant in respect of any of the "representations" which he declares to be *a priori* except in so far as it is coupled with, or has as a consequence, the thesis that the manifestation of the corresponding feature in experience, its presence in the world, is attributable solely to our cognitive constitution, the nature of our faculties, and not to the character of those things, as they are in themselves, which affect our constitution to yield experience, to yield, indeed, our world. Kant would have no interest in a thesis to the effect that the *ideas* of space and time were "in us prior to experience" which did not carry with it the thesis that space and time themselves were in us prior to experience. *Mutatis mutandis*, he later explicitly makes a parallel point in rejecting a parallel suggestion regarding the categories, the *a priori* elements in experience supposed to be contributed by understanding.[1]

6. CONCLUDING REMARKS

[1] The Aesthetic contains or implies a number of theses which, if we were invited simply to pronounce upon their truth without commitment as to their logical character, we should be ready enough to declare to be true, or at least to accept as faithful reflections of our actual working conception of experience and the world. They include the following: (*a*) that particular states of consciousness are temporally ordered; (*b*) that such states include sense-perceptions of particular items, conceived of as existing independently of states of consciousness, which are both temporally and spatially ordered; (*c*) that the space in which these particular items are ordered is unitary, i.e. that each such item is spatially related to every other; (*d*) that the time in which both these items and the states of consciousness which include sense-

[1] B 167–8.

perceptions of them are ordered is unitary, i.e. that every particular item constituting, or encountered in, experience is temporally related to every other.

[2]   Intertwined with these unexceptionable theses is the complex doctrine of transcendental idealism, its complexity reflected in the connected theses that space and time are *a priori* forms of empirical intuition, that they are themselves pure intuitions and that we have the faculty of pure or *a priori* spatial and temporal intuition. This striking doctrine, in all its complexity, rests on no discernible support in the Transcendental Aesthetic other than the argument from geometry in the case of space and perfunctory suggestions of parallel argument in the case of time. The vital premise of the argument from geometry is that geometrical propositions are known to hold necessarily of physical objects in space.

[3]   With regard to the unexceptionable theses listed at [1], the question arises which of them embody *a priori* features of our conception of experience in the relatively austere sense of that expression which I have alluded to. It is very far from obvious that all of them do. Though perhaps everyone would be prepared to acknowledge, for example, that the idea of a unitary physical space forms part of our actual working conception of reality, there is plenty of evidence, in the shape of literary and philosophical fantasy, of preparedness to challenge the thesis that we can form no coherent alternative conception which lacks this feature. Now a major part of our interest in the *Critique* is to be interest in the question, how far Kant succeeds in establishing that certain features are, in the austere sense, *a priori* features of our conception of experience. Wherever he may be taken to be claiming this character for some feature of that conception, we must, of course, be prepared for his linking the claim to, and explaining it by, the further claim that the feature in question has its source in our cognitive faculties alone. But it would be a mistake to think that, because a feature of our conception of experience figures prominently in the Aesthetic, we may conclude that Kant assigns its provenance exclusively to sensibility and hence that no further argument is to be expected tending to establish its claim as an *a priori* feature of our conception of experience. To lapse into the

idiom of Kant's own model: the co-operation of the faculty of sensibility with another faculty, that of understanding, is essential to experience. We may confidently expect further elaboration of the model of our faculties responding to things as they are in themselves to yield experience. We may also at least hope for further analytical argument tending, perhaps, to secure to some features already mentioned, as well as to features yet to be mentioned, the status of *a priori* elements in our conception of experience.

II

OBJECTIVITY AND UNITY

1. PROGRAMME FOR THE ANALYTIC

Against the background of transcendental idealism, the rich idiom of faculties provides a simple-sounding statement of the aims of the next stage of the critical inquiry. The co-operation of sensibility and understanding is essential to experience, as is also the excitement of these faculties by things as they are in themselves. What sensibility brings *a priori* to experience has already been declared in a Transcendental Aesthetic. It is for a Transcendental Logic to determine the *a priori* contribution of understanding. This science "will concern itself with the laws of understanding ... solely in so far as they relate *a priori* to objects".[1]

If we attempt to detach this statement of aims from the transcendental idealist background, and to re-phrase it in our austerer idiom, we may seem to be faced with a fairly blank prospect. For experience to be possible at all, we must become aware of particular items and become aware of them as falling under general concepts. Thus we render the duality of intuitions and concepts, the necessary co-operation of sensibility and understanding. We can conceive of no form of experience which does not involve a temporal ordering of the particular items of which we become aware; and perhaps (though this has still to be argued) we cannot coherently conceive of any form of experience which does not involve a spatial ordering of at least some of those items. Thus we render the thesis of the Aesthetic regarding the *a priori* contributions of sensibility. What question now confronts us? It seems that the question must run something like this: abstracting from the forms of particularity, from the temporal and spatial ordering of particular items encountered in experience, what features can we find to be necessarily involved in any coherent conception of experience solely in virtue of the fact that the particular items of which we become aware must fall under (be brought under) general concepts?

[1] A 57/B 81–2.

The question seems to offer us rather little to work on: nothing, indeed, as Kant blandly puts it, but "the form of the thought of an object in general".[1] As the investigation proceeds, however, we become aware that the word "object" is to be taken more weightily than we might at first have thought. It means something more than merely a particular instance of a general concept. It carries connotations of "objectivity". To know something about an object, e.g. that it falls under such-and-such a general concept, is to know something that holds irrespective of the occurrence of any particular state of consciousness, irrespective of the occurrence of any particular experience of awareness of the object as falling under the general concept in question. Judgements about objects, if valid, are objectively valid, valid independently of the occurrence of the particular state of awareness, of the particular experience, which issues in the judgement.

If we are to view Kant as analyst of the structure of the conception of experience in general, then it must be with mixed feelings that we recognize the weight of the word "object". On the one hand we are offered the hope that the inquiry into the "*a priori* contribution of understanding" may be more fruitful than at first seemed likely. It may very well be that we can form no conception of experience, understood as including knowledge of objects in this weighty sense, except one which involves the employment of certain identifiable general concepts, or types of general concept, over and above such merely temporal or merely spatial concepts as we presumably must be equipped with if the austerely interpreted doctrine of the Aesthetic is true. If this is so, it will be the task of the Analytic to identify such concepts, or concept-types, and to show that they have this status. Clearly Kant thinks there are such concepts and has his name for them ready: they are the categories, the pure concepts of the understanding.

Recognition of the weight of the word "object", then, may encourage our hopes in one way. But it may seem to disappoint them in another and more important way. If it is to be a matter of the definition of the word "experience" that experience necessarily includes knowledge of objects in the weighty sense, then some interest evaporates from the analytical enterprise. At first the inquiry may seem to proceed as if it *is* a matter of definition,

[1] A 51/B 75.

as if the thesis that experience includes knowledge of objects in this sense is to be treated as a fundamental *premise* of the analytical argument. But as the argument develops, it becomes happily clear that this is not so, that this thesis is to yield its place as a premise to a more fundamental principle from which it is itself derived, a principle which we shall now simply name as that of the necessary unity of consciousness. This surrender, on the part of the principle of objective knowledge, of its status as a premise of the inquiry restores to the latter all the depth and interest which we were threatened with the loss of. What we have to do, then, is to follow and interpret the argument as best we can, acquiescing in the temporary usurpation, prepared for the moment at which the truly sovereign premise asserts its supremacy.

2. FORMAL LOGIC AND TRANSCENDENTAL LOGIC

Kant turns first to formal logic for a clue to the discovery of categories. I shall try to reconstruct, without dependence on the model associated with transcendental subjectivity, the reasoning which leads to this step—a line of reasoning initially not unattractive, which collapses, however, on closer examination.

We begin with a re-affirmation of the already familiar point that all experience, all empirical knowledge, requires the co-operation of sensibility and understanding, i.e. the awareness of particular objects as falling under general concepts; only the point is modified by the provision that the word "objects" is to be taken in the weighty sense I have just alluded to. What is now to engage our attention is what is involved in the recognition of objects as falling under *concepts*, the "bringing of them under concepts". This is identical with making *judgements* about objects. "The only use which the understanding can make . . . of concepts is to judge by means of them."[1] To bring an object under a concept involves thinking that a certain proposition is true of the object or is objectively valid. Empirical knowledge, like all knowledge, is essentially expressible in propositions.

Now we have already available, in formal logic, a complete and completely general classification of the general forms of the proposition. Formal logic supplies us, as it were, with the complete

[1] A 68/B 93.

theory of the general forms of thought. Any proposition or judgement whatever must possess one or other of the general forms recognized and classified in formal logic. This does not mean that formal logic supplies us directly with what we are seeking, i.e. general concepts which must have application to objects of experience. For in formal logic proper, as Kant repeatedly insists, no account is taken of the conditions which objects must satisfy in order for the different "functions of judgement" discriminated in formal logic to be exercised in the making of objectively valid judgements. General logic, as he calls it, is not concerned with the relations of its forms to objects, but with the logical relations which hold between the forms themselves. "General logic abstracts from all content of knowledge, i.e. from all relation of knowledge to an object, and considers only the logical form in the relation of any knowledge to any other knowledge."[1] General logic makes use of such concepts as those of truth, subject, predicate, hypothetical proposition, etc. It tells us, for example, that given the truth of a hypothetical proposition and the truth of its antecedent, then the truth of its consequent necessarily follows. But it has nothing directly to say about the conditions under which the hypothetical form of proposition can itself be used to make true or valid judgements about objects, about the conditions, that is to say, under which we can truly or validly affirm that one possible state of affairs is so related to another that, given the first, we may conclude to the existence of the second. Again, general logic offers us, in the case of singular propositions, the idea of something which appears as the subject of predication but not itself as a predicate; but it says nothing about the conditions under which we can make use of this idea in judgements about objects.

Nevertheless, although formal logic abstracts in this way from all relation of its forms to objects of empirical judgement, it is surely possible to form the idea of another parallel "logic" (transcendental logic) which does not abstract from this relation. For experience or empirical knowledge to be possible, we must make empirical judgements. The forms which logic isolates are the forms we must use in making such judgements. So much is a necessity of thought, of the whole business of bringing objects under concepts. Therefore we must have some conception of the

[1] A 55/B 79.

general conditions of applying these forms in making true empirical judgements, valid judgements about objects of experience; and the general conditions of applying these forms to objects must be objectively satisfied, otherwise we could never make objectively valid judgements, and empirical knowledge, or experience, would be impossible. So if, for every fundamental form of logic, we frame the idea of the general condition of its application to objects of experience, the result in each case will be a pure concept or category – i.e. a general concept which has necessary application to the world of experience.

Such is the general line of the (reconstructed) reasoning. The statement of Kant's own which approximates most closely to the form in which I have just stated it is probably that found in the Prolegomena. At Section 39 of that work we have: "The work of the logicians lay before me, finished. . . . I referred these functions of judging [i.e. forms, or formal features, of propositions] to objects in general, or rather to the conditions of determining judgements as objectively valid, and there arose pure concepts of the understanding. . . ." It must be admitted that when we look at the Table of Categories and compare it with the logical Table of Judgements, the former in general do not seem to us to "arise" from the latter in quite the effortless and inevitable manner which Kant's wording suggests. But that is another matter which we will put on one side for the time being.

Before we consider more closely the nature of the general argument underlying this derivation, we should ask how far Kant is remaining faithful to the announced intention of eliciting the *a priori* contribution to experience of understanding alone. That is to say, is the argument so far really to be understood as abstracting from the necessity of a temporal (and perhaps also a spatial) ordering of particular items encountered in experience? There is a section of the *Critique* which prompts the question and the opening sentences of which may suggest a negative answer to it. The passage, which immediately precedes the actual derivation of the categories, begins:

> General logic, as has been repeatedly said, abstracts from all content of knowledge and looks to some other source, whatever that may be, for the representations which it is to transform into concepts. . . . Transcendental logic, on the other

hand, has lying before it a manifold of *a priori* sensibility, presented by transcendental aesthetic. . . . Space and time contain a manifold of pure, *a priori* intuition.[1]

As the passage proceeds, however, it becomes clear that the specifically spatial and temporal character of our forms of intuition is not to be invoked at this stage. What is to be invoked is the notion of "the synthetic unity of the manifold in an intuition *in general*".[2] This is an anticipatory reference to doctrines to be developed in the Transcendental Deduction. For the moment we must be content with the declaration that this "synthetic unity of the manifold" is required for knowledge of objects and is the product of the understanding.

There are, moreover, decisive independent reasons for holding that the spatio-temporality of experience is not being invoked at this stage. The categories as now derived are "unschematized". The schematized categories are held to be concepts which must have application if the forms of general logic are to be used in making judgements about objects of an experience which *is* specifically *temporal* in character. They are derived from the unschematized categories by the *addition* of this condition; and it is when we consider what their necessary applicability involves that we come to appreciate the necessity of their having application to *spatial* objects, objects of outer sense. Hence the original derivation of the categories in the sections we are now considering – the "Metaphysical Deduction" of the categories – cannot be held to rest on the spatio-temporal character of experience. We must take it that the categories are here derived simply by adding to the forms of logic the idea of applying those forms in making true judgements about objects of awareness (intuition) in general, whatever the character of our modes of awareness of these objects may be.

It is, of course, easier to say this than to understand what it means. But in a sense we can understand it. We can see Kant here as pushing to the limit the distinction between intuitions and concepts, sensibility and understanding, trying to extract as much as he can of the *a priori* conditions of empirical knowledge or experience from a consideration merely of one half of this distinction, namely the necessity of bringing particular objects of

[1] A 76–7/B 102.   [2] A 79/B 105.

experience – whatever the "forms of particularity" may be – under general concepts. To do this – and here I outline again the argument – we must use the forms distinguished in logic. Logic offers us analytic truths about the logical relations between these forms, tells us, e.g. that if a judgement of one form is true, then a related judgement of another form must be true (or false). But it tells us nothing about the conditions under which individual judgements of different forms are empirically true, true of objects of experience. To have empirical knowledge, it is not enough that we should be able to calculate, to infer, given the truth of a judgement of one form, the truth of a judgement of another. We must know the empirical truth of individual judgements. If, whatever our experience of objects may in fact be like, there is some condition which must be satisfied, some concept which must have application, for one or another of these forms to be applied so as to yield a true judgement about objects of experience, then that concept will have necessary application in experience, even though the full elucidation of what it means for that concept to have application in experience will have to wait upon adding the condition of spatio-temporality. And the necessity of application of such concepts will be traceable simply to the necessity of bringing objects under concepts, i.e. to pure understanding alone.

So much for the general form of the argument and the assumptions upon which it rests. Serious doubts arise when we look a little more closely. Let us consider first Kant's classification of the "logical functions of judgement", given in the Table of Judgements. The formal features he lists are grouped under four heads, each with three sub-divisions. Universal, particular, and singular forms are distinguished under the head of *quantity*; affirmative, negative, and "infinite" under the head of *quality*; categorical, hypothetical, and disjunctive under that of *relation*; and under the head of *modality* a distinction is drawn between judgements to the effect that something is possibly, actually, or necessarily the case. We may note that it is not entirely clear what this is a list of. It is certainly not, nor does Kant regard it as, a list of logical forms co-ordinate with one another; a categorical proposition might, for example, be universal or singular. Nor is it exactly, though perhaps Kant does regard it as, a list of four sets of features such that the logical form of any proposition is determined when it is specified which of three mutually exclusive features from each of four sets the proposition possesses. A hypothetical proposition, for example, might have a universal antecedent and a singular consequent. Is it then universal or singular? Clearly the relations between the classifications are at least a little more complex than this suggestion would allow; and there are oddities of inclusion and arrangement which set a pattern to be repeated with persistent artificiality throughout the Transcendental Logic.

It would be pointless to dwell on imperfections of detail in Kant's Table of Judgements. He has made, at least, a list of features for which it is claimed that they are all fundamental to the classification of logical forms of proposition, and that there are no others which are. The idea is to construct a parallel list of what might be called putative categorial interpretations, one for each feature; i.e. a list of concepts for which it is claimed that the appropriate concept is applied or used whenever a judgement which exhibits the corresponding formal feature is made about objects of experience. Each of the concepts in this parallel list may be held to have necessary application to empirical reality.

But we must pause over this conclusion. It is true that knowledge (in any sense, at least, in which we are concerned with it) is essentially expressible in propositions. But it does not follow that every form, or every formal feature, of propositions which the logician thinks it worth while to distinguish is absolutely necessary in the expression of knowledge. Given a certain indispensable minimum equipment of notions, the logician can, if he chooses, distinguish indefinitely many forms of proposition, all belonging to formal logic. If we allowed a category for each form, we should have indefinitely many categories. But Kant claims that his list of categories is complete and exhaustive. "I knew beyond doubt that exactly these, and only so many of them, neither more nor less, could constitute our whole knowledge of things out of pure understanding."[1]

Now what Kant was here claiming to be complete was not the entire list of all pure concepts of the understanding; for he suggests that it would be a "not unpleasant task" to work out a system of derivative concepts, which would be equally pure or *a priori*, from his fundamental list.[2] He was claiming that he had a complete list of the *primitive* or underived pure concepts of the understanding. Only these deserved the name of categories; for

---

[1] *Prolegomena*, 39.   [2] A 82/B 108.

their derivatives he reserved the name "predicables". And this, especially in the light of post-Kantian developments in logic, should make us more seriously critical of Kant's list of logical forms or formal features. For a form or feature to deserve a place in the list, it is not sufficient that it should be a possible logical form or feature, one which a logician can frame out of his fundamental resources or describe in terms of them. It must be an essential form or feature, one which exhibits, as no other can, some part of those fundamental and indispensable resources themselves. Only under this condition can we safely even try to derive a category, an indispensable conceptual element in our thought about objects, from a logical form or feature of propositions. But it is by no means clear that this condition is satisfied by all the items in Kant's list. For instance, that list includes the hypothetical and disjunctive forms, the analogues of which in modern logic are interdefinable with the help of negation. It is not enough that these are forms which the logician can frame, or even forms which we in fact use. For if the form is derivative, then any pure concept the use of which is involved in the use of the form is derivative also and hence not a category.

If we are to take the clue from formal logic seriously, we must think again. We must ask what is the minimum that the logician must acknowledge in the way of logical forms. This brings us up against the difficulty that, as far as logical forms are concerned, the logician's choice of primitives *is* a choice. For example the idea of quantification in general may be said to be a primitive idea in modern logic in that it cannot, except for an antecedently limited language, be defined in terms of propositional constants, names, and predicates; but it is a matter of choice whether we introduce the existential quantifier without a formal definition and define the universal quantifier in terms of it, or vice versa. So it is better, even as far as a single system of logic is concerned, to think, not of fundamental logical forms, but of fundamental logical ideas – the basic equipment of notions out of which the logical system is built. Even to proceed in this way is to make a choice; for it is to choose one system of logic rather than another. Perhaps this last point is not very serious. For it seems certain that there is some set of fundamental notions which must be represented in one way or another in anything we could properly recognize as a comprehensive and adequate logic of statements. And it seems unlikely that we shall go very far astray if we take current logic, in which economy of primitive concepts has been so assiduously pursued, as our guide. Current logic is usually presented in two parts: propositional logic, or the logic of truth-functions; and predicate logic, or the logic of quantification. At its basis there lie, correspondingly, two fundamental and underived ideas: first, the idea of truth-functional composition in general; second, the general idea of quantification.

Neither idea seems likely to yield much of a harvest in the way of categories. There can be no particular way in which we *must* conceive of objects of experience in order for truth-functional composition of statements about such objects to be possible. Granted that the necessary conditions of making *atomic* objective judgements are fulfilled, the possibility of truth-functionally compounding such judgements cannot turn on our possession of any further *a priori* concepts of an object in general. Similarly for quantification. Granted that we are ever able to make a particular objective judgement to the effect that a certain *specified* thing has a certain predicate, it is difficult to believe that any further assumptions about how we must conceive of objects can be necessary in order to explain the possibility of a judgement to the effect that something or other, *unspecified*, has that predicate – i.e. in order to explain the possibility of quantification.

The points here are two. The first is that all the special forms of truth-functional composition can be defined in terms of the idea of truth-functional composition in general, which itself can be fully explained in terms of the notion of a proposition as something which is true or false but not both, while all forms involving quantification can be defined in terms either of existential or of universal quantification, together with truth-functional composition. The second is that "referring" the general notions of truth-functional composition and of quantification "to the conditions of determining judgements as objectively valid" can yield nothing in the way of "*a priori* concepts of an object in general" *which is not already contained in the notion of a singular subject–predicate proposition*, i.e. a formally atomic proposition in which a one-or-more-place predicate is applied to one or more specified objects of reference. If, then, we are to make *any* use of the clue provided by formal logic, it is to this single notion that we must turn.

The formally atomic proposition is something which is

F

essentially determinable as true or false and which essentially involves the introduction of general concepts and their application to specified or identified instances; it essentially involves predicating concepts of identified objects of reference. Following the clue from logic, then, will consist in asking the following question: How in general must we conceive of objects if we are to make empirical judgements, determinable as true or false, in which we predicate concepts of identified objects of reference? or: What in general must be true of a world of objects of which we make such judgements? But now it seems that the question adds little or nothing to the question we set out with: viz. what is involved in bringing objects of experience under concepts, i.e. in making judgements, determinable as true or false, about objects of experience? The excursion through the forms of logic has not advanced us a single step. We are left merely with the notion of unschematized categories, if any, corresponding to the logical distinction of individual "name" (definite referring expression) and predicate-expression. Referring this logical distinction to the conditions of making objective judgements of experience seems to give us at most the notions of particular object and universal kind or character as "categories" which must have application in a world in which such judgements can be made. But this meagre result we might have attained directly from the original distinction between intuitions and concepts, sensibility and understanding.

3. SKETCH OF AN OVER-HASTY ARGUMENT

The results of the appeal to formal logic are not merely meagre. Their meagreness is such as to render almost pointless any critical consideration of the detail of Kant's derivation of the categories from the Table of Judgements. Yet it might be urged that, even with this drastically diminished result, progress can still be made. For, it might be said, the shift to the question of the conditions of making atomic subject–predicate judgements about objects, though not a big shift, really does make it easier to see a possible line of development, granted that we are prepared to fill out this question by adding to it, as assumptions, *all* those theses of the Transcendental Aesthetic which can be detached from the doctrine of transcendental idealism.

The question will then run: How in general must we conceive of objects if we are to be able to make judgements, determinable as true or false, in which we predicate concepts of identified objects of reference, *conceived of as related in a single unified spatio-temporal system*? This question again will be the same as the question: What in general must be true of a world of objects, so conceived, of which we make such judgements? In answering these questions, we shall simultaneously find our *a priori* concepts or categories and the guarantee of their application. And we shall achieve these results simultaneously because they are not two results, but one result. Of course the resulting categories will not be the unschematized categories which Kant envisaged as discoverable with the help of the clue provided by formal logic and without reference to our actual modes of intuition. They will be the schematized categories we actually employ in our spatio-temporal world.

It is true that if we were prepared to let the inquiry develop along these lines, we could in fact make some progress. First, we might argue that in order to preserve the unity of the spatio-temporal system from one judgement to another, we must conceive of at least some spatial objects of reference as persisting through time and as re-identifiable from one occasion of reference to another. For the unity of the spatio-temporal system requires that there should be only one space at different times. Neither the space itself which objects occupy, nor the parts of that space, are themselves, apart from their occupants, objects, as Kant would say, of empirical intuition. Hence the preservation of the unity of space from judgement to judgement requires the persistence and re-identifiability of occupants of space. Here, in this concept of the space-occupying persistent object, we might be said to have at least a faint analogue of Kant's schematized category of substance – which, significantly enough, he associates with the logical notion of the subject of a categorical proposition.

Further, the requirement of re-identifiability has some consequences regarding the concepts under which these persisting objects of reference must fall. We cannot just re-identify a thing, or recognize it as the same thing, without making use of the notion of its being a thing of a certain *kind*. It is the notion of the kind of thing which gives its meaning, in the particular application, to the expression "the same". That is to say, there must be concepts under which we bring persisting things, such that the concepts in question contain within themselves the idea of the conditions under which we can say that a thing falling under that concept is the same as a previously identified thing falling under that concept. But that there should be concepts of this kind applicable generally and readily enough to make possible the use of the notion of the unified spatio-temporal system of persisting things seems to require, to say the least, that the world should exhibit a certain regularity in its operations. If things change or move, as they do, they must change or move in ways which their concept can provide for. Our concepts of persisting things must be concepts of things which change or move in regular or explicable ways – or, as Kant would say, according to causal laws. Hence, if these concepts are to be readily applicable, as they must be if knowledge of a unified world is to be possible, then at least much of the change in the world must be subject to causal law.

This second result, of course, echoes Kant even more strongly. The necessary applicability of the concept of cause was one of the theses that he most strongly argued for, though on different grounds. But, though the grounds were different, he was well aware of the connexion between the category of substance and that of cause; and there are passages, even in the Transcendental Deduction, which seem to involve similar considerations to those which I have just sketched.

The above is no more than the outline of an argument. It is meant to suggest that, even though the appeal to formal logic produced virtually no result, even though the attempt to derive categories from the notion of an objective judgement was a failure, yet progress towards the discovery of categories might be made *if* we were prepared to assume as premises certain theses advanced in the Transcendental Aesthetic. But it is clear, first, that this is not the line which Kant's own argument follows; and, second, that it is not a line which it is desirable that any argument should follow. The first point is clear from the fact that it is not until we reach the Principles that we find any detailed argument to the effect that this or that particular category (e.g. substance or cause) is a necessary element in our conception of experience or a necessary feature of experience. Indeed it is not until we reach the Schematism that we learn what the interpretation of the categories in their application to an essentially temporal experience actually is (e.g. that the interpretation of the category of substance is in terms of the permanence of the real in time). In between the Metaphysical Deduction of the categories from the forms of judgement and this interpretation and demonstration of particular categories lies the whole mystery of the Transcendental Deduction.

As for the second point – that it is in any case undesirable that the argument should immediately follow the lines I have just sketched – it is sufficient to refer to some of my earlier remarks. If it would be a disappointment of our analytical hopes to find an argument resting on the assumption (or definition) that experience necessarily involves knowledge of *objects*, the topics of *objective* judgements, how much more would those hopes be disappointed by an argument which assumes that experience is necessarily of an objective and spatio-temporally unitary world. The conclusions of such an argument could have no more strength than belongs to these questionable assumptions.

4. WHY A TRANSCENDENTAL DEDUCTION?

We are not, then, to rush speculatively forward along a path neither attractive nor Kantian. We are, instead, to ask two questions. First, how does the next stage of the inquiry in fact develop in Kant? Second, what might the sympathetic critic hope from the next stage of the inquiry? Little enough, as we have seen, was to be gained from the last stage, the "metaphysical deduction" of the categories from the forms of logic; though this negative thought must, evidently, be set for the moment aside if we are to understand Kant's own conception of the role of the next stage, the Transcendental Deduction of the Categories. Yet setting this thought aside seems at first to deepen the difficulty of understanding the Deduction's role. It is, apparently, designed to supply a general argument to establish the necessary applicability of the categories to appearances, to the objects of experience. Kant says, of the categories: "If we can prove that by their means alone an object can be thought, this will be a sufficient deduction of them and will justify their objective reality."[1] But was not the Metaphysical Deduction held to prove precisely that "by their means alone an object can be thought"? Why should it be

[1] A 97.

necessary to seek another and independent proof of the same conclusion? How indeed, unless the new proof rested on different premises, should it be possible?

The idea of different premises encourages once more those analytical hopes which we seemed forced to suspend so long as the concept of "objectivity" figured among the premised features of experience. Deferring consideration of those hopes a little longer, let us note, first, that though the Transcendental Deduction is indeed an argument, it is not only an argument. It is also an explanation, a description, a story. To understand its role as a story, we must consider again all those elements of the Kantian model which we eschew in our austerer interpretation. We must remember the subjective implications which the phrase *"a priori"* has for Kant and the seriousness with which he takes the division between the faculties of sensibility and understanding. To say that a form of intuition or a concept of an object in general is *a priori* is, for him, not primarily to say that it embodies a limiting condition of any experience of which we can form a coherent notion. It is primarily to say something about the source or origin of the corresponding feature of experience. Our awareness of objects must be spatio-temporal in character *because* this is how our faculty of sensibility is constituted. We must think about objects in accordance with the categories *because* so much is demanded by the constitution of our faculty of understanding. If this is so, it is indeed true that no further *proof* is required that only by means of the categories an object can be thought. But something else may well seem to be required – viz. an *explanation*. We have before us the materials of a transcendental drama; and we wish to know how the drama is played out. In the mind we have the pure forms of sensible intuition and the pure concepts of an object in general. Extraneous to the mind we have the unknown and unknowable source of the matter for these forms, the source of that out of which our contentful experience is made. Nature, the subject-matter of our objective judgements, is the outcome. But if the mind makes Nature, we want to know as much as we can of the story of its making, we want to understand in particular how such disparate faculties can co-operate to make it. In the Transcendental Deduction the story is told, the explanation is given. This *explanatory* role of the Transcendental Deduction – which has a more prominent place in the first than in the second edition – is announced in the very passage which contains the sentence which I quoted in the last paragraph and which I now return to its context:

> The concepts which thus contain *a priori* the pure thought involved in every experience, we find in the categories. If we can prove that by their means alone an object can be thought, this will be a sufficient deduction of them and will justify their objective validity. But since in such a thought more than merely the faculty of thought, the understanding, is brought into play, and since this faculty itself, as a faculty of *knowledge* that is meant to relate to objects, calls for explanation in regard to the possibility of such relation, we must first of all consider, not in their empirical but in their transcendental constitution, the subjective sources which form the *a priori* foundation of the possibility of experience.[1]

Again, in a retrospective passage at the end of the first edition version of the Deduction, its task is said to have been "to render *comprehensible* this relation of understanding to sensibility" and thereby to "make intelligible" the objective validity of the categories.[2]

Now to return to the role of the Transcendental Deduction as an argument. We shall find that its fundamental premise is that experience contains a diversity of elements (intuitions) which, in the case of each subject of experience, must somehow be united in a single consciousness capable of judgement, capable, that is, of conceptualizing the elements so united. We shall find that its general conclusion is that this unity requires another kind of unity or connectedness on the part of the multifarious elements of experience, namely just such a unity as is also required for experience to have the character of experience of a unified objective world and hence to be capable of being articulated in objective empirical judgements. So far as this general conclusion is concerned, it remains a largely open question precisely what specific concepts or concept-types, if any, are essential if the conceptualization of experience is to satisfy these general requirements of objectivity and unity. But Kant, on the basis of the Metaphysical Deduction, will think himself justified in identifying the "pure

[1] A 96–7.   [2] A 128.

concepts" there derived from the forms of logic, as precisely such conceptual elements.

If this outline is correct, then Kant's sense of the need for a Transcendental Deduction not merely as explanation but as proof – a need which he himself clearly feels, but never very clearly explains – accords very satisfactorily with our suspended analytical hopes. A major part of the role of the Deduction will be to *establish* that experience necessarily involves knowledge of *objects*, in the weighty sense, and hence to displace that thesis from the status of prior definition, or premised assumption, of the inquiry. Of course, even if we are satisfied with the general argument of the Deduction, we shall not follow Kant in stepping from its highly general conclusions to the further specific conclusion that the listed "pure concepts" have necessary application to experience. For we have no such faith in the Metaphysical Deduction as would warrant this step. Instead we may reasonably look forward with the hope that a further working out, in the Principles, of these highly general conclusions will be at least partly independent of any assumption of the correctness of the Table of Categories.

But we shall not be surprised to observe that Kant's own plan for the post-Deduction development of the argument of the *Critique* includes an extra step. Since the Deduction, as he understands it, is a deduction not merely of the highly general conclusions I mentioned but of the pure categories – concepts previously derived in abstraction from our actual, temporal, mode of intuition – he naturally finds it desirable to provide, in the Schematism, yet another list of concepts – filling out the meaning of the unschematized categories by adding to them the temporal condition of their application – before he passes on, in the Principles, to demonstrate in detail the application of each.

So now to consider the Transcendental Deduction, remembering that we have to see it as two things at once: both as an argument about the implications of the concept of experience in general, and also as a description of the transcendental workings of the subjective faculties, whereby experience is produced. It would no doubt be satisfactory if we could reduce the latter aspect altogether to the former, interpreting all the transcendental psychology in terms of the analytical argument. Any effort to do so, though it might be heroic, would certainly be misplaced.

Rather we must try to disentangle the two elements, while remaining aware of them both; for it seems probable that we cannot fully understand the exposition of the argument without some attention to the exigencies of the model. It is, I think, a more serious obstacle to understanding that, partly because of the demands of transcendental psychology, partly because of a typically Kantian straining towards the maximum of generality and abstractness at every stage of the inquiry, Kant postpones until the Principles some of the considerations which really give substance to the highly general arguments and conclusions of the Deduction.

5. OBJECTIVITY AND UNITY

We begin by taking as provisionally premissed the thesis that experience necessarily includes awareness of objects conceived as distinct from particular subjective states of awareness of them, from particular "representations" or "experiences". Kant maintains that for representations thus to have an objective reference, it is necessary that they should possess or exhibit a certain unity or connectedness among themselves. We could not employ any ordinary empirical concepts of objects unless our manifold perceptual experiences possessed the kind of coherence and interconnexion which is required for the application of such concepts. Kant speaks of concepts of objects as rules governing the connexion of experiences. We may illustrate the point – Kant does not do so in the Deduction, though he does in the Principles – by remarking that any particular "unruly" perception, which fails to cohere with the general course of experience as articulated in judgements embodying these concepts, is rated as merely subjective, an illusion or a "seeming", not a true representation of how the world objectively is. Kant thinks of this requirement of unity and connectedness of representations as extending to the whole course of our experience. No breaks can be allowed in it. A particular unruly perception is not reckoned as a glimpse of another objective world, but is relegated to the status of subjective illusion. Similarly, if any phase of experience is to count as a phase of experience of the objective, we must be able to integrate it with other phases as part of a single unified experience of a single objective world.

Doubts about this last generalization of the requirement of

connectedness will be set aside now and considered much later on. A more fundamental objection might be raised even to the beginning of this account of what is involved in experience of objects conceived as distinct from particular subjective states of awareness of them. It might be conceded that the employment of ordinary empirical concepts of objects does indeed imply the kind of rule-governed connectedness of perceptions of which Kant speaks, yet denied that the employment of any such concepts was necessary to experience of objects conceived of as distinct from particular subjective states of awareness of them. Why should not objects of awareness be conceived of as items possessing an existence distinct from experiences of awareness of them even though the concepts under which they fell were not such as could give occasion for rejecting any particular putative perception as "unruly" and hence as not a true representation of an object? Again, the employment of ordinary empirical concepts of objects goes hand in hand with the conception of objects and their particular characteristics as existing in an order and arrangement of their own which is not only theoretically distinguishable from, but is actually distinct from, the order and arrangement of a subject's experiences of awareness of them. But why should this feature be conceived of as essential to experience conceived of as experience of objects? Why should not objects of awareness be conceived of as items possessing an existence distinct from experiences of awareness of them even though the order and arrangement in which they were conceived of as independently existing reflected exactly, point for point, the order and arrangement of a subject's experiences of awareness of them?

Apart from any argument of Kant's, there may seen sufficient ground for rejecting these suggestions. There is, however, one passage in the first edition version of the Deduction which might almost be construed as an answer to such objections from the point of view of transcendental idealism. It is by way of allusion to a part of the latter doctrine that Kant, in this edition, introduces this topic of objectivity. Objects in general are conceived of as those independently existing items to which our sensible experience is due. But objects *as they really are*, or are in themselves, lie entirely outside our experience. We are never aware of them. All we are aware of is appearances, and "appearances are themselves nothing but sensible representations which, as such and in themselves, must not be taken as objects existing outside our power of representation".[1] If, therefore, our experience is to have for us the character of objectivity required for empirical knowledge, our "sensible representations" must contain some substitute or surrogate for awareness of the real, unknown object. This surrogate is precisely that rule-governed connectedness of our representations which is reflected in our employment of concepts of *empirical* objects conceived of as together forming a unified natural world, with its own order, distinct from, and controlling, the subjective order of perceptions. *Really*, nothing comes within the scope of our experience but those subjective perceptions themselves; so all that can be really understood by empirical knowledge of objects is the existence of such rule and order among those perceptions as is involved in our being able to count them as perceptions of an objective world, having its own independent order, to which we can ascribe, as a consequence, the order of our perceptions. The notion of *experience of objects* can have no more meaning than this; but, for the same reason, it can have no less.

This is a revealing argument. The claim that for experience to count as experience of the objective, it must exhibit just the features of which the necessity was questioned by our imaginary objector, is represented as resting on that part of the doctrine of transcendental idealism according to which we are not *really* aware of independently existing objects at all, but only of appearances which "are themselves nothing but sensible representations". But this foundation seems superfluous. We do not need to premise that what we ordinarily conceive of as objects existing independently of our experiences of awareness of them are *really* no such things in order to make the point that this conception would be empty unless experience contained such a ground for it as it does in that connectedness which makes possible the employment of ordinary empirical concepts of objects. Here is a recurrent feature of Kant's transcendental subjectivism. It is regularly invoked to support theses which can stand on their own feet; and this is the reason why we are sometimes tempted to put such innocuous interpretations on the theses of transcendental subjectivism. But such interpretations do not really stand up to the impact of the work as a whole.

[1] A 104.

My reference to this passage is really parenthetical. We were primarily to note what Kant regarded as implied by the provisional premise of objectivity in experience. Now we are to note the point at which the provisional premise yields up its place, the point at which it becomes apparent that it is by no means simply a matter of the definition of "experience" that experience involves knowledge of objects. When this becomes apparent, something else becomes apparent too: that the argument from the fundamental premise is an argument not just to the provisional premise stated generally but to all that is held to be implied by the provisional premise. So it becomes unnecessary to discuss whether what is held to be implied by the provisional premise really is implied by it.

Our sensible experience may, and does in fact, exhibit that connectedness which enables us to employ empirical concepts of objects, to count our sensible representations – apart from a few unruly exceptions – as veridical perceptions of states of affairs in an objective world. But might not that experience have been of a quite different character? Might not sensible representations have succeeded one another in consciousness, possessing none of that connectedness which makes possible the employment of ordinary concepts of the objective? Kant answers that no experience of such a disconnected character would be possible. He does not base his answer on a definition which writes "knowledge of objects" into the meaning of "experience". He bases his answer on a quite different principle. One might almost say, as he does himself, that he bases it on a tautology. When we entertain the thought of a possible experience in which sensible representations succeed one another but possess none of that connectedness necessary for employment of concepts of the objective, we are at least thinking of such a succession of representations as belonging to a single consciousness. The tautology on which Kant bases his declaration that no such experience is possible is the tautology that experiences or representations belonging to a single consciousness must satisfy the conditions of belonging to a single consciousness.

Then what are those conditions? Given the state of the argument, Kant's answer must be admitted to have a certain sublimity. What is required for a series of experiences to belong to a single consciousness is that they should possess precisely that rule-governed connectedness which is also required for them collectively to constitute a temporally extended experience of a single objective world. The burden of the entire argument is thus shifted to the necessary unity of consciousness.

Evidently this answer raises questions, suggests objections. Before we try to evaluate it, however, we must turn to face that other aspect of the Transcendental Deduction – the story of the activity of our faculties – with which the argument now becomes entwined. I shall not try to penetrate to every point of this jungle; rather, to hover over it long enough to note its principal features.

6. SYNTHESIS, SELF-CONSCIOUSNESS, AND NATURE AS MADE BY THE MIND

Kant sometimes expresses the thesis of the necessary unity of consciousness by saying that it must be possible for the "I think" to accompany all my representations, if they are to be anything to me. The thought appears to be a complex one, a fusion of two thoughts. (Later we shall see that Kant regards the one as implying the other.) One is the old thought that intuitions must be brought under concepts to yield experience. Hence, in Kant's terms, the faculty of understanding (of thought, of concepts, of rules) must be brought into play. But, further, if different experiences are to belong to a single consciousness, there must be the possibility of *self*-consciousness on the part of the subject of those experiences. It must be one and the same understanding which is busy at its conceptualizing work on all the intuitions belonging to a single consciousness, and it must be possible for this identity to be *known* to the subject of these experiences.

It is useless to look for an explanation of the satisfaction of this condition to what might be called ordinary empirical self-consciousness. "Consciousness of self according to the determinations of our state in inner perception is merely empirical and always changing. No fixed and abiding self can present itself in this flux of inner appearances."[1] The point is a familiar one in all discussions of personal identity, though neither here, by Kant, nor elsewhere, by Hume, is it made with its full force. The problem would not be solved if the "determinations" of our inner state were not "always changing", if some, say, were constant or

[1] A 107.

relatively so; they would still be *states* of ourselves. The point is that to refer simply to the fact of empirical self-awareness (aware-ness of one's inner states as such) is not to solve the problem but to state it. What we are in quest of is precisely the fundamental ground of the possibility of empirical self-ascription of diverse states of consciousness on the part of a consciousness capable of knowledge of its own identity throughout its changing (or its constant) determinations.

At times Kant seems to turn for an answer to a special kind of "transcendental self-consciousness" associated with the *activity* of the faculty of understanding. The key to the unity of conscious-ness, it seems, is to be sought in the fact that the connectedness of our perceptions is *produced* by the *activity* of the mind. The process of producing such connectedness or unity is called synthesis; and our consciousness of the identity of ourselves is fundamentally nothing but our consciousness of this power of synthesis, or combination, and of its exercise. I can count a given representa-tion as *mine* solely because *I* have combined or synthesized it with others. Now the only modes of synthesis for given intuitions which are possible for an understanding like ours are those represented by the categories; and the combination of repre-sentations in accordance with the categories is their combination in judgements as to what is objectively the case. Hence the fact that my experience is of a unified objective world is a necessary consequence of the fact that only under this condition could I be conscious of my diverse experiences as one and all my own. And hence also, Kant concludes, we are ourselves the source of what-ever general order and connexion in Nature is necessary to satisfying this requirement of objectivity and unity.

Here many theses are linked together. The suggestion which immediately concerns us is the suggestion that our consciousness of our own identity is fundamentally nothing but our conscious-ness of the power of synthesis or combination, and of its exercise. Such a view seems to find expression in several of Kant's remarks. Thus, in the second edition, he writes that relation of different representations to the identity of the subject comes about "only in so far as I can conjoin one representation with another and *am conscious of the synthesis* of them";[1] or, more poignantly, in the first edition, that "the mind could never think its identity in the

[1] B 133.

manifoldness of its representations . . . if it did not *have before its eyes the identity of its act* whereby it subordinates all synthesis of apprehension . . . to a transcendental unity".[1] Elsewhere, however, the emphasis is placed, not on consciousness of the *activity* of synthesizing or combining but on consciousness of the *power* of doing so. In the second edition we have: "The thought that the representations given in intuition one and all belong to me is . . . equivalent to the thought that I unite them in one self-consciousness or *can* at least so unite them."[2] Later he writes: "I exist as an intelligence which is conscious only of its power of combination."[3]

The cautious character of the last two remarks should warn us against reading too much into the first two. Kant does not, after all, think that we have a special kind of experience or awareness of the self or its activity, distinct from that empirical self-consciousness in which, as he holds, we are aware only of appearances of ourselves. He remarks, in the second edition: "In the synthetic original unity of apperception I am conscious of myself not as I appear to myself, nor as I am in myself, but only that I am. This representation is a thought, not an intuition."[4] Again, in the first edition, he says, of the "bare representation 'I'", which is "transcendental consciousness" and which "makes possible the collective unity of all other representations", that "whether this representation is clear or obscure, or even whether it ever actually occurs, does not here concern us."[5]

We may begin to wonder precisely in what way a reference to the combining or synthesizing activities of the understanding is supposed to elucidate the conditions under which self-consciousness is possible, these being also the conditions under which diverse experiences may be said to be united in a single consciousness. The supreme principle of synthetic unity "says no more than that all *my* representations in any given intuition must be subject to that condition under which alone I can ascribe them to the identical self as *my* representations".[6] This is clear enough in itself. The condition under which diverse representations may be said to be united in a single consciousness is precisely the condition, whatever that may be, under which a subject of experiences may ascribe different experiences to himself, conscious

[1] A 108.   [2] B 134.   [3] B 158–9.
[4] B 157.   [5] A 117, footnote.   [6] B 138.

of the identity of that to which these different experiences, at different times, belong. The fulfilment of this condition is said to be dependent on the synthesizing activities of the mind. But since these synthesizing activities do not, after all, yield any kind of self-knowledge or self-awareness other than that which ordinary empirical self-consciousness supplies, it seems that we may have to look for the explanation of the possibility of self-ascription of experiences in the nature of the *outcome* of the synthesizing activities rather than in any special awareness of those activities themselves or of the powers exercised in performing them. Perhaps that very connectedness of experiences, under concepts of the objective, which synthesis is held to *produce*, is itself the condition – or the fundamental condition – under which alone self-ascription of experiences is possible. The possibilities of this shift of emphasis we shall explore in the next section.

Kant, then, does not really make it clear in the Deduction how the doctrine of the mind's activity explains the possibility of acribing experiences to the one self and thereby explains the unity of diverse representations in a single consciousness. What is clearly *affirmed* is the necessary connexion, by way of synthesis, between the unity of consciousness on the one hand and the relation of representations to an objective (empirical) world on the other; and it remains to be seen whether this connexion can be made out independently of the doctrine of synthesis. What is also clearly *affirmed* is the subjectivity of the source of such order in Nature as is necessary to yielding the unified objective world of our experience – an affirmation which parallels, on the side of the active faculty of understanding, the thesis of the subjective source of the spatial and temporal modes of relation in the passive faculty of sensibility. But the only support for this affirmation lies in the doctrine of synthesis, and that doctrine may perhaps be by-passed by establishing a direct analytical connexion between the unity of consciousness and the unified objectivity of the world of our experience.

In the hope of by-passing the doctrine of synthesis altogether, I shall not linger now over that elaboration of it in the *Critique* which provides such inexhaustible matter for commentators. Some subsequent references to the doctrine will indeed be necessary to make clear the bearing of later remarks. Here I confine myself to the barest outline and the briefest comment.

The doctrine of synthesis rests firmly on the distinction of faculties. What is given in sense alone, in mere receptivity, is one thing; what is made out of it by understanding, the active faculty, with the help of its no less active lieutenant, imagination, the go-between of sense and understanding, is quite another. The data of sense alone are discrete, single, separate, without complexity. All combination, all connexion, is produced by imagination which assembles and reproduces as necessary the discrete data of sense, acting always under the control of understanding, the source of concepts. Experience is the outcome of this activity of combination or synthesis. Not that the activity of synthesis is confined to the data of empirical intuition. "Pure" synthesis is involved also in the generation of the unity of the "pure manifold" of space and time and in the constructions of pure mathematics.

It is useless to puzzle over the status of these propositions. They belong neither to empirical (including physiological) psychology nor to an analytical philosophy of mind, *though some of them may have near or remote analogues in both.* They belong to the imaginary subject of transcendental psychology, a part of the Kantian model. There are, of course, points enough at which we have to refer to the model if we are to follow the line taken by Kant's exposition.

7. UNITY AND OBJECTIVITY

We are now to consider, without dependence on the doctrines of transcendental psychology, the thesis that for a series of diverse experiences to belong to a single consciousness it is necessary that they should be so connected as to constitute a temporally extended experience of a unified objective world. In the process we shall come to perceive that the thesis of the necessary unity of consciousness can itself be represented as resting on a yet more fundamental premise – on nothing more than the necessity, for any experience at all to be possible, of the original duality of intuition and concept. But first we must recall what is to be understood by the notion of a unitary consciousness on the one hand, and by the notion of experience, or of empirical knowledge of objects, on the other.

G

The notion of a single consciousness to which different experiences belong is linked to the notion of self-consciousness, of the ascription of an experience or state of consciousness to oneself. It is not necessary, in order for different experiences to belong to a single consciousness, that the subject of those experiences should be constantly thinking of them as *his* experiences; but it is necessary that those experiences should be subject to whatever condition is required for it to be *possible* for him to ascribe them to himself as *his* experiences. "All *my* representations . . . must be subject to that condition under which alone I can ascribe them to the identical self as *my* representations."[1] This holds of "all my representations (even if I am not conscious of them as such [sc. as mine])".[2] Unity of the consciousness to which a series of experiences belong implies, then, the *possibility* of self-ascription of experiences on the part of a subject of those experiences; it implies the *possibility* of consciousness, on the part of the subject, of the numerical identity of that to which those different experiences are by him ascribed.

We have already discussed what is to be taken to be implied by experience or awareness of *objects*, conceived of as distinct from any particular states of awareness of them.[3] A judgement which claims objective validity purports to be true "no matter what the state of the subject may be";[4] experience of objects is possible only if objectively valid judgements are possible. The possibility of objectively valid judgements implies that rule-governed connectedness of perceptions which is reflected in our employment of empirical concepts of objects conceived of as possessing an order and arrangement of their own, distinct from the order and arrangement of the subject's experiences of awareness of them.[5]

Unity of diverse experiences in a single consciousness requires experience of objects. We can test the strength of the thesis by seeing how it stands up to attack. Let us begin with the most obvious line of attack. No doubt, it might be said, the contents of a possible experience must be unified in some way and must be brought under concepts. But why should not the objects (accusatives) of awareness of such a consciousness be a succession of

---

[1] B 138.   [2] B 132.
[3] See Section 5 of this chapter.   [4] B 142.
[5] This last element in the notion of objectivity is not clearly stated till the Principles are reached. It is necessary to anticipate them to this extent.

items such that there was no distinction to be drawn between the
order and arrangement of the objects (and of their particular
features and characteristics) and the order and arrangement of the
subject's experiences of awareness of them – items, therefore,
which would not be the topics of objective judgements in Kant's
sense? Such objects might be of the sort which the earlier sense-
datum theorists spoke of – red, round patches, brown oblongs,
flashes, whistles, tickling sensations, smells. Certainly concepts,
recognition, some span of memory would be necessary to a
consciousness with any experience at all; and all these would
involve one another. But why should the concepts not be simply
such sensory quality concepts as figure in the early and limited
sense-datum vocabulary? The claim that a possible experience
might have this limited character is in no way inconsistent with
the acknowledgement that in fact it has not merely a more complex but a quite different character. That is to say, it may consistently be admitted that it is impossible in fact to give an
adequate account of the character of our actual perceptual experience, even considered solely in its subjective aspect, without
the employment of concepts of substantial objects. The claim is
only that this is not a necessary feature of any possible experience,
that it is quite conceivable that experience should have as its
contents precisely the sort of essentially disconnected impressions
we have been speaking of – impressions which neither require,
nor permit of, being "united in the concept of an object" in the
sense in which Kant understands this phrase.

There are passages in the first edition version of the Deduction
which might almost be read as comments on such a suggestion.
If appearances were not such as to allow of knowledge expressible in objective judgements, they would be "for us as good
as nothing";[1] they would be merely "a blind play of representations, less even than a dream".[2] Or again, in an awkwardly expressed passage, Kant says that if it were accidental that appearances should fit into a connected whole of human knowledge,
then it might be that they did not so fit together, were not
"associable" in the required way; and "should they not be
associable, there might exist a multitude of perceptions, and
indeed an entire sensibility, in which much empirical consciousness would arise in my mind, but in a state of separation, and

[1] A 111.   [2] A 112.

without belonging to a consciousness of myself. This however is impossible."[1]

Comments are not arguments; and in any case these comments may not seem very happily expressed. The difficulty which Kant must find in the hypothesis advanced as an objection to his thesis – let us call it the hypothesis of a purely sense-datum experience – really goes very deep. Approaching it first at a comparatively superficial level, we very soon find ourselves at a deeper level. First, we ask: how can we attach a sense to the notion of the single consciousness to which the successive "experiences" are supposed to belong? We seem to add nothing but a form of words to the hypothesis of a succession of essentially disconnected impressions by stipulating that they all *belong* to an identical consciousness. Nor do we seem to add anything more by saying: the unitary consciousness is that which is successively *aware* of them all. The trouble with such "objects of awareness" as those offered by the hypothesis is that just as their esse is, to all intents and purposes, their percipi – i.e. there is no effective ground of distinction between the two – so their percipi seems to be nothing but their esse. The hypothesis seems to contain no ground of distinction between the supposed experience of awareness and the particular item which the awareness is awareness of. Given the word "experience" we are apt to overlook this because of the tenacious implications of our vocabulary, its covert retention of attachments which have been formally given up in philosophical speculation. But if we are to take the hypothesis seriously, we must not overlook it.

We have already reached the deeper level of difficulty. It was agreed at the outset that experience requires both particular intuitions and general concepts. There can be no experience at all which does not involve the recognition of particular items *as* being of such and such a general kind. It seems that it must be possible, even in the most fleeting and purely subjective of impressions, to distinguish a component of recognition, or judgement, which is not simply identical with, or wholly absorbed by, the particular item which is recognized, which forms the topic of judgement. Yet at the same time we seem forced to concede that there are particular subjective experiences (e.g. a momentary tickling sensation) of which the objects (accusatives) have no

[1] A 122.

existence independently of the awareness of them. It is clear what Kant must regard as being the way out of this difficulty. The way out is to acknowledge that the recognitional component, necessary to experience, can be present in experience only because of the *possibility* of referring different experiences to one identical subject of them all. Recognition implies the *potential* acknowledgement of the experience into which recognition necessarily enters as being one's own, as sharing with others this relation to the identical self. It is the fact that this potentiality is implicit in recognition which saves the recognitional component in a particular experience from absorption into the item recognized (and hence saves the character of the particular experience as an *experience*) even when that item cannot be conceived of as having an existence independent of the particular experience of it.

What then is implied by the potentiality of such an acknowledgement, by the potentiality – which must be present in every experience – of awareness of oneself as having it? The very minimum that is implied, Kant must reply, is precisely what the hypothesis of the purely sense-datum "experience" attempts to exclude. The minimum implied is that some at least of the concepts under which particular experienced items are recognized as falling should be such that the experiences themselves contain the basis for certain allied distinctions: individually, the distinction of a subjective component *within* a judgement of experience (as "it seems to me as if this is a heavy stone" is distinguishable within "this is a heavy stone"); collectively, the distinction *between* the subjective order and arrangement of a series of such experiences on the one hand and the objective order and arrangement of the items of which they are experiences on the other. Granted that these distinctions are implicit in the conceptual character of some experiences – of which a few perhaps have to be dismissed as subjective illusion on the ground of failure of connectedness with others – we are free to allow that there are *also* experiences which lack this conceptual character altogether, i.e. the objects (accusatives) of which are not such as must be conceived of as existing independently of the experience of them. What is excluded is that experiences should be entirely of the latter class. For if, *per impossibile*, they were so, even the basis of the idea of the referring of such experiences to an identical subject of a series of them by such a subject would be altogether lacking;

and if the basis of this idea were lacking, it would be impossible to distinguish the recognitional components in such "experiences" as components not wholly absorbed by their sensible accusatives; and if this were impossible, they would not rate as experiences at all. Here we have the force of the doctrine that the "I think" (with an identical reference for "I") must be *capable* of accompanying all the perceptions of a single subject of experience; and here we have also its implications regarding the necessary objectivity of experience. But its force and its implications are here detached from the doctrine of synthesis, from the theses of transcendental psychology.

Let us now see how the Kantian thesis might be attacked from another direction. It might be urged that the Kantian requirements for "a possible experience" are simply not met by Kant's own provisions for meeting them. Let it be provisionally granted that the possibility of experience in general is bound up with the possibility of self-ascription of experiences. It is a quite general truth that the ascription of different states or determinations to an identical subject turns on the existence of some means of distinguishing or identifying the subject of such ascriptions as one object among others. Applying this general truth to the case before us, we may say, in Kant's terminology, that the possibility of ascribing experiences to a subject of experiences and hence the possibility of self-ascription of experiences requires that there be some "determinate intuition" corresponding to the concept of a subject of experiences; or, substituting a later terminology for Kant's, we may say that this possibility requires that there be empirically applicable criteria of identity for subjects of experience.[1] In actual practice this condition is satisfied by the fact that each of us is a corporeal object among corporeal objects, is indeed a man among men. Our personal pronouns, the pronoun "I" included, have an empirical reference; and in some way such a reference must be secured if the general notion of ascribing experiences to a subject of them is to make sense.

But Kant's provisions for the possibility of self-ascription of experiences (the objection continues) includes no reference to these facts. He speaks of the "abiding self" of transcendental apperception; but he certainly does not mean by this the (at least

---

[1] Which is *not* to say that such criteria *must* be invoked in self-ascription of experiences. See the discussion of the Paralogisms, Part III, Chapter 2 below.

relatively) abiding man, an object among others in the world, a point of application for empirical criteria of personal identity. Yet if he rejects this interpretation of the "abiding self", does he not evacuate the notion of ascription of experiences to a subject of its ordinary meaning, without producing anything to fill the vacuum? He is really in no *better* position than the theorist of sense-data who maintains that a possible experience, the contents of a consciousness, could theoretically consist of a succession of intrinsically disconnected sensory data somehow linked by memory and expectation. It is true that Kant is in a *different* position from this theorist. For he maintains that in order for there to exist a series of experiences belonging to a unitary consciousness, it must be the case that some (though not all) members of the series are conceptualized in such a way that they fit together to form a coherent picture of an objective world. Thus Kant holds an intermediate position between that of the theorist of sense-data and that of one who insists that the notion of a series of experiences belonging to a consciousness depends for its sense on the existence of empirically applicable criteria for the identity of a subject of experiences.

But really (the objection concludes) this intermediate position is an impossible one. If Kant's essentially connected experiences, which together form a picture of an objective world, can meaningfully be said to be the possible contents of one consciousness, why cannot this also be meaningfully said of the essentially disconnected experiences of the sense-datum theorist? If, on the other hand, it is objected that no meaning has been given to talk of such disconnected "experiences" belonging to one consciousness, because none has been given to their being ascribed to himself by a subject of them, i.e. to the notion of self-consciousness, then does not the very same objection hold against the Kantian position? The Kantian must either give a fuller weight to the notion of self-consciousness or he must abandon his objections to the sense-datum conception of a possible experience.

The bark of this objection is worse, it might be answered, than its bite. For its main point may be conceded without detriment to the Kantian position. It is not essential for Kant to maintain that his provisions are *sufficient* to explain the actual occurrence of self-ascription of experiences. It is enough if they are *necessary* to its possibility. It may be that they do not represent the full conditions we need to make satisfactory sense of the notion of self-consciousness; and yet that Kant has successfully performed a difficult feat of abstraction of the more fundamental part of those full conditions.

Let us, then, view the matter from this angle. We may consider the history of a normal human being, a "case" in which there is no question but that the conditions of self-ascription of experiences are fulfilled, no possible objection, therefore, to speaking of a series of experiences which belong to a unitary consciousness. Not all the members of such a series are in fact self-ascribed: a man may be more prone to forget himself in contemplation of the world (or in transactions with it) than he is to be conscious of, or to think of, himself as perceiving (or doing) what he perceives (or does). But it is a shining fact about such a series of experiences, whether self-ascribed or not, that its members collectively build up or yield, though not all of them contribute to, a picture of a unified objective world through which the experiences themselves collectively constitute a single, subjective, experiential route, one among other possible subjective routes through the same objective world. The point of the objection just outlined is that the notion of the *identity of the subject* of such a series of experiences is dependent upon the complex notion of the identity of a man. The more fundamental point of the Kantian provisions is that the experiences of such a subject must themselves be so conceptualized as to determine a distinction between the subjective route of his experiences and the objective world through which it is a route. The history of a man, we might say, is – among much else – an embodiment of a temporally extended *point of view* on the world. We need not hold that we could fully explain the notion of self-ascription of experiences solely in terms of the notion of such a temporally extended point of view abstracted from all else. All we need to maintain is that we could not explain the former notion at all without providing for the latter.

There are here implications – which I interrupt the argument to mention, but over which I shall not linger – regarding the causal involvement of a perceiving subject with the objective world of his perception. A series of experiences builds up a picture of an objective world in which the order and arrangement of the objects of which they are experiences must be conceived of as distinct from the order and arrangement of the experiences which form the series. But the experiences which form the series cannot come in any order whatever. That such a series yields the objective picture it does yield is partly a matter of the possession by its members of their own order. There is a certain necessary interdependence between the two types of order and arrangement, the subjective and the objective. Of course, we cannot specify, on these very general grounds, any particular forms of interdependence. We can only point, on these very general grounds, to the general fact that our pictures of the objective world and our picture of possible perceptual routes through it cannot be independent of each other. Further investigation of this interdependence is a desideratum in the theory of knowledge. I mention the matter now in order to bring out more clearly the implications of the notion of a temporally extended point of view on an objective world.

To return to the main contention. The point of the objection to be considered was that the notion of ascribing experiences to a subject of them is dependent upon the conception of subjects of experience as distinguishable "objects of intuition". Such subjects, if a plurality is in question, must be conceived of as perceptibly belonging to a common world. The point of the reply was that if such subjects must be conceived of as perceptibly belonging to a common world, they must also be conceived of as each having his own experience of that world. Properly understood, the objector's point does not contradict the Kantian point; it includes it. If we abstract from the fact that the subject is an intuitable item in the objective world of his experience, we leave the fact that the world is an objective world; and this fact must be provided for in the nature of the subject's experience of it. This is what Kant provides for. A series of experiences satisfying the Kantian provision has a certain double aspect. On the one hand it cumulatively builds up a picture of the world in which objects and happenings (with their particular characteristics) are presented as possessing an objective order, an order which is logically independent of any particular experiential route through the world. On the other hand it possesses its own order as a series of experiences of objects. If we thought of such a series of experiences as continuously articulated in a series of detailed judgements, then, taking their order and content together, those judgements would be such as to yield, on the one hand, a (partial) description of an objective world and on the other a chart of the course of a single subjective experience of that world. Not only the series as a whole, but each member of the series, has a double aspect. This explicitly emerges when one objective judgement is corrected by another: what remains unaltered when the correction is made is the subjective experience, the "seeming". In this duplicity of aspects lies the fundamental ground of the possibility, though not, it may be conceded, the full conditions of the actuality, of self-ascription of experiences in general, including such as have no contribution at all, or no concordant contribution, to make to the picture of the objective world.

The critic who argues for the necessity of empirically applicable criteria for the identity of a subject of experience might well feel, when faced with this answer, that the finer point of his criticism had been missed. For suppose it granted that the employment of concepts of the objective is a necessary condition of the possibility of experience. Yet must it not be conceded that the necessity of the fulfilment of the objectivity-condition was incorrectly, or inadequately, explained in the original argument? For the necessity of the objectivity-condition was explained as required for the possibility of self-consciousness, of self-ascription of experiences. Yet it has in effect been conceded to the critic that the fulfilment of the objectivity-condition is not sufficient to make self-ascription of experiences possible, i.e. to make fully intelligible the notion of self-ascription of experiences on the part of a subject capable of consciousness of his own numerical identity throughout the series of his experiences. But if the fulfilment of the objectivity-condition does not, by itself, make such self-ascription possible, it cannot be *as* making such self-ascription possible that the fulfilment of the objectivity-condition is a necessary element in a coherent conception of a possible experience. An adequate explanation would involve referring to the full conditions of the possibility of self-ascription of experiences (including the existence of the subject as an intuitable object in the world); and *then* pointing out that the full conditions involve the objectivity-condition. But there is no suggestion in Kant's work that the possibility of experience requires that a subject of experience be an intuitable object in the world.

To rebut this final form of the criticism, it will be sufficient to show that the requirement which underlies the objectivity-condition can be explained, and is explained, as something less than, though entailed by, the satisfaction of the full conditions of the possibility of empirical self-ascription of experiences. The only concession called for is that the statement of this requirement has some obscurity. The objection we have been considering turned, in its original form, on the point that the ascription of states to a *subject* required the subject itself to be an intuitable object for which there existed empirically applicable criteria of identity. The requirement which underlies the objectivity-condition, however, is not exactly that experience should be ascribable to such a subject, but that it should have a certain character of self-reflexiveness *which is expressed by Kant in terms of the notion of self-consciousness*. The expression is not altogether happy because we are immediately led by it to think in terms of *personal* self-consciousness and hence in terms of the full conditions for ordinary empirical self-ascription of experiences. But what is intended by it is something less than this, which yet really does constitute the essential core of personal self-consciousness.

What is meant by the necessary self-reflexiveness of a possible experience in general could be otherwise expressed by saying that experience must be such as to provide room for the thought of experience itself. The point of the objectivity-condition is that it provides room for this thought. It provides room, on the one hand, for "Thus and so is how things objectively are" and, on the other, for "This is how things are experienced as being"; and it provides room for the second thought *because* it provides room for the first. This is the point that is made – not, as we see, entirely happily – by reference to the separable component of subjective experience in any particular objective judgement of experience and by reference to one subjective experiential route (among other possible routes) through an objective world. What is necessary is that there be a *distinction*, though not (usually) an *opposition*, implicit in the concepts employed in experience, between how things are in the world which experience is of and how they are experienced as being, between the order of the world and the order of experience. This necessary doubleness is the real point of connexion between what Kant refers to as "original (or transcendental) self-consciousness" on the one hand and the objectivity-condition on the other. It is legitimate, though it may be misleading, to express the former conception in terms of *self*-consciousness, of *self*-ascription of experiences, because, while it is not equivalent to the possibility of self-ascription of experiences (i.e. is not the conception of the full conditions of giving sense to the notion of the identity of a subject of experiences), yet it really does represent the fundamental basis of the possibility of self-ascription of experiences. For "This is how things are (have been) experienced *by me* as being" presupposes "This is how things are (have been) *experienced* as being"; and the latter in turn presupposes a distinction, though not (usually) an opposition, between "This is how things are experienced as being" and "Thus and so is how things are".

Thus transcendental self-consciousness is not to be *identified* with the possibility of empirical self-ascription of experiences. But it must be recognized as the basic condition of that possibility. And it is shown to require the fulfilment of the objectivity condition.

This reply to the final form of the criticism has an important consequence. It leaves it an open question whether the conditions of "a possible experience in general" include, or do not include, the satisfaction of the full conditions for empirical self-ascription of experiences, i.e. the existence of empirically applicable criteria for the identity of a subject of experience. If they do, then the requirement of transcendental self-consciousness is derived from the requirement of the possibility of empirical self-ascription, and ultimately derives its intelligibility from the latter. If they do not, then the requirement of transcendental self-consciousness is derived from nothing but the thought of a possible experience in general, and is intelligible quite independently of the empirically applicable concept of the identity of a subject of experience. Since Kant never explicitly confronted this alternative, it cannot be entirely clear what his answer to the question would have been. But it is clear that either answer to it is compatible with the claim that the argument of the Deduction establishes the most general features of any conception of experience which we can make intelligible to ourselves.[1]

This reply also shows the need for care in reading the exposition

[1] At this point reference is desirable to Kant's treatment of the subject of self-knowledge in the Paralogisms – a treatment which complements the argument of the Deduction. See Part III below.

at many points at which the notion of "self-consciousness" is invoked. It does not show a need for so much care that a total abandonment of the language of the exposition is demanded.

I conclude with a few remarks which do not themselves add anything to the argument but which it may be helpful to make before this section is brought to an end.

[1]   First, let us return briefly to the sense-datum theorist's conception of a possible experience. If such an experience were possible, then a series of corresponding judgements of experience would be possible. But a set of such judgements would yield no picture of a world of objects the relations of which are distinct from the relations of experiences of them. Hence it would provide no basis either for the conception of an experiential route through such a world or for the isolation of the subjective, experiential component in individual judgements. Hence it would provide no basis for the necessary self-reflexiveness of experience, which is in its turn the essential core of the possibility of self-ascription of experiences. Hence the theorist has not succeeded in producing a description of a possible experience.

Even in the face of the argument, we might still be tempted by the final objection that each one of us can perfectly well imagine a stretch of *his own* experience as being such as the sense-datum theorist describes, and hence can perfectly well conceive of a plurality of other similar stretches, not his own. What more could be required to demonstrate the possibility of an entire experience having, throughout the whole of its temporal extent, the character of such a stretch? And this is precisely the sense-datum theorist's conception of a possible experience. But of course it is not enough that, equipped with the conceptual resources we are equipped with, we can form such a picture. What has to be shown is that the picture contains in itself the materials for the conception of itself as experience. What *has* been shown is that it does not. Nor must we suppose that the objections to this conception of a possible experience could be met simply by providing for its elaboration to such a point as to permit of the "logical construction" of an objective world, while retaining for sense-datum judgements the status of basic judgements of experience. For if the elaborated conception of a possible experience made sense, then so would the simpler conception of which it is an elaboration.

Or, if this consequence does not hold, then no true alternative has been advanced to the Kantian requirement that the
fundamental or basic judgements of experience should themselves
be objective judgements. (It would be a great misunderstanding
to suppose that the doctrine of synthesis implies anything contrary to this requirement: however we interpret that doctrine, it
is clear that synthesis is not an operation performed on the basis
of experience, but a precondition of experience.)

[2]   The study of the argument of the Deduction in this section
has been an evolving study; and this fact perhaps calls for a retrospective glance at an earlier phase of it, to make explicit something implicit in the evolution. If any thesis of the Deduction
seemed at first central, it was this: that the possibility of experience requires the satisfaction of the basic condition of self-
consciousness, where by the latter is understood the possibility of
self-ascription of diverse experiences on the part of a subject
capable of consciousness of the numerical identity of that to
which these diverse experiences are ascribed. This central thesis
is then argued to have as a consequence the necessity of such
concept-carried connectedness of (at least some of) the experiences
which the subject is to be capable of ascribing to himself as constitutes them experiences of a unified objective world. Now it is
possible, as was shown at an early point in my exposition, to
represent the central thesis itself as a consequence of the more
general thesis that any experience whatever must contain a conceptual component or component of recognition. But this connexion was there presented without anticipating the difficulty
which subsequently arose concerning the notion of self-consciousness.[1] How is this phase of the argument to be re-cast to take
account of that difficulty?

The operation is very simple. For the necessity of saving the
recognitional component in an experience from absorption into
its sensible accusative (and thereby saving the status of the
experience as experience) is simply identical with the necessity of
providing room, in experience, for the thought of experience
itself; and it is just this necessity which calls directly for the
distinction between how things are and how they are experienced

[1] See p. 102 and ff. above.

as being and hence for the employment, in judgements of experience (though not in *every* such judgement) of concepts of the objective. In this re-casting, reference to empirical consciousness, on the part of the subject, of his own numerical identity is short-circuited. But it can then be re-introduced by pointing out that the condition required for the self-reflexiveness of experience is also the basic condition required for empirical self-ascription of experiences, that "transcendental self-consciousness" is the core of empirical self-consciousness.

To present the argument for the objectivity condition in this form is to present it in its boldest possible form. In setting out the alternatives which Kant never explicitly confronted,[1] we saw that a less bold form of argument is available.

It will be seen that, as the study of the argument of the Deduction has evolved in this section, the simple-seeming notion of "a unitary consciousness to which diverse experiences belong" appears less and less adequate to express the fundamental thought on which the argument rests. It yields its place, first, to that of the possibility of empirical (personal) self-consciousness, then to that profounder notion of transcendental self-consciousness, the necessary reflexiveness of experience, which appears as the basic condition of the possibility of empirical self-consciousness. And it must do so; for it only expresses a coherent thought when interpreted in these terms.

[3] My final remark concerns memory. It may seem odd that I have treated of the topics of this section with so little explicit reference to this important factor in experience. Does not the notion of a temporally extended series of experiences belonging to a single consciousness essentially involve memory, whatever else it involves? Does not the notion of the conceptual component in experience involve recognition and therefore memory? How *can* this faculty be so neglected? Now of course memory is involved in experience, recognition, consciousness of identity of self through diversity of experience. But it is far too deeply and essentially involved to be capable of being safely handled as if it were a separable and detachable factor which can, say, be conveniently invoked to link up temporally successive or separated

---

[1] See p. 108 above.

episodes into an experiential sequence. If experience is impossible without memory, memory also is impossible without experience. From whatever obscure levels they emerge they emerge together.

8. TRANSCENDENTAL SUBJECTIVITY AND THE LIMITATION OF THE CATEGORIES TO EXPERIENCE

There are strands in the Deduction to which I have so far given scant attention or none. Most are connected with the subjectivity thesis regarding the order of Nature, the thesis that we ourselves are the source of order and objectivity in the natural world, the thesis which corresponds on the side of understanding to the thesis of transcendental idealism on the side of sensibility. We must, of course, recognize that Kant makes two distinct uses of the notion of subjectivity, just as he employs in two distinct senses the contrast between what is "in us" and what is "outside us". The subjectivity thesis regarding the order of Nature is not a *retraction* of the distinction between the subjective order of self-ascribed or self-ascribable experiences, on the one hand, and the objective order of the world which some of these experiences must be conceived as experiences of, on the other. The subjective source of that objective order is not the self as it appears in ordinary empirical self-consciousness, but that mystery, the self as it is in itself.

The two theses of transcendental subjectivity, that of the Aesthetic and that of the Deduction, are not merely parallel. In Kant's eyes the latter rests on, and presupposes, the former. There is some reasoning, which seems to go as follows.[1] Granted that, simply as being in space and time, all natural objects are, like space and time themselves, *in us* (appearances only, mere modifications of sensibility, having no existence outside our power of representation), then it is intelligible that they should necessarily conform to the understanding's conditions for their being objects of empirical knowledge, objects of a possible experience. What can exist only as appearances (i.e. things in space and time) *must* satisfy *all* the conditions (those imposed by understanding as well as those imposed by sensibility) for existing as appearances. If, on the other hand, things in space and time had an existence of their own, then it would be in no way necessary that they should

[1] See A 128–30, B 164.

satisfy the understanding's conditions for their being objects of knowledge (i.e. that they should conform to the categories); and, unless we were prepared to regard the categories as empirical in origin, it would merely be an accident that they did so, a fluke of pre-established harmony.[1] Of this reasoning it is enough to remark that it is respectable in its own terms; but the terms are those of the model.

There is another point, in the second edition version of the Deduction, at which a link is explicitly established with the doctrine of the Aesthetic. Thus we note that, though, at the end of Section 20, Kant claims to have proved that "the manifold of a given intuition in general" is necessarily subject to the categories, he calls this only a beginning of the deduction of the categories and does not report the task as completed until, in Section 26, he has appealed to the fact that space and time, as well as being our *forms* of sensible intuition, are themselves intuitions. Up to Section 20 the argument concerning the necessary synthetic unity of understanding is supposed to have proceeded in abstraction from the actual modes of sensible intuition, the temporal and the spatial. When we do refer to these, we are supposed to be able to appreciate just how the general conclusion harmonizes with the nature of these modes of intuition, how, in a general way, it works out in connexion with them. Space and time may be considered apart from actual empirical intuition, apart from the matter of sensation, as is done, in the case of space, in the constructions of pure geometry. Even in such constructions in pure intuition, we are dealing with a manifold, having diverse parts which have to be considered together, i.e. synthesized or unified. But what is thus synthesized in pure intuition is, from another point of view, just the system of relations in which items encountered in empirical intuition, and hence subject to the categories (themselves functions of synthesis), necessarily present themselves. Space and time are both pure intuitions and the forms of empirical intuition. Hence being empirically encountered in a *unified* space and time and being subject to the general principles of unity imposed by the understanding on "the manifold of a given intuition in general" (i.e. to the categories) necessarily go together. Of this passage it is sufficient to remark that it may be seen, in part, as an anticipation of the Principles, in which the categories

[1] B 166–8.

are brought into relation with the sensible modes of intuition, in part, as another manifestation of the complex requirements of the theory of synthesis.

Next, we must notice the connexion which Kant supposed to exist between the subjectivity thesis regarding the order of nature and another important doctrine, indeed another supposed conclusion, of the Transcendental Deduction. This is the doctrine that the application of the categories is limited to objects of possible sensible experience. It is a doctrine which receives particularly strong emphasis in the second edition version of the Deduction.[1] Of it, and its connexion with the Kantian theses of transcendental subjectivity, I shall speak more fully hereafter when I come to treat of the metaphysics of transcendental idealism in general. But something must be said now of the treatment which these themes receive in the Deduction.

The conclusions which, in the previous section, I tentatively extracted from a reconstructed version of the analytical argument of the Deduction were of an extremely general nature. Anything we could understand by a possible experience must be, potentially, the experience of a self-conscious subject and must therefore have the internal connectedness, carried by concepts of the objective, which is necessary to constitute it a single course of experience of an objective world. There is no mention in this of any particular concepts or concept-types which must have application if experience is to be possible. Kant, relying on the Metaphysical Deduction, thinks himself entitled to draw the more specific conclusion that the listed categories are just such concepts; for they are, he thinks, the concepts we must apply in experience if we are to employ, in making objectively valid judgements, the forms of judgement we must employ if we are to make any judgements at all.

At our point in philosophical time, it may seem unnecessary to give special emphasis to the thesis that a concept which has necessary application in experience has no possible use in the expression of knowledge except in association with empirical criteria for its application, i.e. except in application to objects of possible experience. No one, we think, would ever entertain the idea that the use of ordinary empirical concepts could be divorced from the conditions of their empirical application without loss of

---

[1] See B 146–8, B 148–9, B 165–6.

significance. There would seem to be no more reason for supposing this in the case of categories – if analysis of the notion of
experience shows there to be such concepts – than in the case of
ordinary empirical concepts. For what distinguishes a category,
if there are any, from an ordinary empirical concept is that when
we push our notion of experience to the limits of coherent
abstraction, we still find that this notion implies the applicability
of the concept in question. We call a concept merely empirical
when we can say: If experience had been different in *these* or *these*
respects, we should have had no use for this concept. We call a
concept non-empirical (*a priori*) when we can frame no coherent
counter-factual antecedent from which we could derive such a
consequent relating to that concept. There is nothing in this to
suggest that we could detach such a concept altogether from
empirical conditions of its application and still use it to make
significant assertions.

But to present the matter simply in these terms is to ignore
altogether the doublesidedness which the notion of the *a priori*
has for Kant. Whatever is a *necessary* feature of experience is so
because of the *subjectivity* of its source. These two ideas are, for
him, indissolubly linked.[1] Moreover, there are two distinct subjective sources of necessary features of experience: sensibility on
the one hand, understanding on the other. The categories are
thought of as derived by attending to the requirements of understanding in abstraction from sensibility. If this derivation is to be
more than a pretence, the concepts so derived must be supposed
to have *some* significance, considered apart from sensible intuition.
And indeed Kant has other reasons, connected with the topic of
morality, for wishing to secure non-sensible significance to the
categories. We must be allowed to *think*, for example, of causes
not limited to the conditions of space and time.[2] All this makes it

---

[1] The linkage, in the case of the categories, can be more forcibly shown by
quoting a single sentence than by any amount of elucidating comment:
"This unity of nature has to be a necessary one, that is has to be an *a priori*
certain unity of the connexion of appearances; and such synthetic unity
could not be established *a priori* if there were not subjective grounds of such
unity contained *a priori* in the original cognitive powers of our mind, and if
these subjective conditions, inasmuch as they are the grounds of the possibility of knowing any object whatsoever in experience, were not at the same
time objectively valid" (A 125–6).

[2] Cf. B 166, footnote.

the more urgent for him to state emphatically, in terms of his theory of cognitive facilities, the reasons for the restriction on the significant use of these concepts as far as knowledge is concerned. This he does. The categories are "merely rules for an understanding whose whole power consists in thought . . . a faculty, therefore, which by itself knows nothing whatever but merely combines and arranges the material of knowledge, that is, the intuition which must be given to it by the object".[1]

On the one hand, then, "the order and regularity in the appearances which we entitle nature we ourselves introduce. We could never find them in appearances had not we ourselves, or the nature of our mind, originally set them there".[2] On the other hand, this ordering function of the categories is their sole function in knowledge. Thus the thesis of the limits of the application of the categories is presented as the reverse side of the thesis that the understanding is responsible for the fundamental order of Nature.

Only, however, for the fundamental order. Kant is emphatic that though we can know *a priori* the necessary conformity of Nature to law in general – so much being a condition of the possibility of experience – this does not mean that the methods of ordinary scientific investigation into Nature can be anything but empirical. The point is very clearly stated in both editions.[3] We have yet to discuss, of course, the question of what exactly Kant regards as involved in the necessary conformity of Nature to law in general. Even this vague conception may seem to exceed anything we can regard as established by the analytical argument of the Transcendental Deduction.

---

[1] B 145.   [2] A 125.

[3] In the first: "Certainly, empirical laws as such can never derive their origin from pure understanding. That is as little possible as to understand completely the inexhaustible multiplicity of appearances merely by reference to the pure forms of sensible intuition" (A 127).

In the second: "Pure understanding is not in a position to prescribe to appearances any *a priori* laws other than those involved in a nature in general, i.e. in the conformity to law of all appearances in space and time. Special laws cannot in their specific nature be derived from the categories, although they are one and all subject to them. To obtain any knowledge whatsoever of these special laws we must resort to experience" (B 165).

9. CONCLUDING REMARK

What are we actually left with at the end of this long discussion? Such analytical argument as we can find is conducted at dizzying heights of abstractness and generality; it is intertwined with the elaboration of the subjectivity thesis, the transcendental psychology of faculties; for anything detailed or specific by way of conclusion, it depends entirely on the derivation of a list of categories from the forms of judgement. We can place no reliance on this derivation. We have no faith in the theory of synthesis. Yet we are left with something; if not with proof, yet with reason for entertaining favourably an exceedingly general conclusion: viz. that any course of experience of which we can form a coherent conception must be, potentially, the experience of a self-conscious subject and, as such, must have such internal, concept-carried connectedness as to constitute it (at least in part) a course of experience of an objective world, conceived of as determining the course of that experience itself. Whether this general conclusion entails the necessary applicability in experience of any further concepts or principles and, if so, what these are, are questions open to further argument. The principal arguments which Kant will use will turn on relating the general notion of objectivity to that of temporal order. We may expect them to be of a less abstract nature than the arguments of the Deduction and we may accordingly hope, not only for more specific conclusions, but for a better grasp of, perhaps a strengthened confidence in, the general conclusion – which the Deduction leaves us favourably entertaining rather than wholly possessed or persuaded of.

III
PERMANENCE AND CAUSALITY

We turn from the Transcendental Deduction to the Principles
with the fairly definite hope that the significance of the general
conclusions argued for in the Deduction will be made clearer and
that, in the process, those conclusions themselves will be more
firmly established. For really the argument of the Deduction as I
have interpreted it is too general and too obscure to have more
than a precarious hold on our minds. We have the doctrine that
some form of concept-carried connectedness among experiences
such as to constitute them experiences of an objective world is a
necessary condition of the possibility of experience in general.
The hold of the doctrine would undoubtedly be strengthened by
definite and acceptable arguments to the effect that certain *specific*
forms of concept-carried connectedness are necessarily involved
in a possible experience. And such arguments, it is understood,
are to be looked for in the Principles.

1. AN "HISTORICAL" VIEW OF THE PRINCIPLES
CONSIDERED AND REJECTED

It is only with qualifications that our fairly definite hope can be
said to be fulfilled. The qualifications are serious. They are so
serious as to make it unsurprising that many philosophers have
taken a quite different view of the Principles from the hopeful
one which I have just mentioned. This quite different view, which
I must outline before proceeding, is itself an application of a
certain general doctrine regarding the nature of metaphysics; and
the application of this doctrine to the Principles rests upon the
fact that what Kant actually offers as the explicit conclusions of
the arguments of the Principles can, in a number of cases, be
reasonably viewed as fundamental assumptions of physical
theory as it existed in Kant's day and for some time before and
after his day. Thus he argues for a quantitative conservation
principle; for a principle of continuity of alteration; for the

principle that every alteration of state has a cause; for the principle of the reciprocal interaction of all parts of matter at any time. The connexion of all these principles with Newtonian physics is an easy one to make. And the connexion was certainly in Kant's mind – as we can see, if from nowhere else, from a footnote to B 252, in which, speaking of the principle that every alteration has a cause, he is careful to say that he does not count uniform motion of a body as a case of alteration of state. But though Kant viewed his conclusions as presuppositions of physical science, he did not, and could not consistently with the declared aims of the Principles, so view them under that historical perspective implied by the phrase "assumptions of physical theory as it existed in his day". On us, however, that historical perspective is imposed; for, it is authoritatively said, the framework of basic ideas contained in some of the explicit conclusions of the Principles is increasingly discarded, or at least challenged, in contemporary physics.

According to the conception of metaphysics which I have just alluded to, this position is in no way unsatisfactory. It is indeed precisely what we should expect. For on this view of metaphysics the whole function of the enterprise is precisely to articulate the buried, basic framework of ideas within which the scientific thinking – and, some would add, the social and moral thinking – of an epoch or society is conducted. Such a framework of ideas is not itself to be thought of as a theory or set of principles consciously adopted by scientists (or moralists) as a solution to some definite problem, but rather as supplying the very terms in which, in the epoch or society in question, problems are raised and competing theories constructed. Hence such sets of ideas are not to be thought of as open to direct refutation; rather, they are silently abandoned when scientific (or social) thinking enters a new phase. The whole task of the metaphysician, however *he* may conceive it, is really to make clear to us the character of our thinking, both now and in the past, by making clear what these sets of ideas actually are, or have been.

The distinctions implied in this account of metaphysics are not altogether clear. But clearly there is something in them. One who accepts not only the distinctions, but the accompanying account of metaphysics, might be supposed to congratulate Kant on having done quite a good job for the presuppositions of

Newtonian physics and even to recommend him as a model for any
successor-metaphysician willing to undertake the same job for
quantum and relativity physics. It is substantially this view of the
Analytic of Principles which we find expressed by Collingwood[1]
and by Körner.[2] Körner indeed suggests that the whole *Critique*
needs a thoroughgoing reconstruction by a philosophical physicist.

> Its doctrine of space and time as *a priori* particulars and forms of
> perception might need replacing by a new notion of space-
> time; and its three analogies by a different set. Whitehead's
> *Concept of Nature* and other works of his could be regarded . . .
> as attempts in this direction. Any philosophical physicist under-
> taking this task could learn a good deal not only from Kant's
> general approach, but also from the results of his examination
> of the science of his day.[3]

This is one view of the matter. If it were the only possible view,
the *Critique* as a whole would be a less interesting work than we
hoped. Accepting this view would amount to giving up the idea
that we may find in the Principles further elaboration of the general
conclusions of the Transcendental Deduction into more detailed
statements of generally necessary conditions of the possibility
of any experience of objective reality such as we can render
intelligible to ourselves. Instead we should have to look at the
Transcendental Deduction itself in a new light, knowing that in
general we have to be content with historical metaphysics:
accounts of the fundamental framework of ideas within which
scientific thinking has been conducted at this or that period, or is
conducted now.

This is so very far from Kant's intentions, and from what he
supposed himself to have achieved, that we should at least
hesitate over the matter. Suppose we grant, as Collingwood
held, that deficiency of historical sense led Kant into the mistake
of supposing that the fundamental assumptions of the scientific
thinking of his day were the absolutely necessary assumptions of
scientific thinking in general. It does not follow, from his making
this mistake, that there are no statable necessary conditions of the
possibility of experience in general, nor does it follow that Kant
at no point in the Principles comes anywhere near stating such
conditions. What does follow, perhaps, is that he might be more

[1] *Metaphysics*, III B.   [2] *Kant*, Chapter 4.   [3] *Op. cit.*, p. 87.

liable to misstate them, that he might be more liable to mis-identify what he took to be the necessary presuppositions of physical science as just those necessary conditions of the possibility of experience in general which he was in search of. He would be especially liable to this mistake if there were certain types of formal relation between the two: if the presuppositions of a particular kind of science were, for instance, rather specific forms of the necessary conditions of experience.

The character of the conclusions which Kant explicitly advances in the Principles is, then, no absolute bar to our hopes. We can reasonably reject the invitation to surrender in advance to a merely historical view and can persevere, with reservations, in the attempt to remain true to a conception of the Principles which corresponds more closely to Kant's own. The reservations, indeed, are important. In the first place, we are not to be bound by the Table of Categories which Kant invokes to justify his own selection and presentation of the Principles. In the second place, we are to avoid the traps set by Kant's own preoccupation with what were in fact the presuppositions of contemporary physical science. This means that we have to take as our sole and precious clue such general conclusions as we can regard as established, or at least impressively argued for, in the Transcendental Deduction. These conclusions I have expressed in a number of ways. One of them was this: that what Kant above all insisted on in the Transcendental Deduction was the necessity of a certain unity or connectedness of experiences, just that connectedness which involves and is involved by the employment of concepts of objects conceived of as together constituting an objective world. The conception of an objective world is bound up with the conception of alternative possible experiential routes through it, with the distinction between subjective experience and the world of which it *is* experience, and with the very possibility of empirical self-consciousness. The link, then, between objectivity and the necessary unity or connectedness of experience – this conception is the very heart of our precious clue, and what we are to look for in the Principles is the exposition of what is necessarily involved in this conception.

2. OBJECTIVE AND SUBJECTIVE TIME-RELATIONS

It is in the section of the Principles entitled the Analogies of Experience that there seems to be best hope of finding this exposition. We do not find it in the Axioms of Intuition or in the Anticipations of Perception. They are largely concerned with the applicability of mathematics, first, to empirically given spatial and temporal quantities – extents and durations – second, to those properties of physical objects of which the measurability is reflected in variations of degree or intensive magnitude in the sensations they excite. Nor do we find what we seek in the Postulates of Empirical Thought, which consist largely of instructions and warnings about the employment of the concepts of possibility and necessity, in application to the natural world, in senses other than the narrowly logical. But the Analogies seem to promise something of what we are looking for. The general principle of the Analogies is declared to be that "experience is possible only through the representation of a necessary connection of perceptions";[1] and Kant's own retrospective description of them runs as follows:

> Our analogies really portray the unity of nature in the connection of all appearances under certain exponents which express nothing save the relation of time . . . to the unity of apperception. . . . Taken together the analogies declare that all appearances lie, and must lie, in *one* nature, because without this *a priori* unity no unity of experience, and therefore no determination of objects in it, would be possible.[2]

It is not quite true that it is to the Analogies alone that we must turn at this stage in the argument. There are two other passages in the Principles, both added in the second edition, which deserve our attention now. The first is the Refutation of Idealism, not very strategically placed in the middle of the Postulates of Empirical Thought;[3] and the second is the General Note on the System of Principles which concludes the whole chapter.[4] Both relate to the necessity of outer intuition, of awareness of objects in space – a point from which Kant severely, though for good reason, abstracts in the description of the Analogies which I have just quoted. The first of these passages is in part – though it is also

[1] B 218.   [2] A 216/B 263.
[3] B 274-9, cf. also B xxxix-xli, footnote.   [4] B 291-3.

more than this – an anti-Cartesian argument to the effect that self-consciousness is possible only through the perception of outer objects. In the second passage, Kant, having argued in the Analogies that the applicability of the concepts of substance, cause and community (or reciprocal interaction) is a necessary condition of the possibility of objective experience, adds that a condition of our being able to attach any meaning to these notions or make any use of them is that we should be able to apply them to objects of outer or spatial intuition, i.e. to objects which we are aware of as being objects in space.

Both passages are important as underlining once more how little Kant depends on the theses of the Transcendental Aesthetic as premises for his arguments in the Analytic – a point foreshadowed in my earlier discussion of the relation between the theses of the Analytic and those of the Aesthetic. It has been argued in the Deduction that there must be some form of connexion among experiences such as to constitute them experiences of an objective world. We might have expected that in the argument now before us, Kant would draw on the theses of the Aesthetic to the extent of taking as premissed the spatiality of the world of objects. Then the problem to be solved in the Analogies could be stated as follows. For the world to be conceived as objective, it must be possible to distinguish between the order of perceptions occurring in one experiential route through it and the order and relation which the objective constituents of the world independently possess. That order and those relations cannot be determined by reference to the pure spatio-temporal framework itself, which is not a possible object of perception. Somehow or other, therefore, that objective order must be represented in the concepts which we apply to, or under which we bring, the contents of our perceptions themselves – concepts, as Kant says, of necessary connexion of perceptions. The problem of the Analogies is to show how that order is, and must be, represented.

But Kant does not in fact pose the problem in this form. Throughout the Analogies the problem is represented solely as that of ascertaining the necessary conditions of determining objective *time*-relations. That this involves determining objective relations not merely in a temporal, but in a *spatio*-temporal, order is not something assumed by the argument, but something that, in a manner, emerges from it. In the two passages I have just mentioned we come as near as anywhere to an explicit statement of the point.

I have just said that Kant represents his problem in the Analogies as that of ascertaining the necessary conditions of determining objective time-relations. Nowhere, I think, is Kant's generalizing genius more clearly shown than in his reduction of the problem to this form. It is perhaps evident enough, given the arguments of the Transcendental Deduction, that the problem is to discover what is necessary to make a temporal succession of experiences (or perceptions) perceptions *of* an objective reality, a reality of which other temporal series of perceptions are also possible. But it was a great insight to perceive that this problem can be reduced to that of discovering the necessary conditions of the possibility of distinguishing two sets of relations: (1) the time-relations between the objects which the perceptions are to be taken as perceptions of; (2) the time-relations between the members of the (subjective) series of perceptions themselves. If there were no way of making this distinction, then no meaning would attach to the distinction between objects and perceptions of objects; and all the attendant notions would collapse too: i.e. the notion of a subjective or experiential route through an objective world, the possibility of empirical self-consciousness, the necessary self-reflexiveness of experience, hence the very notion of experience itself. If, on the other hand, the distinction can be made, then any necessary conditions of making it are necessary conditions of the possibility of experience. The Transcendental Deduction has argued in general terms for the necessity of *some* forms of concept-carried connexion or unity among experiences in order to constitute them experiences of a reality describable in objective judgements. What these forms of connexion and unity are we may hope to discover among the conditions of determining objective time-relations, as opposed to merely subjective time-relations, among experiences.

The elements we may still find acceptable in Kant's solution to his problem really together form a single complex structure of argument. But no such unified argument is presented by Kant. We have to pick it out as best we can from the several arguments of the three Analogies and the Refutation of Idealism. I begin by considering, in a conflated form, the arguments of the Refutation and of the first Analogy.

3. PERMANENCE: THE REFUTATION OF IDEALISM AND THE FIRST ANALOGY

The announced achievement of the Refutation is "to turn the game played by idealism against itself" by proving that empirical self-consciousness is only possible through an immediate awareness of objects in space. The announced, though not actual, achievement of the first Analogy is to prove a quantitative conservation principle to the effect that the quantum of substance in Nature is neither increased nor diminished. The latter, however, is simply Kant's surprising gloss on a more promising idea which figures prominently in both arguments: that of the necessity of something permanent in perception. One argument is explicitly concerned with the general conditions of the possibility of self-consciousness; the other is explicitly concerned with the general conditions of determining time-relations among the objects of experience. In view of what has been said about the connexion between these problems, it would not be surprising if both arguments should point towards a common conclusion.

Unfortunately, they only waveringly do so. A course of argument we might have hoped for, rather than any we actually find, could be set out as follows. It is impossible to draw the necessary distinctions between (1) the time-relations of the members of a subjective series of perceptions and (2) the time-relations of at least some objects which the perceptions are perceptions of, unless the objects in question are seen as belonging to an enduring framework of relations in which the objects themselves enjoy their temporal relations (of co-existence or succession) with each other independently of the order of our perceptions of them. This enduring framework of relations is spatial. Space is the necessary permanent framework for objective time-relations. As Kant himself puts it emphatically at B 291, "space alone is determined as permanent". But there is no question of perceiving the necessary framework itself, of perceiving, as it were, pure spatial permanence. So we must perceive some *objects* as enduring objects, even if our perceptions of them do not endure, must see them as falling under concepts of persistent objects, even though objects of non-persistent perceptions. The idea of a subjective experiential route through an objective world depends on the idea of the identity of that world through and in spite of the changes in our experience;

and this idea in turn depends on our perceiving objects as having a permanence independent of our perceptions of them, and hence being able to identify objects as numerically the same in different perceptual situations.

Neither argument follows just this course. The first Analogy argues obscurely for the necessity of a permanent and then leaps to the conservation-principle already mentioned. The Refutation argues by way of the idea of a permanent for the necessity of immediate awareness of outer objects. Let us consider the latter a little more closely. Kant begins: "I am conscious of my own existence as determined in time" and moves straight to "All determination of time presupposes something permanent in perception", thereby echoing the first Analogy. Then he proceeds to argue that this permanent must be something which I perceive outside me. He was clearly not very happy, however, about the statement of the argument in the main text. As he justly remarks, "there is some obscurity in the expressions used in the proof"; and he wrestles with the argument again in a long footnote in the Preface, several times the length of the proof as originally stated. Perhaps it is possible to get somewhat nearer to the actual movement of his thought than I have done in the course of argument I have just set out. I shall make the attempt.

Suppose we think first simply of a temporal series of representations or experiences, abstracting momentarily from the fact that what we really mean by an experience's membership of such a series is really nothing different from its being an experience of a potentially self-conscious subject. We may then simply think of the members of the series as temporally ordered in relation to each other, as having each a determinate temporal position in the series relatively to the others. But, recalling now what we momentarily abstracted from, we see that these internal temporal relations of the members of the series are quite inadequate to sustain or give any content to the idea of *the subject's awareness of himself as having* such-and-such an experience at such-and-such a time (i.e. at such-and-such a position in a temporal order). To give content to this idea we need, at least, the idea of a system of temporal relations which comprehends more than those experiences themselves. But there is, for the subject himself, no access to this wider system of temporal relations except through his own experiences. Those experiences, therefore, or some of them, must be taken by him to be experiences *of* things (other than the experiences themselves) which possess among themselves the temporal relations of this wider system. But there is only one way in which perceived things or processes can supply a system of temporal relations independent of the order of the subject's perceptions of them – viz. by *lasting* and being *re*-encounterable in temporally different perceptual experiences. Awareness of permanent things distinct from myself is therefore indispensable to my assigning experiences to myself, to my being conscious of myself as having, at different times, different experiences.[1]

What we have here, evidently, is a form of the argument for the objectivity thesis, with particular emphasis on the point that abidingness or permanence must somehow be represented in the objective order. There is, as usual, no independent argument to the effect that the objective order must be a spatial order. Instead there is the usual transition from "things distinct from our representations of them" through "outer things" or "objects of outer intuition" to "spatial things" or "things in space". If directly challenged on the point, Kant would no doubt, and reasonably, reply that, endowed with the kind of experience we are endowed with, we cannot really make intelligible to ourselves the idea of any alternative to an objective spatial order; or, at least, that if we can conceive of an alternative, we can conceive of it only on analogy with space. Perhaps it is worth while briefly re-plotting the course of the argument in such a way as to bring out the force of this reply.

The thought which lies at the core of all argument for the objectivity thesis is one which we have encountered before and which I first introduced in connexion with the Transcendental Deduction. It is that the fundamental condition of the possibility of empirical self-consciousness is that experience should contain

---

[1] The argument, being expressly anti-Cartesian in aim, takes empirical self-consciousness as an unquestioned element in any possible experience. It could be re-framed on the basis of the perhaps less demanding requirement of self-reflexiveness in experience. The required distinction between "things being thus-and-so" and "things being *experienced* as being thus-and-so" must be provided for within the temporal series of experiences themselves, and can be so provided for only if some of the latter are taken to be experiences *of* things which possess among themselves temporal relations independent of the order in which they are actually experienced. From this point the argument proceeds as before.

at least the seeds of the idea of one experiential or subjective route through an objective world. The idea of a mere temporal succession of representations, of the form "Now A, now B, now C", etc., does not by itself contain the seeds of this idea. If and only if we enlarge the form to "*Here* now A", etc., and dwell on the implications of this addition, do we find the seeds of this idea. For the addition of "here" to "now" is completely otiose unless it carries with it the possibility of such contrasts as "somewhere else now" and "here again later on"; i.e. unless it carries with it the implications of a wider and enduring spatial (or quasi-spatial) framework through which *one* experiential route is possible just because different experiential routes are possible. Therefore, since the "pure" framework itself is not a possible object of perception, the fundamental condition of the possibility of empirical self-consciousness in time is the awareness of enduring objects in space (or, at least, in some analogue of space which we can make intelligible to ourselves only *as* an analogue of space).

And now we must return to the actual claims Kant makes for the argument of the first Analogy. We must face the contrast, that is, between what he thought he had established and what he can be held actually to have established by these arguments to the effect that permanence or abidingness must somehow be represented in the objective (spatial) order. The announced conclusion of the first Analogy is, in effect, the scientific principle of the conservation of mass or of some other measurable essence of matter. The theorem to be proved is stated as follows: "In all change of appearances substance is permanent; its *quantum* in nature is neither increased nor diminished."[1] Again, at the end of the first brief run-through of the proof, we have the conclusion:

> The permanent, in relation to which alone all time-relations of appearances can be determined, is substance in the field of appearance, that is, the real in appearance; and as the substrate of all change, remains ever the same. And as it is thus unchangeable in its existence, its *quantity* in nature can be neither increased nor diminished.[2]

This interpretation by Kant of his own results is quite inexplicable except on the hypothesis I have already mentioned, viz. that Kant was exposed to a very strong temptation to identify

[1] B 224.   [2] B 225.

whatever he succeeded in establishing as necessary conditions of the possibility of experience of an objective world with what he already conceived to be the fundamental, unquestionable assumptions of physical science. On this hypothesis it is not altogether unintelligible that the temptation should operate in the present case. Kant, we may say, has succeeded in establishing a metaphysical conservation-principle of some kind. He has established the principle of the necessary conservation of the identity of the world of things in space. This is what must be conceived as absolutely permanent and abiding: the spatio-temporal frame of things at large. It is also perfectly true that this absolutely permanent and abiding frame is not itself, as it were, a pure object of perception and that its abidingness must therefore somehow be empirically represented for us in our actual perception of objects. But all that is required is that we should in principle be able to locate in the enduring framework everything objective that we encounter, i.e. to relate everything that we count as objective to everything else that we count as objective in one system of spatio-temporal relations. And for this to be possible it is certainly not necessary either that we should operate with (or even dream of) any scientific conservation principle or that any such principle should in fact apply to the world of our experience. What is necessary, no doubt, is that we should be able to identify places, and hence objects or processes, as the same at different times. Given the limitations of our actual perceptual experience, this in turn requires that we should *perceive* some objects *as* having a permanence which our perceptions of them do not have. It requires that our perceptual experience be such as is only adequately describable by the application of concepts of certain kinds – of precisely such kinds (e.g. concepts of material bodies) as those our actual application of which the sense-datum theorist tries to justify in other ways. But none of this implies any necessity for any absolute permanence either of particular objects or of any such quantitative aspects of matter as physicists once did, or now do, refer to under such names as "mass" or "energy".

Kant's radical confusions on the matter appear in such a passage as the following:

Substances, in appearance, are the substrate of all determinations of time. If some of these substances could come into being and

I

others cease to be, the one condition of the empirical unity of time would be removed. The appearances would then relate to two different times and existence would flow in two parallel streams – which is absurd. There is only one time in which all different times must be located, not as coexistent but as in succession to one another.[1]

The shift from "substance" in the singular (in the original statement of the proof) to "substances" in the plural is puzzling enough. Kant has said, of substance in the singular, that *its* quantum in Nature can neither be increased nor diminished. By supposing substance to be divided into equal units (ultimate particles perhaps), to be called substances, we could indeed derive from this dictum the conclusion that the *number* of substances in Nature can be neither increased nor diminished. We should still not have the consequence that substances could not go out of, or come into, existence, but merely the consequence that losses and gains must always and simultaneously offset each other. But whatever we understand by "substances", it seems obvious that our conceptual scheme (or our myths) could allow for the endings and beginnings of existence of particular items of any class, however conceived, without destroying our grasp of the continuing unity and identity of the spatio-temporal framework of the world to which those items belong. If it has been, or is, a presupposition of some scientific view or theory, that there are permanent and indestructible elementary constituents of matter, then this fact shows only that the presupposition of such a view or theory is by no means a necessary precondition of the possibility of experience of an objective world.

Perhaps we can come a little nearer to explaining, though not to justifying, the passage in question. Kant, let us say, has shown the necessity of something abiding and permanent, viz. the whole frame of Nature; and if the word "substance" is to be linked with the concept of absolute permanence, it is to the whole frame of Nature that it should be applied – as it was by Spinoza. At the same time, he is at least partially aware that what represents this permanence for us in experience is not any one absolutely permanent thing, but rather those merely relatively permanent objects of perception which, in their relations to each other, yield

[1] A 188–9/B 231–2.

the one enduring framework.[1] It might, therefore, be natural enough to apply the word "substance" in a transferred sense to these objects too. Then we should have substances – in the plural; and, of course, at least some kinds of relatively persisting spatio-temporal particulars have an historical, indeed an Aristotelian, claim to the title. If we now suppose a conflation of the two ideas of absolute permanence and plurality, belonging respectively to these two uses of the word, and – under the influence of the temptation I have already mentioned – an identification of the result with a third and scientific application of the word, then we have the outcome we set out to explain.

It is clear that Kant was not only confused in, but also uneasy about, his doctrine of substance. At the end of the first Analogy, after repeating its general conclusion, "Permanence is thus a necessary condition under which alone objects are determinable as things or objects in a possible experience", he goes on: "We shall have occasion in what follows to make such observations as may seem necessary *in regard to the empirical criterion* of this necessary permanence – the criterion, consequently, of the substantiality of appearances."[2] That Kant should have felt the need for further observations on this point is natural enough. He has to reckon here not only with the general, and admirable, Kantian principle that we can attach sense to a concept only in terms of the conditions of its empirical employment. There is also the fact that the concept in question is supposed to be a category, i.e. a concept such that our making an empirical use of it is a necessary condition of our having any experience of an objective world. The necessity of its having application to the objective world is indeed identical with *this* necessity. Now no doubt a description can be given of the use, in application to objects of experience, of some scientific principle of quantitative constancy in matter. Rules can be given for the empirical employment of the concept. But it is quite unplausible to suggest that the employment of this concept is necessarily implicit in any non-scientific person's judgements of experience. The pre-scientifically-minded person is quite able to see or think of something's going up in smoke or being reduced to ashes without in any way supposing that anything quantitatively identical persists

[1] Cf. B 277, Note 2 to the Refutation of Idealism.
[2] A 189/B 232. We find the passage concerned at A 204–6/B 249–51.

throughout the transaction. If we are really dealing with a category, then we are dealing with a concept which anyone capable of objective experience *must*, at least implicitly, apply; but the doctrine of implicit application would be quite unplausible in this case. Kant, therefore, does not in fact tell us anything about the use made by scientists of conservation principles. He postpones the whole question of "the empirical criterion of a substance" to that late passage I referred to, in which he says that "substance appears to manifest itself not through permanence of appearance but more adequately and easily through action",[1] and, again, "action is a sufficient empirical criterion to establish the substantiality of a subject without my requiring first to go in quest of its permanence through the comparison of perceptions".[2] But though he says that "acting" is a criterion of permanence, he does not tell us what is the, or a, criterion of acting, except to say that action signifies the relation of a subject of causality to its effect. I mention this passage mainly as a symptom of uneasiness, and shall not examine it further.

As regards the first Analogy, taken together with the Refutation of Idealism, then, we can, I think, say this. Kant does not succeed in proving the scientific conservation principle which he affirms as its conclusion. But he does prove something important. Experience of the objective demands the possibility of determining objective time-relations. To say that objective time-determination is possible is to say that we can assign to objects and happenings temporal relations of co-existence and succession and that we can, where necessary, distinguish these relations from the temporal relations of our perceptions, though, of course, we assign them fundamentally on the strength of our perceptions. For this to be possible we must see objects as belonging to, and events as occurring in, an identical, enduring spatial framework. For this in turn to be possible, we must have empirically applicable criteria of persistence and identity, embodied in concepts under which we bring objects of non-persistent perceptions. If we choose to call such concepts "concepts of substances", then we must have and apply concepts of substances.

[1] A 204/B 249.   [2] A 205/B 250–1.

4. CAUSALITY: THE ARGUMENTS OF THE SECOND AND THIRD ANALOGIES

In the first Analogy Kant has been professedly concerned with the general conditions of objective time-determination; and he has held that any such determination involves objective permanence being somehow represented in perceptions which are themselves constantly changing. Now any time-relations whatever, and hence any objective time-relations, are fundamentally of two kinds: relations of succession and relations of simultaneous existence or, as Kant says, of co-existence. (The relation of temporal overlap can be analysed in terms of the two others.) In the second and third Analogies Kant appears to turn from the question of the general conditions of the possibility of determination of objective time-relations to what he appears to treat as the separate questions of the special conditions, respectively, of empirical knowledge of objective succession and of empirical knowledge of objective co-existence. It may well look as if there must be something odd about the idea of further *independent* proofs of conditions for these two cases. For any account, or any complete account, of the conditions of determining objective time-relations in general must surely be an account of the conditions of determining just these two kinds of relations. It might seem, therefore, that the natural procedure would be to take the conclusion of the first Analogy as the premise of any further argument; to inquire, that is, what further conditions must be satisfied if objective permanence is to be represented in changing perceptions. But these are no more than preliminary doubts. Let us put them aside while we turn to the examination of the arguments themselves.

The central thought of both the second and the third Analogies may be expressed as follows. In respect of all successive perceptions which are taken to be perceptions of the objective, there arises a certain question. This is the question whether those perceptions could or could not have occurred in the opposite order to that in which they in fact occurred, whether they possess or lack a feature which might be called "order-indifference". The sense of the question is not immediately obvious. But it is at least partially clarified by Kant's answer to it; which runs as follows. If what we perceive is an objective alteration, an event, a case of one objective state of affairs giving place to another, then our successive perceptions of these objectively successive states *lack* the feature of order-indifference.[1] Our successive perceptions could not have occurred in the opposite order to that in which they in fact occurred. To put it more positively, the order they have is a necessary order. If, on the other hand, what we successively perceive are objectively co-existent things or parts of a thing (i.e. things or parts of a thing which exist simultaneously throughout the time taken by our successive perceptions), then our successive perceptions of these objectively co-existent items *possess* the feature of order-indifference. They could have occurred in the opposite order to that in which they in fact occurred.

Kant, particularly in the case of objective succession, expresses these connexions with a particular direction of epistemological emphasis. Any use we may make in experience of the concept of an objective event depends upon our implicit use of the notion of a necessary order of the relevant perceptions. Similarly, our knowledge, through perception, of the co-existence of things depends upon our implicit recognition of the order-indifference of the relevant perceptions. Lack or possession of order-indifference on the part of our perceptions is, he seems to say, our criterion – whether we reflectively realize the fact or not – of objective succession or co-existence.[2]

Before we consider how Kant proceeds to exploit these connexions, we must inquire whether they in fact hold. It seems that, suitably and reasonably interpreted and qualified, they do. The basic interpretation runs as follows. Given a period of co-existence of two particular, independently perceptible objects, A and B, then it is possible that during the period of their co-existence we should perceive them either in the order A, B, or in the order B, A; and if in that period we do perceive them in the order A, B, it is possible that we might instead have perceived them in the

---

[1] It should be noted that the concept of objective succession in general is wider than that of one objective state of affairs *giving place* to another in a single event or change. One state (S_2) may begin to exist at the time when another state (S_1) ceases to exist without its being the case that there is a *change* from S_1 to S_2 or that the succession of S_2 upon S_1 constitutes a single event. Yet such a succession of states may fall within the perception of a single observer. Kant is concerned only with the narrower application of the concept.

[2] See further Part IV, Section 3, pp. 244–5 below.

order B, A. On the other hand, given that a change occurs which consists in one objective state of affairs, A, giving place to another objective state of affairs, B, then it is possible that we should perceive those states of affairs in the order A, B, but not possible that we should perceive them in the order B, A; and if we do perceive them in the order A, B, it is not possible that we might instead have perceived them in the order B, A.

The first part of the doctrine calls for little comment. Of course, the supposition that we might have perceived two co-existent objects in the opposite order to that in which we in fact perceived them will normally involve some supposition of a further difference in the situation as a whole: a different order of appearance of the objects in procession, a different direction of scanning on our part, etc. These suppositions of difference may be quite radical but may legitimately be made, so long as the given condition, of the co-existence of the particular objects, A and B, is not upset.

This requirement, that the given condition be not upset, preserves the second part of the doctrine from the simple-minded objection that we might have perceived the objective state of affairs B (the ship downstream) before the objective state of affairs A (the ship upstream) if the ship had been sailing, with engines reversed, in the opposite direction to that in which it sailed in fact. More sophisticated objections remain. Suppose the state of affairs A was such as we might properly be said to *hear* and the state of affairs B such as we might properly be said to *see*. Then might it not be supposed that we perceived (saw) B before we perceived (heard) A? Or again, without exploiting any differences of sensory modes of perception, might it not be supposed that whereas we saw (or heard) B directly, we saw (or heard) A only very indirectly through some complex delaying mechanism for the transmission of light (or sound), so that our perception of B preceded our perception of A, though in the same sensory mode?

Evidently these particular objections can be met by stipulating that the doctrine is to be understood as applying only to perceptions of A and B which are equally direct and in the same sensory mode. Any further objections of a similar general kind could be met by further stipulations of a similar general kind. Or, better, the general principle of such qualifications can be incorporated in the doctrine. There is, as we shall see in a moment, no difficulty about stating that principle.

Suitably understood and qualified, then, the doctrine appears to hold in both its parts, i.e. both as regards the perception of objective events and as regards the perception of co-existent objects. Kant, we know, proposes to use these truths to prove that certain principles of causality hold of any objects or objective events of which we can have any empirical knowledge through perception. Before we examine the course of his argument for these principles, it may be worth raising, in a preliminary way, the question what prima facie connexions, if any, are to be found between these truths and the topic of causality. That there are such connexions can scarcely be doubted. But they seem to have to do not so much with causal transactions or dependencies relating objects of subjective perception to one another as with the causal dependencies of subjective perceptions themselves upon their objects. That an effect cannot precede its cause in time Kant would perhaps acknowledge as a conceptual truth requiring no special mode of proof. That any experience conceived of as a perception of some objective item is thereby conceived of as causally dependent upon (an effect of) the existence of that item is a truth contained in the very concept of sense-perception of objects whose existence is independent of our awareness of them. If these truths are taken together with the suppositions (1) that A and B are objective states of affairs of which A precedes B in time, this succession constituting a single event (the event of A's being succeeded by B), (2) α is a perception of A and β of B, (3) there is no relevant difference in the modes of causal dependence of α on A and β on B (a relevant difference being any which affects the time taken by the causal process whereby the object (A or B) produces its effect (α or β) to complete itself), then there follows, with *logical* necessity, the consequence that α precedes β. The substitution for (1), however, of the supposition that A and B are co-existent objects leaves it a logically open question which, of α and β, comes first. The necessary order of perceptions in the one case, their order-indifference in the other, reduce, it seems, to just this logical necessity and this logical indifference. Causality figures, indeed, in the argument; but in no other way than that indicated.

It is not in this way that causality figures in Kant's argument.

His idea is not that causation of perceptions by their objects serves as a bridge linking the notions of objective change and objective co-existence to the notions of a determined (necessary) or undetermined (indifferent) order of perceptions. His idea is, rather, that these latter notions are themselves to serve as a bridge linking the notions of objective change and objective co-existence to certain general principles regarding causal relations between the objects of perception. The role of the linking notions is to provide a demonstration that we could claim no empirical knowledge of those objective time-relations without presupposing the application of these principles to the objective world. The idea is that we could not empirically apply (and hence could have no real grasp of) the concepts of objective change and objective co-existence without implicitly using the notions of a necessary order, and of order-indifference, of perceptions, and that these notions in turn could have no application unless the relevant causal principles applied to the objects of the perceptions to which these notions are implicitly applied.

In the light of the preceding discussion of the doctrine of necessary and indifferent orders of perception, this general description of Kant's argument may seem already to constitute a tolerably firm ground for scepticism regarding its worth. But we cannot condemn the arguments without hearing them.

In the second Analogy Kant expresses in a number of ways the thought that the order of perceptions of those objective states of affairs the succession of one upon the other of which constitutes an objective change is – as, in the sense examined and with the qualifications mentioned, we see it is – a necessary order. The order of perceptions is characterized not only as a *necessary*, but as a *determined* order,[1] an order to which our apprehension is *bound down*,[2] or which we are *compelled* to observe.[3] These may all perhaps be admitted as legitimate ways of expressing the denial of order-indifference. But from this point the argument proceeds by a *non sequitur* of numbing grossness. Suppose the objective succession in question consists in the succession of state of affairs B upon state of affairs A, in the change, that is to say, from A to B. It is admitted, in the sense and with the qualifications mentioned, as *necessary* that the perception of the second state (B) follows and does not precede the perception of the first state (A). To conceive the

---

[1] A 192/B 237.   [2] A 192/B 237.   [3] A 196/B 242.

sequence of perceptions as the perception of an objective change is implicitly to conceive the order of the perceptions as, in this sense, necessary. But – and here comes the step – to conceive this order of perceptions as necessary is equivalent to conceiving the transition or change from A to B as *itself* necessary, as falling, that is to say, under a rule or law of causal determination; it is equivalent to conceiving the event of change or transition as preceded by some condition such that an event of that type invariably and necessarily follows upon a condition of that type. (It should be noticed that Kant does not say that to conceive the order of perceptions of A and B as necessary is equivalent to conceiving A as causally necessitating B. He says it is equivalent to conceiving the change from A to B as causally necessitated by *some* unspecified antecedent conditions.) Briefly, any succession of perceptions is a perception of objective change only if the order of those perceptions is necessary; but the order of the perceptions can be necessary only if the change is necessary, i.e. causally determined. Any objective change which is an object of possible experience for us, i.e. an object of possible perception, is causally determined. Hence the Law of Universal Causality is valid for all possible experience.

The character of the fallacy should be clear from our previous discussion of the notion of necessity or indifference of the order of perceptions. Kant is under the impression that he is dealing with a single application of a single notion of necessity. In fact, he not only shifts the *application* of the word "necessary", but also changes its *sense*, substituting one type of necessity for another. It is conceptually necessary, given that what is observed is in fact a change from A to B, and that there is no such difference in the causal conditions of the perception of these two states as to introduce a differential time-lag into the perception of A, that the observer's perceptions should have the order: perception of A, perception of B – and not the reverse order. But the necessity invoked in the conclusion of the argument is not a conceptual necessity at all; it is the causal necessity of the change occurring, given some antecedent state of affairs. It is a very curious contortion indeed whereby a conceptual necessity based on the fact of a change is equated with the causal necessity of that very change.

If the use which Kant makes of the notion of a necessary order of perceptions in the sense of the second Analogy is illegitimate, it might still be inquired whether any legitimate use, for purposes at least akin to his, can be made of it. The answer is, I think, that none can, that the notion of a necessary order, in the sense in question, is useless for these purposes. This does not mean that we cannot establish any conclusion akin to his, regarding change in the objective world, with the help of other notions considered in the Analogies. But we must go less directly to work.

Before we undertake this, however, we must consider the official argument of the third Analogy. It is, if anything, even less persuasive than that of the second, in which we have at least the play on the notion of necessity to confuse us. There is a certain formal parallelism between the two arguments. Just as in the second Analogy the necessary order of perceptions is equated with the causal determination of objective change, so in the third the order-indifference of perceptions is equated with the mutual causal influence of co-existent objects. The thought that at the very moment at which we are actually perceiving the object A we might instead be perceiving the object B and vice versa is held to contain implicitly the thought that the two objects are in reciprocal causal interaction. The thought of objects as co-existing during a certain period is identical with the thought of our perceptions of them during that period as being reversible or order-indifferent. Hence knowledge of objective co-existence implies the truth of whatever is implied by the latter thought. Hence a law of mutual interaction between co-existent objects holds for all possible experience.

Such play as there is in this argument is mainly on the notion of "reciprocity": a possible "reciprocity of perceptions" reflects an actual reciprocity of causal influence; or the possibility of "reciprocal perceptions" of objects reflects the existence of reciprocal causal influence of objects. The relevant senses of the words "reciprocal" and "reciprocity" are here so widely different that the mere repetition of the word lacks the confusing power of the second Analogy's shift in sense and application of the word "necessity". A little later on the words "determine" and "community" are also pressed into equivocal service. We have – at the opening of some remarks which Kant says "may be helpful", as indeed they are, though not quite in the way he intends – the following sentence: "In so far as objects are to be represented as co-existing in connexion with each other they must mutually determine their position in one time and thereby constitute a whole."[1] This sentence may be juxtaposed with one which in fact occurs on an earlier page but which, without any distortion of Kant's argument, could just as well have followed it, viz. "Now only that which is the *cause* of another, or of its determinations, determines the position of the other in time." Hence "each substance . . . must contain in itself the causality of certain determinations in the other substance and at the same time the effect of the causality of that other".[2] The transition calls for only the barest comment. Let it be granted that the thought of an object of possible perception which is not currently being perceived as co-existing with another which *is* currently being perceived involves the thought of their being mutually related in some way other than that of mere co-existence. Thus they may (perhaps must – it is a question we have to discuss further) be thought of as being related to each other in a common space. In so far as the position of each in a common space can be specified by relating it to the other, they might be said mutually to determine their positions. That they also causally interact, if they do, however, is an additional truth which it would require something better than an equivocation to derive from mutual determination of position in the sense just mentioned.

5. CAUSALITY: ANOTHER ATTEMPT

If the direct arguments of both second and third Analogies fail, however, it does not follow that the problem of the Analogies cannot be advanced at all, and advanced in something like a Kantian direction, with the help of materials which Kant puts at our disposal. We will here reverse the order of the Analogies and start with themes prominent in the third. In spite of Kant's disreputable play with the notions of reciprocity and mutual determination, it is possible that the ideas underlying these notions can be put to some more legitimate use. Let us recall what the general problem of the Analogies is. It is the problem of the conditions of the possibility of objective time-determination; and the importance of the problem resides in the fact that only if it is possible to distinguish between the subjective time-order of perceptions

[1] A 241/B 261.   [2] A 212/B 259.

and the time-relations of objects which the perceptions are perceptions of, is it possible to give content to the general notion of experience of an objective reality, hence to make intelligible the possibility of experience itself. Evidently a, or the, key notion in this problem is that of currently unperceived objects which are nevertheless objects of possible perception, co-existing with, or existing at the same time as, objects of actual perception. If there were no such co-existence of objects of possible with objects of actual perception, there would be no effective distinction to be drawn between objective and subjective time-orders. Again, the mere idea of such objects as objects of possible perception is not enough for the distinction to have any effective employment. It is effectively employed only if we think of objects actually encountered in experience, objects which we actually perceive, as existing not only when we perceive them, but also at other times, when we perceive, not them, but other objects. Now this is the thought which underlies the notion of order-indifference of perceptions. This notion involves that of the possession by objects which we actually perceive of a relative permanence or persistence which our perceptions of them do not possess. It gives prominence to the notion of particular or numerical identity of objects: the identity of an object actually perceived at a certain moment with an object which the perceiver might have perceived at an earlier or later moment.

Evidently we are not here far removed from the governing conception of the first Analogy. The question is how much more we can make of that conception. We have asserted already, but can now see more clearly, the link between the idea of a permanent in perception and two further thoughts, both Kantian in spirit and not independent of each other. We *perceive successively* objects which we nevertheless *know* to be *co-existent*. But how can we know this? Kant asks this question, and answers it by invoking the reversibility or order-indifference of perceptions.[1] He then proceeds to what appears to be a mere equivocation with the notion of reciprocity. Nevertheless there is something right about Kant's answer; and what is right about it is the suggestion it seems to carry that it is the character of our perceptions themselves that enables us to count perceptions which succeed each other as perceptions of objects which do not. This character of the perceptions

[1] A 211/B 258.

themselves can be expressed by saying that we *perceive* (some of) the things we do perceive *as* things of certain general kinds, *as* things falling under general concepts of relatively persistent and re-identifiable objects. We cannot, that is to say, characterize those perceptions themselves except with the help of concepts of persistent things which we perceive the objects of those perceptions as instances of. That is the first and by now familiar thought. The second is that we must conceive of such objects as *ordered in some system or framework of relations such as alone can give sense to the notion of particular identity of such objects*. I say that these two thoughts are not independent of each other; for the notion of having general concepts of the kind required and perceiving objects as falling under them without, however, having any idea of how questions of particular identity regarding such objects might be settled is a senseless one.

It has been sufficiently remarked already that the most natural way, and perhaps the only way, for us to conceive of a possible framework or system of relations of the kind required is to conceive of it as spatial. To this we may now add two further points, also wholly Kantian in topic, though not both equally Kantian in spirit. The first is that we must conceive ourselves, as perceivers, as having at any moment a determinable position in the system of relations to which the perceived objects belong. For only under this condition can the subjective series of our experiences be conceived as a series of *perceptions* of objects existing independently and enjoying their mutual relations in the system. The second point is in the nature of a query or a caution. I have spoken of the necessity of objects belonging to, or being ordered in, a system of relations in which we, as perceivers, also have a position. But is it necessary that there should be just *one* such system? Of course the easiest and most natural way for us to conceive of the satisfaction of this condition is simply the way in which we do in fact conceive of it: every natural object whatever is thought of as located, in a more or less direct sense, in one abiding and all-comprehensive space. But is it really impossible to conceive any coherent alternative to this? Would it not be possible, for example, that, in order to give our position as perceivers at any moment, we had to refer to two independent systems of relations – one, perhaps, the space of sight and touch that we know and the other an unrelated quasi-space involving different modes of perception?

Or again might we not, by imagining certain kinds of radical discontinuity in our experience, suppose ourselves at different times inhabitants of different spatial worlds, spatially unrelated to each other? To pursue these questions in this section would take us too far from our immediate objective. I shall recur to them briefly a little later on. Kant, of course, would have denied any such possibility; on the ground that unity of consciousness implies thoroughgoing unity of the objective world. But accepting that unity of consciousness implies unity of *an* objective world, one might still feel that further argument is required to show that the idea of a unified consciousness having access to a plurality of unified objective worlds is incoherent. For the time being, however, we will set this doubt aside. There are still further results to be achieved regarding the conditions of the possibility of knowledge of (any) *one* objective world.

So far we have established the necessity of concepts of persistent and re-identifiable objects locatable in a common spatial (or quasi-spatial) framework. We must have such concepts and apply them to objects of perception if we are to make use of the crucial notion of simultaneous existence of objects not simultaneously perceived – a notion which is crucial because without it we can make no use of the distinction between objective and subjective time-determinations. But now suppose we add to the idea of *unperceived* objective co-existence (the key notion of the third Analogy) the idea of *perceived* objective succession or change (the key notion of the second Analogy). Does the addition of this idea carry with it any further necessities? The two ideas are clearly different in a most important respect. The first invites us to consider the conditions of our making a distinction between the way our perceptions are ordered (i.e. as successive) and the way their objects are ordered (i.e. as co-existent). But the second cannot invite us to consider the conditions of making any such distinction; for no such distinction is in question. It does, indeed, invite us to consider something new, viz. the conditions of conceiving a change in our perceptions as the perception of a change. A perceived change *in* objects is certainly something different from a change *of* objects perceived. But on this we might be inclined to comment that all that is required is that the concepts of persistent objects, which, as has already been sufficiently argued, we must have and apply, should be concepts of objects which are capable of change: e.g. of qualitative change; or of change of relative position in the common framework; or of change in the relative positions of their parts.

We must pause, however, over the implications of this answer. We are to acknowledge that changes in the ever-changing subjective series of perceptions may be attributable not only to changes in the viewpoint of the perceiver, but also to changes in the world of objects he perceives. The point is allowed for, it is said, by the requirement that his concepts of persistent objects must be concepts of changeable objects – of objects that can change, that is to say, both while being perceived and while not being perceived. Yet these concepts must still be – for this is the fundamental condition of all knowledge of the objective – concepts of persistent objects such that it is possible for the observer empirically to apply criteria of re-identification to those objects. Objects may change; but they must not, so to speak, change out of all recognition. If they did, we could not know they had; for we could not recognize *them* as having changed. Objects may retain, or alter, their positions relative to each other; but not in such a way that it is impossible for us to tell which have retained and which have altered their relative positions. Tentatively, then, we may suppose that while perceptions of the world may reveal *some* objective changes which we can characterize as inexplicable, quite unpredictable or utterly random, they can do so only against a background of persistences and alterations which we recognize as explicable, predictable, and regular.

Let us return for a moment to those changes in our perceptions which are attributable to changes in the viewpoint of the observer. Such changes are associated in a law-like way with movement of the observer's body or parts of his body relative to other persistent objects. More generally, they exhibit a regular correlation with change of the observer's position and his sense-orientation in relation to objects in the world. Without some such correlation it is impossible to see how notions of enduring and re-identifiable objects of changing perception could secure application in the observer's experience. But the possibility of this correlation in turn seems to depend upon changes and persistences in the world of objects being themselves subject to some kind and degree of order and regularity.

These limitations must somehow be reflected in the character of our concepts themselves. That is to say, our concepts of objects, and the criteria of re-identification which they embody, must allow for changes in the objective world subject to the limitation that change must be consistent with the possibility of applying those concepts and criteria in experience. How is this requirement satisfied? The answer seems to lie in the fact that our concepts of objects are linked with sets of conditional expectations about the things which we perceive as falling under them. For every kind of object, we can draw up lists of ways in which we shall expect it not to change unless . . ., lists of ways in which we shall expect it to change if . . ., and lists of ways in which we shall expect it to change unless . . .; where, with respect to every type of change or non-change listed, the subordinate clauses introduce further and indefinite lists of clauses each of which would constitute an explanatory condition of the change or absence of change in question.

But, it may be said, such conditional expectations are precisely the sort of thing we learn *from* experience of the objective world. How, then, can the existence of any such links between concepts and expectations be a condition of the possibility of experience of the objective? To this it is not enough to reply that it is not the existence of any specific link between concept and conditional expectation that has been declared to be a necessary feature of concepts of objects, but rather the existence, for each such concept, of some such links. For the point of the objection must be to suggest that each such concept comes to be established independently of any such links, the latter in every case being established empirically after the establishment of the concept. Now here we may be tempted in reply to press a too sharp distinction and say simply that such links fall into two classes, viz. those which are thus established empirically and those which are not, which enter rather into the formation of the concept itself. But it is better to recognize, as many have insisted, a certain indeterminacy in our concepts. We need not be concerned with the detail of this controversy. The point is that in contradistinction to concepts of simple sensory *qualities*, and in contradistinction, too, to any concepts there may be of particular sensory *items* which are quite fully describable in terms of simple sensory qualities ("sense-data", perhaps, in one sense of the term), concepts of *objects* are always and necessarily compendia of causal law or law-likeness, carry

K

implications of causal power or dependence. Powers, as Locke remarked – and under "powers" he included passive liabilities, and dispositions generally – make up a great part of our idea of substances.[1] More generally, they must make up a great part of our concepts of any persisting and re-identifiable objective items. And without some such concepts as these, no experience of an objective world is possible.

Kant argued, as we have seen, by a short, invalid step, for the conclusion that the Law of Universal Causality held for all possible experience, i.e. for the conclusion that there existed strictly sufficient conditions for absolutely every change that we can take cognizance of. Of course we cannot regard any such absolute conclusion as established by the considerations just put forward. We do not have to suppose that explanatory conditions, fully stated, of every change or absence of change must be strictly sufficient conditions. We do not have to suppose that there must always be an explanatory condition if only we could find it. We could accommodate some inexplicable objective change, and some mere exceptions to our law-like expectations, without damage to the necessary but loosely woven mesh of our concepts of the objective. The most we can say about these two absolute thoughts – of *strictly sufficient* conditions for *every* objective change – is not that they are necessary thoughts, but that they are natural hopes. They do not represent, in our equipment of concepts, absolutely indispensable elements in terms of which we must see the world if we are to see an objective world at all. They represent, rather, a heightening, an elevation, a pressing to the limit of those truly indispensable but altogether looser conditions which I have argued for.

6. AN ELEMENT OF DECEPTIVE LOGIC

We have seen that by starting from Kantian premises and by following a path of argument which partially coincides and partially diverges from his, we can arrive at conclusions which exhibit certain analogies to his: we have, as it were, looser substitutes for his principles of permanence and causality. The initial clues Kant offers we have followed, indeed, in a direction he scarcely considered: the direction of inquiring what conclusions

[1] *Essay*, Book II, Chapter 23.

can be drawn, from the general necessity of distinguishing objective and subjective time-orders, regarding necessary general features of our ordinary classificatory (empirical) concepts. He did not follow his clues in this direction because he thought he could take shorter steps to more impressive results. Each of these steps is so easily seen to be invalid that we may wonder at Kant's making it. But our wonder may be a little diminished by noting a general feature of Kant's thinking in the Analogies which I have not commented on in respect of all three of them and which helps to make this section of the work more intelligible if not, as it stands, more acceptable.

The fundamental thought of the Analogies is that of the connexion between objectivity of experience and unity of the spatio-temporal framework of experience. To this is added the clear realization that there is no question of pure objective Space–Time itself being an object of perception to which we can directly relate other objects of perception. And from these two thoughts together there follows the general conclusion that the necessary unity of Space–Time must somehow be represented by a system of connexions between our ordinary empirical perceptions. Then, as we have seen, Kant's thought veers away from the facts – from the facts about how this system of connexions is actually secured, how indeed it must be secured. It veers away, beckoned by the lure of establishing the three scientific super-principles. But there is just one element of deceptive logic in this veering, and in its direction, which is present in the Analogies and which I have not fully brought out. Kant seems at times to think that certain formal properties of the unified space–time frame must have direct correlates in the objects of perception themselves or in the connexions between those objects. This I have already remarked on in the case of the first Analogy. There it is plain enough that Kant thinks that there must be some absolutely permanent objects of perception to represent the permanence of the space–time frame itself. He is not content to allow that a merely relative permanence of particular objects of perception is sufficient to secure the abiding identity of the whole system of such objects.

The other formal properties for which he attempts to find correlates in the other two Analogies might be expressed, with the help of one of Kant's favourite words, as follows: "the parts of space mutually determine one another at any instant" and "the preceding time necessarily determines the succeeding". It will be noted that the latter remark – an actual quotation[1] – is not as general as the former. Generalizing, and dropping the word "determine", we have: "a given part of space necessarily is *where* it is in relation to other parts of space" and "a given time necessarily is *when* it is in relation to other times". What these thoughts come to is simply this: that we may regard space (or a sector of space) as divided into spaces and time (or a stretch of time) as divided into times; and when, as we do, we import names or descriptions for the results of such division, we generate indefinitely many necessary relational propositions. The hour between 3 and 4 necessarily follows the hour between 2 and 3. Square A 10 necessarily has the relation it has to squares A 9 and B 10 and indeed to squares A 1 and C 3. One army might surround another and it would not be a necessary truth that it surrounded it; but one part of space cannot surround another without its being a necessary truth that it surrounds it.

As before, we have the thought that pure space and time and their divisions are not themselves objects of empirical perception, hence that these necessary relationships between the parts of space and time must somehow be represented by objects of perception, if the latter are to be perceived as objects, i.e. as belonging to the unified framework. And it is concluded that all such objects must stand in relations of necessary connexion which are the analogues and representatives of these formal relationships between spaces and times. Thus all parts of matter – which fills and represents space so far as all possible perception of it by us is concerned – are in reciprocal interaction, mutually determining their states to be what they are. Or again:

> If, then, it is a necessary law of our sensibility, and therefore a *formal condition* of all perceptions, that the preceding time necessarily determines the succeeding (since I cannot advance to the succeeding time save through the preceding), it is also an indispensable law of *empirical representation* of the time-series that the appearances of past time determine all existences in the succeeding time, and that these latter, as events, can take place only in so far as the appearances of past time determine their existence in time, that is, determine them according to a rule.[2]

[1] A 199/B 244.   [2] A 199/B 244.

No doubt it was the attractiveness of the conclusions which made attractive these transitions from the necessary formal properties of a space–time system to their representation in necessary connexions between alterations and previous states, and between simultaneously existing states. No doubt, also, this explains why Kant makes the correlations less than complete and does not say, for example, that all subsequent states contain, and must contain, sufficient conditions of previous events.

7. VERIDICAL AND NON-VERIDICAL PERCEPTION

There is one more problem which must be mentioned in connexion with the Analogies, if only because the latter have been some-times thought to be largely concerned with it, though they are not, or are only indirectly, so concerned. This is the problem, not of the general conditions of distinguishing between objective and subjective time-relations, but of how we in fact distinguish, among those experiences which present themselves as percep-tions of the objective, the veridical from the non-veridical. There is indeed a fleeting reference to this distinction in the second Analogy[1] but none at all in the first or third. Now this form of problem is a familiar one in the history of philosophy and might seem to be one which Kant could turn to some account for the purposes of the Analogies. Even "the good Berkeley", as Kant patronizingly calls him, gave attention to this form of problem when he considered what he misleadingly calls the distinction between ideas of sense and ideas of imagination; and his answer, in terms of the coherence and order which the former exhibited and the latter did not, besides being a generally popular answer, looks as if it might be plausibly connected with the notions of causal regularities which Kant is anxious to introduce as pre-suppositions of experience in general.

Nevertheless it is clear that a direct consideration of this ques-tion can at most yield confirmation of results already achieved by investigating the general conditions of the possibility of know-ledge of the objective. It is true, and important, that we are able to make the distinction between the veridical and the non-veridical in putative perceptions of the objective only if the general conditions of objective time-determination, hence of objective

[1] A 201–2/B 247.

experience, are satisfied. But, equally, if they are satisfied, we are able to make the distinction. Something may present itself – momentarily at least – as a perceptual experience of an object, or of an objective change, and then be relegated to the sphere of mistake or illusion as showing no congruence at all with the general body of our objective judgements. Kant deals very adequately with the matter in a Note to the Refutation of Idealism.[1] After remarking that it is not the case "that every intuitive representation of outer things involves the existence of these things, for their representation can very well be the product merely of the imagination (as in dreams or delusions)", he goes on:

> Whether this or that supposed experience be not purely imaginary, must be ascertained from its special determinations, and through its congruence with the criteria of all real experience.

The only objection to this sentence is that it perhaps makes the matter appear more reflective than it usually is. We do not generally calculate that it would put too much strain on our concepts to suppose that the bush turned into a bear and back again. It is rather that what we saw fleetingly and unsteadily as a bear we see now, and steadily, as a bush. Of course, the types of case which Kant, like Berkeley, assigns all together to "imagination" are very various, very different among themselves. But it is unnecessary for us now to discuss these differences.

8. WHY ONLY ONE OBJECTIVE WORLD?

"Our analogies," I earlier quoted Kant as saying, "portray the unity of nature"; and again, "the analogies declare that all appearances lie, and must lie, in *one* nature, because without this *a priori* unity no unity of experience and therefore no determination of objects in it would be possible". Before leaving the Analogies, I must recur to that previously mentioned doubt which attacks this very notion of the necessity of *one* unified nature. We are to suppose granted the interdependence of certain ideas: viz. the possibility of empirical self-consciousness, the objective reference of empirical judgements, and the reference of such judgements to items belonging to a unified spatio-temporal world.

[1] Note 3, B 278-9.

The question raised is: Why only *one* unified objective world? The two rival possibilities that I suggested might be advanced were, first, simultaneous membership both of a spatial world such as we know and of an unrelated quasi-space involving different modes of perception, and, second, successive or alternating membership of different and spatially unrelated spatial worlds. Familiar fantasies, both literary and philosophical, make us more at home with the second suggestion than with the first. A generous objector might concede that the unity of consciousness demands an original context of a single unified spatio-temporal world and ask whether, granted this original context, empirical self-consciousness does not then possess a potentially wider scope. We can easily enough imagine, tell ourselves stories about, worlds different enough from that of our experience, though no doubt imagined on the basis of the latter; and we do not have to include in these imaginings any details about the location of these worlds relative to that which we know. Of course, in fact, admitting that such a world is *nowhere* relative to anything we know is admitting that it is unreal, merely imaginary. But might not this be merely a limitation of fact? Could we not further imagine that without loss of continuity of empirical self-consciousness, there occurred certain radical discontinuities in experience such that no experienced item in the period following such a gap could be spatially related to any experienced item in the period preceding it, though all gap-sequent items, like all gap-precedent items, were spatially related to each other in their own unified systems? In other words, can we not conceive of the unity of consciousness carrying over from one unified objective world to another? and back again perhaps?

We should remember that all Kant's treatment of objectivity is managed under a considerable limitation, almost, it might be said, a handicap. He nowhere depends upon, or even refers to, the factor on which Wittgenstein, for example, insists so strongly: the *social* character of our concepts, the links between thought and speech, speech and communication, communication and social communities. If fantasies of the kind I speak of are to have any chance of getting us to admit the conceivability of a multiplicity of objective worlds, they must at least take account of this factor; they must at least allow for the point that another name for the *objective* is the *public*. Otherwise, though the individual consciousness may be imagined to claim what it likes about independent objective worlds, the world, in another sense, must be supposed to adhere to its own and unsympathetically exclusive standard of objectivity.

A necessary condition, then, of admitting spatially independent worlds of experience is that the members of a cultural community should be able to claim a shared membership of such another world or, rather, should find such a claim more compelling than the diagnosis of their mutually cohering stories as a kind of harmonious dreaming. It is safe to say that such a claim would have a greater chance of being found compelling if there were any way in which transactions in the putative other world could be represented as influencing and being influenced by transactions in the original world. Since physical interaction is ruled out by hypothesis, it seems that the reciprocal influence of worlds, if conceivable at all, could be best conceived as operating at the level of interpersonal and social arrangements and relationships. There would be, to say the least, considerable difficulties in the way of elaborating a coherent, let alone a compelling, scheme on these lines. It would be an interesting, though some would say an idle, exercise, to attempt it. I shall not attempt it; but will content myself with remarking again that the exercise would have to be controlled by the wholly Kantian thought that the degree of our readiness to allow a single concept of the objectively real to range over spatially independent worlds will be directly proportional to the degree to which it seems possible to represent those worlds as systematically integrated in ways other than the (by hypothesis forbidden) spatial way. Thus the general Kantian emphasis on the connexion between objective reality and systematic unity is preserved.

PART THREE

Transcendent Metaphysics

I

THE LOGIC OF ILLUSION

With the end of the Transcendental Analytic comes the end of Kant's positive or constructive metaphysics of experience. The exhibition of that necessary structure of fundamental ideas which constitutes the framework of our thinking about the world is now complete. What follows, in the Dialectic, is the work of demolition, the exposure of the illusions of transcendent metaphysics. This negative description by itself, however, scarcely gives an adequate conception of the role of the Dialectic in the grand strategy of the *Critique*. A number of interdependent objectives are to be secured by this great division of the work. The attempt to gain knowledge, transcending all possible experience, of God, the soul, and the cosmos is indeed to be repulsed, the confinement of knowledge to the empirical re-affirmed. But the defeat of this presumptuous attempt is not to be seen as frustration. First, it is to be effected in such a way as to secure the simultaneous defeat of the counter-thrusts of materialism and atheism. Second, the territory thus denied to speculative inquiry is left open for possible occupation under a different kind of authority, viz. that of morality. Third, by a curious harmony of the interests of knowledge and morality, some of the ideas which we cannot, as inquirers, know – though we may, as moral agents, confidently believe – to have counterparts in non-sensible reality, turn out nevertheless to have a necessary part to play in the direction of our theoretical inquiries in their proper field, that of sensible experience. Finally, if there should be any doubt as to whether there really is any territory beyond the empirical for theoretical reason to be repulsed from, the doubt is to be triumphantly dispelled by a new and independent proof of the thesis of transcendental idealism, a proof arrived at by following pure reason, in the attempt to gain experience-transcending knowledge of the cosmos, into the conflicts of the mathematical antinomies.

Such, at least, is the plan. These bright prospects are, as we shall see, considerably clouded in the outcome. All that is actually achieved is negative: the exposure of the illusion in the Cartesian concept of the soul; the refutation of the proofs of God's existence; the exhibition of certain cosmological questions as at least highly problematic in character. The rest is unplausible claim and fallacious argument. But for the moment we are concerned with the general structure of the Dialectic rather than the detail of its arguments.

The reader of the *Critique* is already very thoroughly prepared by the discussions of the Transcendental Analytic for the general topic of metaphysical illusion. For any employment of concepts in propositions purporting to give knowledge of objects to be a significant employment, that employment must be tied to a possible intuition, to empirical conditions of the concept's application. Any employment of a concept not subject to this limitation, the limitation to objects of possible experience, is illegitimate. Here is the principle of significance; and we are reminded, in the last chapter of the Analytic, of temptations to violate it in the shape of the existence of formal or categorial concepts on the one hand and of things as they are in themselves on the other. We might expect a series of more or less connected illustrations of such violations, such excursions into transcendent metaphysics. But this would scarcely be systematic enough to satisfy Kant. He seeks to show that there is at least a certain range of topics within which the illusions of transcendent metaphysics are no less systematic and, in a sense, necessary than the non-illusory necessities of non-transcendent metaphysics. The basis of the systematic structure of illusion, as of knowledge, is held to lie in formal logic. Just as the experience-ordering concepts of understanding are correlated with the fundamental logical forms of statement, so the illusion-begetting ideas of reason are correlated with the fundamental forms of mediate deductive inference. Of these forms, Kant thinks, there are three – the categorical, hypothetical, and disjunctive syllogisms; and there are three corresponding types of dialectical illusion. Just as in formal reasoning we expect completeness in the premises of a given conclusion, so, in all inquiry concerning given objects, we presume completeness in the conditions under which the objects are given. The typical demand of reason in this field is the demand for completeness in the series of conditions, and hence for "the unconditioned"; and this demand takes three main directions, each exhibiting a fourfold division in accordance with the fourfold division of the categories.

This logical framework, in its connexion with the topics of the Dialectic and its elaboration under the guidance of the fourfold division of the categories, is altogether too strained and artificial to be taken seriously, and I shall dispense myself from discussing it further. This is not too say that everything which goes into its construction is worthless or irrelevant. Under the general heading, "the demand of reason for the unconditioned", Kant does in fact note genuine analogies between certain types of ordinary and scientific thinking; and the features in respect of which the analogy holds can, in fact, it seems, at least in certain cases, lead straight to metaphysical illusion, to our employing concepts in an apparently legitimate and significant way without in fact specifying any conditions for their application when so employed. He notes the in itself legitimate and natural tendency to seek for ever greater generality of explanation, whereby ever wider ranges of phenomena can be brought within the scope of a single type of theory – which might indeed be held to be a species of search for more and more comprehensive premises or principles of reasoning. This search exhibits broad analogies with other tendencies of scientific thinking which Kant notes as equally legitimate and natural: such as the tendency to press our investigations farther and farther into remoter regions of space and of past time, and to inquire ever more minutely into the composition of matter. These connected tendencies of sophisticated inquiry are continuous with simpler re-iterations of "Why?", of "And what is beyond *that*?" or "before *that*?", of "And what is *that* made of?" – though Kant does not explicitly speak of these particular childish manifestations of the natural dialectic of human reason. Whether we think of them in their sophisticated or in a more primitive form, it seems at least possible to assimilate to each other these serial types of inquiry, as Kant does, with the help of the idea of one thing's being "conditioned" by another. Whenever we get an answer to a question forming part of such a series, that which the question is asked about is said to be conditioned by what is mentioned in the answer to it. Clearly we must not ascribe to this expression any meaning beyond what this explanation gives it. It is simply a way of speaking in general about these different types of serial inquiry.

Kant's central thought about such serial inquiries develops as follows. The items disclosed at successive stages of the inquiries themselves form a series, each member of which stands in a typical (e.g. temporal) relation to the item disclosed at the following stage, and is said to be conditioned by that item. Inevitably, in each case, we form the idea of the series of such items *as a whole*; and with this idea there comes the idea of something which, unlike the typical member of the series, is not itself conditioned by any member of the series. This is the idea of the "absolutely unconditioned"; and metaphysical illusion arises from assuming, in each type of case, that there must be something answering to this idea. This unconditioned something is necessarily conceived in one of two ways. The more natural and less sophisticated way is to conceive of it, in each case, as an absolutely ultimate member of the series: that of which no explanation is necessary or possible but which contains the ultimate ground of explanation of everything else; the outer limits of the world in space, which are beyond everything else and which nothing is beyond; the first beginning of things in time; the ultimate and absolutely simple particles of matter, of which everything is composed. The less natural and more sophisticated way is to conceive of it not as an unconditioned and ultimate member of a series of conditioned things, but as the unconditioned totality of an *infinite* series all of whose members are conditioned. For neither type of concept, however, Kant says, is it possible to specify any empirical conditions of its application, i.e. no possible experience or intuition could warrant the application of either type of concept. Hence both violate the conditions of significant employment. Yet the disposition to suppose that one or the other must apply is endemic in human reason, committed as the latter is to these serial inquiries. When we contemplate the thought of such a series, it seems that we cannot escape the idea of the absolutely unconditioned; it must be the case *either* that there is a final term *or* that there is not, in which case there is an infinite totality of the members of the series. But, in forcing this alternative, we are allowing ourselves to assume an application for the concept of *the series as a whole*, without considering whether we may legitimately do so. If we could talk significantly about objects *without considering them as objects of possible experience* – without in general considering the conditions of intuition or awareness of them – it would be perfectly legitimate to insist on the disjunction in each case. But we may not; and it is not.

But now it must be pointed out that in permitting the description of the dialectical process to develop in just this way, to just this point of resolution, I have in effect restricted the description to the Antinomies and, even, to the first two of them. (Though the solution to the first two implicitly carries with it a solution to the second two, it is not that solution, as we shall see, which Kant adopts.) This point is of great importance. For it is precisely in the field of the Antinomies that we find, or may seem to find, a brilliant example of the necessary interconnectedness of those features which Kant represents as systematically interconnected over the whole area of systematic metaphysical illusion. First, it seems that we are *inevitably* led, in the pursuit of complete and systematic knowledge in the cosmological field, to entertain the idea of each relevant series as a whole, whether finite or infinite. Second, these ideas, in either form, seem to have the character of *absoluteness* or *ultimacy* which Kant attributed to all the metaphysical ideas which he treats of in the Dialectic: they are ideas of absolute totalities, of ultimate constituents of matter, of an absolutely first beginning of the universe, etc. Third, it must have seemed plausible enough at the time at which Kant wrote, though it seems less clear now, that there could never be adequate empirical grounds for opting for either the finite or the infinite alternative in the case of any of the cosmological questions, i.e. that the ideas in question are essentially *transcendent* of any possible experience. Fourth, and by the same token, it would seem entirely reasonable to claim for the idea of the infinite alternative in each case the status of a necessary *directive* or *regulative* idea in science, thus setting ourselves a task of inquiry which we could never declare to be completed.

In theoretical inquiries in the cosmological field, then, the notion of "the demand of reason for the unconditioned" does have a definite sense; and in this field, too, the four features of inevitability, absoluteness, transcendence, and regulative utility do seem jointly to characterize certain of the ideas to which this demand gives rise. But Kant thought that the phrase "the demand of reason for the unconditioned" embodied a description, both precise and general, of the sources of *all* the metaphysical ideas discussed in the Dialectic. Perhaps it was for this reason that he was encouraged to generalize those features, to find them jointly characterizing the ideas of speculative theology and of rational psychology as well as the cosmological ideas. In the case of speculative theology the parallel goes, indeed, some little way. In the case of rational psychology it scarcely starts. It is true that the Cartesian conception of the soul can be shown to be such that we cannot specify empirical criteria for its application. If this is enough to make it a transcendent idea, then a transcendent idea it is. It is true, too – or so the history of philosophy seems to suggest – that it is an idea we are naturally led to entertain. But when the sources of the illusion are traced, as Kant traces them in the Paralogisms, it becomes quite clear that they have nothing to do with reason's demand for completeness and systematic unity in empirical investigations; and there is no case at all for maintaining, as Kant does, that the idea has any directive utility in the systematic empirical study of psychology.

The parallel, as I remarked, seems to go a little farther in the case of speculative theology. The topic of God certainly gives plenty of scope for the notions of the absolute and the ultimate. God is absolutely necessary existence, absolute perfection, etc. Moreover, there is plenty of traditional authority for connecting the notion of God with that of ultimate ground or explanation of everything, and hence with reason's demand for finality in explanation. But a tradition is not the same thing as a compulsion of reason. It seems at least an exaggeration to say that we are *inevitably* led, by the search for systematic unity in theoretical explanation, to entertain such an idea. In so far as the contention is plausible at all, it is so just to the extent to which the idea of God rests upon notions treated of in the Antinomies; and, as Kant recognizes, this basis is inadequate to sustain the idea of God. Finally, the claim of directive utility for the idea of an intelligent and all-powerful extra-mundane creator – or the even stronger claim, which Kant makes, that the enterprise of natural science is *necessarily* conducted under the aegis of this idea – has no more plausibility than the thesis that we are inevitably led to this idea by the search for systematic unity in explanation.

The supposed unity of the logic of illusion, then, is itself largely illusory. The Paralogisms are really quite independent of the other two main divisions of the Dialectic. Between the cosmological and the theological ideas, on the other hand, though Kant exaggerates the *parallels* between them there are certain *connexions* – as we shall see more fully hereafter.

II

SOUL

Kant's exposure of the illusions of rational psychology is both brilliant and profound. It is philosophical criticism of the highest order. Yet it must be confessed that the development of the thought in the text is often dark and involved; and much of its obscurity is due to a certain incompleteness in the exposure, an inadequate consideration of a matter of central importance. I begin by noting, crudely and briefly, (1) the nature of the doctrine to be attacked, (2) the main line of Kant's attack upon it, and (3) the diagnosis which Kant offers of the sources of the illusion. Then I proceed to explain and elaborate and, where necessary, to criticize and to supplement, Kant's doctrine.

The doctrine to be attacked is the doctrine that each of us, by the mere fact of conscious experience, knows that he exists as a Cartesian thinking substance, i.e. as an immaterial, persisting, non-composite, individual subject of thoughts and experiences, capable of existence in total independence of body or matter.

The main line of attack is in accordance with the principle of significance. In order to claim knowledge of the existence of an object falling under a certain concept, we must have, and must have occasion to make use of, empirical criteria for the application of that concept. Sensible intuition, in Kant's terminology, must offer us an object which satisfies those criteria. A crucial concept in the present case is that of numerical identity through time, the persistence of an identical thing;[1] but there neither is, nor could be, any intuition (empirical awareness) of a persisting immaterial subject of experiences.

The diagnosis of the sources of the illusion is that the rational psychologist, the Cartesian philosopher of the soul, confuses the unity of experiences with the experience of unity. It is indeed a necessary condition of the possibility of representations constituting *experience* that there should be such unity and connexion between the members of a temporally extended series of ex-

[1] A 365.

162

periences as to provide the basis of the possibility of that ascription of experiences to oneself in which we express our empirical self-consciousness. This does not mean that there is any such thing as awareness of an immaterial object which is the unitary subject of all those experiences; though only such awareness would justify the Cartesian conception of the soul. Yet by a natural and powerful illusion we mistake the necessary unity of consciousness for just such an awareness of a unitary subject.

Set out as above, the diagnosis may well puzzle us. Why should unity of consciousness, a certain connectedness of experiences, be misunderstood in just this way? There seems, at least, to be a step missing. There are, in fact, several steps missing. We must try to fill them in; and since the matter is not uncomplicated, the exposition shall proceed, in the next section, by numbered paragraphs.

I. THE EXPOSURE OF THE ILLUSION: A RECONSTRUCTION

[1]   *The transcendental unity of apperception.* It will be helpful first to remind ourselves of the significance of the idea of the necessary unity of consciousness, or the unity of apperception, as this emerged from the discussion of the Transcendental Deduction. What was the transcendental unity of consciousness required for, and what did it require? It required that a temporally extended series of experiences should have a certain character of connectedness and unity, secured to it by concepts of the objective, and it required this as a fundamental condition of the possibility of empirical self-consciousness. That experience should be experience of a unified objective world at least makes room for the idea of *one* subjective or experiential route through the world, traced out by *one* series of experiences which together yield *one* unified experience of the world – a potential autobiography. We have here, as it were, the basic ground for the possibility of an empirical use for the concept of the subject of such an autobiography, the concept of the self.

[2]   *The empirical concept of a subject of experience: a person.* This necessary unity, however, supplies only the basic ground, not the full conditions, for the use of such a concept. It is quite clearly

implicit in Kant's position that any use of the concept of a numerically identical subject of experiences persisting through time requires empirically applicable criteria of identity, and that none such are supplied merely by the kind of connectedness of inner experiences provided for by the necessary unity of apperception. On the second point we shall have more to say later. On the first point we must remark now that it is one of the weaknesses of Kant's exposition that he barely alludes to the fact that our ordinary concept of *personal* identity does carry with it empirically applicable criteria for the numerical identity through time of a subject of experiences (a man or human being) and that these criteria, though not the same as those for bodily identity, involve an essential reference to the human body.[1] Kant does not pass the point over entirely in silence. He alludes to it, though obscurely, in the sentence: "Its [the soul's] permanence during life is of course evident, since the thinking being (as man) is itself likewise an object of the outer senses."[2]

The point to which Kant thus alludes in passing is surely of the first importance. It means that we have, after all, a concept, which satisfies the most stringent critical requirements, of a persisting subject of experiences (a man). This concept supplies an absolutely firm basis for a genuinely object-referring use of personal names, and of personal pronouns, in sentences in which states of consciousness, inner experiences, are ascribed to the objects referred to by the names or pronouns. A man is something perceptibly (if only relatively) permanent, a persistent and identifiable object of intuition, a possible subject of a biography or autobiography. Instead of talking, dubiously, of an experiential route through the world, of one series of experiences constituting such a route, we may talk, confidently, of an undeniably persistent object, a man, who perceptibly traces a physical, spatio-temporal route through the world and to whom a series of experiences may be ascribed with no fear that there is nothing persistent to which they are being ascribed.

[3] *No criteria of personal identity invoked in immediate self-ascription of current or recalled experiences.* And now we come to the fact that

---

[1] The topic of personal identity has been well discussed in recent philosophy. I shall take the matter as understood.

[2] B 415.

lies at the root of the Cartesian illusion. It may be put as follows. When a man (a subject of experience) ascribes a current or directly remembered state of consciousness to himself, no use whatever of any criteria of personal identity is required to justify his use of the pronoun "I" to refer to the subject of that experience. It would make no sense to think or say: *This* inner experience is occurring, but is it occurring to *me*? (This feeling is anger; but is it I who am feeling it?) Again, it would make no sense to think or say: I distinctly remember *that* inner experience occurring, but did it occur to me? (I remember that terrible feeling of loss; but was it I who felt it?) There is nothing that one can thus encounter or recall in the field of inner experience such that there can be any question of one's applying criteria of subject-identity to determine whether the encountered or recalled experience belongs to oneself – or to someone else. (I think it could be said, without serious exaggeration, that it is because Kant recognized this truth that his treatment of the subject is so greatly superior to Hume's.)

[4]   *Reference to the empirically identifiable subject not in practice lost in criterionless self-ascription.* When "I" is thus used, without any need or any possibility of its use being justified by empirical criteria of subject-identity, it does not, however, lose its role of referring to a subject. "I" can be used without criteria of subject-identity and yet refer to a subject. It can do so because – perhaps – it issues publicly from the mouth of a man who is recognizable and identifiable as the person he is by the application of empirical criteria of personal identity; or, even if used in soliloquy, is used by a person who would acknowledge the applicability of those criteria in settling questions as to whether he, the very man who now ascribes to himself this experience, was or was not the person who, say, performed such-and-such an action in the past. "I" can be used without criteria of subject-identity and yet refer to a subject because, even in such a use, the links with those criteria are not in practice severed.

[5]   *The illusion of a purely inner reference for "I" (of an independent immaterial individual; of soul as substance).* The links between criterionless self-ascription and empirical criteria of subject-identity are not *in practice* severed. But in philosophical reflection

they may be. It is easy to become intensely aware of the immediate character, of the purely inner basis, of such self-ascription while both retaining the sense of ascription to a subject and forgetting that immediate reports of experience have this character of ascriptions to a subject only because of the links I have mentioned with ordinary criteria of personal identity. Thus there arises a certain illusion: the illusion of a purely inner and yet subject-referring use for "I". If we try to abstract this use, to shake off the connexion with ordinary criteria of personal identity, to arrive at a kind of subject-reference which is wholly and adequately based on nothing but inner experience, what we really do is simply to deprive our use of "I" of any referential force whatever. It will simply express, as Kant would say, "consciousness in general". If we nevertheless continue to think of the "I" as having referential force, as referring to a subject, then, just because we have really nothing left but the bare *form* of reference, it will appear that the object of this reference must be an object of singular purity and simplicity – a pure, individual, immaterial substance.

Kant sees clearly how the key fact, that immediate self-ascription of thoughts and experiences involves no application of criteria of subject-identity, simultaneously explains three things: it explains the temptation to permit ourselves the use of the notion of the subject of experience ("I") while thinking exclusively in terms of the inner contents of consciousness (the contents of "inner sense"); it explains why that notion, so used, is really quite empty of content; and it explains why it *seems*, therefore, to be the notion of an absolutely simple, identical, immaterial individual.

[6]   *Kant's short cut.* Kant's insight was unparalleled, but his exposition is obscure. One of the reasons for its obscurity is that he takes a short cut. As I have remarked, he makes only a minimal reference to the empirical criteria of subject-identity, to the empirical concept of a subject of experience. He does not explicitly say that the delusive use of "I" which has just been discussed results from abstracting it from its ordinary setting, from ignoring its connexion with the empirical concept of a subject. Instead he connects that use with the philosophical employment which he has already made of the first personal pronoun in expounding the doctrine of the necessary unity of consciousness, the transcenden-

tal unity of apperception. He says that the delusive use of "I" merely *expresses* that unity which makes experience possible.

Is this a flaw in his exposition? I think the omission is a flaw. That bits of the diagnosis have to be supplied means that it is, so far, incomplete. But the doctrine that the delusive, non-referential use of "I" (or: the delusive, non-referential thought of the subject) "expresses" the necessary unity of consciousness might, I think, be defended. For any empirical (i.e. legitimate) use to be made of the concept of a subject of experiences it is required, certainly, that there should be such empirically applicable criteria of subject-identity as are supplied by our ordinary concept of a person as something which, *inter alia*, is an object of outer sense. This rule is general. As we have seen, not even the use of the concept of a subject which is made in ascription of immediate experiences to oneself (in consciousness of *oneself* as being in such-and-such a state) would be possible unless this requirement were satisfied. Nevertheless, in the theory of the transcendental unity of apperception, Kant has shown that there are certain necessary conditions of the possibility of self-consciousness which can be described coherently without describing the *full* conditions of this possibility and in particular without referring to our conception of a subject of experiences as himself being an object of outer sense. It is not unreasonable to hold that when we abstract from this last feature of our conception of such a subject, as we certainly do when we entertain the delusive, non-referential thought of a pure subject of experience, we retain in this thought (though no doubt confusedly enough) the idea of that connectedness of experiences which has been shown to be a fundamental necessary condition of the possibility of empirical self-consciousness, a minimal condition of the occurrence of anything that can properly be called experience. Whether we realize it or not, our delusive thought is at least the thought of experiences so connected, so unified. The satisfaction of the conditions required by the transcendental unity of apperception is a necessary condition of our illusion, as it is of the empirical concept of a subject of experience. It is not a sufficient condition of either, not even of the illusion; for in fact we arrive at the illusion by abstraction from the empirical concept. But when we thus abstract from the empirical concept to generate the illusion, we do not also abstract from the conditions required by the transcendental unity of apperception.

So it can, after all, be said that it is, in effect, just this unity of consciousness which, when in the grip of the illusion, we are led to mistake for the consciousness of a unitary subject.

[7]   *The coup de grâce to Cartesianism*. Kant is not content merely to expose the illusion in rational psychology. He underlines its emptiness by pointing out that, if we succumb to the illusion, we are powerless to defend our conclusions against alternative and equally empty theories. The rational psychologist maintains that every man has immediate assurance of the existence of his own soul as immaterial substance, identical throughout the succession of its states. To this we can reply that whatever assurance he expresses by this claim is equally compatible with the hypothesis of a whole series of soul-substances, each of which transmits its states and the consciousness of them to the next in the series, along with all that it has acquired by earlier transmissions of the same kind from earlier members of the series – as motion might be transmitted from one to another of a series of elastic balls.[1] This suggestion is no more, and no less futile than the original claim.

This line of attack could be pressed farther than Kant presses it. Thus when the man (a rational psychologist?) speaks, we could suggest that there are, perhaps, a thousand souls simultaneously thinking the thoughts his words express, having qualitatively indistinguishable experiences such as he, the man, would currently claim. How could the man persuade us that there was only one such soul associated with his body? (How could the – or each – soul persuade itself of its uniqueness?)

The generalized point of such attacks is this. We *have* criteria of singularity and identity for subjects of experience (people, men). If we are to talk of individual souls or consciousnesses as well, we *need* criteria of singularity and identity for them. The only way to guarantee a consequence which must surely rate as an adequacy condition for an admissible concept of an individual soul or consciousness – viz. that a normal man, in the course of a normal life, has at any time just one soul or consciousness which lasts him throughout – is to allow that the notions of singularity and identity of souls or consciousnesses are conceptually dependent on, conceptually derivative from, the notions of singularity and identity of men or people. The rule for deriving the criteria we

[1] A 363–4, footnote.

need from the criteria we have is very simple. It is: *one* person, *one* consciousness; *same* person, *same* consciousness. Acceptance of this rule of derivation, however, is the suicide of rational psychology.

Kant's failure to press this point home is but an aspect of his neglect of the empirical concept of a subject of experience.

2. HUME AND KANT ON THE SELF

Between Kant's treatment of the topic of the self and Hume's there are points of resemblance. There are also profound differences. Kant's repeated point, that there is no inner intuition of the subject itself, that "in inner intuition there is nothing permanent"[1], recalls Hume's famous sentence: "When I enter most intimately into what I call myself, I always stumble on some particular perception or other . . . I never catch myself at any time without a perception, and can never observe anything but the perception."[2] Again, the scantiness of allusion, in Kant, is paralleled by the total absence of allusion, in Hume, to the man as "object of the outer sense", to the role played by bodily identity in the empirical concept of a subject of experience.

Here the resemblance ends. Hume is obliged to give some account of the idea of "what he calls himself". He attempts to do so by finding between the members of the class of his "perceptions" such relations (of resemblance and causation) as will account for the "feigning" of an identical subject to which they all belong. He attempts to reproduce in this field the very same kind of analysis or explanation of the notion of identity as has served him in the discussion of our belief in the continued identity of material objects through discontinuous observation. Distinct perceptions are counted as perceptions of the same body because certain relations obtain between them. Just so, he suggests, distinct perceptions are counted as belonging to the same self because certain relations obtain between *them*. It does not matter much here how we read this "because": whether as introducing a reference to criteria of identity or, in Hume's own anti-rationalist spirit, as introducing a reference to factors which *cause* our

---

[1] B 413, cf. also B 420, A 381, etc.
[2] *Treatise of Human Nature*, Book I, Part IV, Chapter 6.

fictions. Either way we must be struck by the fatal lack of analogy between the two types of case. In so far as such an explanation (or analysis) seems satisfactory for the case of taking distinct perceptions to be perceptions of the same body, it does so because we are able to think of the psychological mechanisms (or criteria) involved as having a field of perceptions to work on, upon which they can operate *selectively*, producing a feigning (a judgement) of identity here, inhibiting one there. Even a fictitious identity needs a contrast. Nothing could induce the thought: Here's (an appearance of) the same *x* as before, unless something could induce the thought: Here's (an appearance of) a different *x*. But in the case of self-identity nothing which belongs to the field in which the mechanisms are supposed to operate can possibly be excluded by those mechanisms from ascription to the one self. The mechanisms are idle; or, rather, it is they that are the fictions. The search for them has the same futility as the search for criteria of subject-identity to be applied in the field of inner experience to determine whether a current experience is or is not one's own.

From the incoherence into which Hume's theory of the self thus lapses, and of which he himself was not unaware, Kant's exposure of the illusion of rational psychology is altogether free. His analysis indeed needs supplementation, as I have tried to show, by a far more explicit acknowledgement than any he makes of the role of empirically applicable criteria of subject-identity. The point is, however, that nothing in Kant's account excludes, and everything in it invites, such supplementation. Hume, on the other hand, does not simply offer to dispel a philosophers' (rational psychologists') illusion. His attempt is to give an adequate explanation of the vulgar conception of the self as subject of experience; but the terms in which he conceives of such an explanation make it impossible for the attempt to succeed.

3. THE COMPLICATIONS OF TRANSCENDENTAL IDEALISM

So far, in this discussion of the Paralogisms, I have completely ignored Kant's commitment to the doctrines of transcendental idealism; and it is an important point that the force of Kant's exposure of the illusions of rational psychology can be conveyed without any reference to those doctrines. To Kant himself, however, the commitment to transcendental idealism seemed to make the exposure of the illusion a matter of particular urgency.

> It would be a great stumbling-block, or rather would be the one unanswerable objection, to our whole critique if there were a possibility of knowing *a priori* that all thinking beings are in themselves simple substances . . . and that they are conscious of their existence as separate and distinct from all matter. For by such procedure we should have taken a step beyond the world of sense and have entered into the field of noumena.[1]

I shall reserve until later a general discussion of the complications of transcendental idealism; and not till then shall I consider fully the first edition version of the fourth paralogism, in which this doctrine figures so largely. But something must be said now to show how Kant views the connexion between that doctrine and the issues I have just been discussing.

Let us begin by noting how it might be possible to read even the cry of alarm I have just quoted in a way consistent with the weakest possible interpretation of transcendental idealism. What is at risk, it might be said, if the doctrine of rational psychology is upheld, is simply the principle that any significant claim to non-analytic knowledge of objects depends on the use of empirical criteria for the application of the concepts in terms of which the claim is expressed. To "enter the field of noumena" would simply be to make good a knowledge-claim of such a kind as to show that this principle could, in at least one case, be violated with impunity. The general methodological importance of dispelling, by careful diagnosis of its sources, the illusion of rational psychology consists in precisely this, that success in dispelling the illusion enables us to re-affirm the principle in the face of the most seductive of all apparent counter-examples to it.

It would be unplausible to hold that this is all Kant means. The doctrine that things in space and time are appearances only, that things are not *in themselves* extended, that I do not, as I am *in myself*, first feel sick, then sorry, is more plausibly held to mean at least that successive feelings and perceptions and their apparent objects are (in an unknown way) dependent for their existence on something of a character completely different (and completely

[1] B 409.

unknown). The "field of noumena" is the field of that upon which these dependent existences are thus dependent.

Among the multitude of naïve questions which spontaneously suggest themselves let us approach the one which it is most relevant to ask now by way of another which seems to present less immediate difficulty. Why, if the character of the noumenal is completely unknown, does Kant speak, on the one hand, of outer objects as *they* are in themselves and, on the other, of ourselves as *we* are in ourselves? Is it at least known that the field of the noumenal contains two distinct types of existence? An at least partially Kantian answer to this question might go as follows. Nothing of the kind is known. It is just that within experience (the field of appearances) a distinction is drawn, without which experience would be impossible, between perceived objects of outer sense (bodies in space) and the successive experiences which human beings count as states of themselves. (On one interpretation of transcendental idealism, indeed, this distinction is not ultimate. For the moment we may disregard this. The fact is that the distinction is drawn, and must be drawn if experience is to be possible at all.) Now the general dependence of both bodies in space and inner states of ourselves on the noumenal unknown is expressed by describing both of the former, in relation to the latter, as "appearances" of "things as they are in themselves". Hence it becomes natural to speak, on the one hand, of outer objects as *they* are in themselves and, on the other, of ourselves as *we* are in ourselves. But this way of speaking reflects nothing more than the distinction which is drawn, and must be drawn, in experience, between outer objects and states of consciousness. It implies no knowledge of any distinction between types of noumenal existence. For all we know the noumenal may be quite homogeneous.[1]

This answer takes account of only some of the features of transcendental idealism. Now let us ask the harder question. Granted that, in the way just indicated, transcendental idealism is much more than a methodological principle of significance, why is Kant so sure that if the pretensions of rational psychology could be made out, we should have entered the field of noumena? Why should the rational psychologist, if successful, have done more than show that a certain principle of significance in knowledge-

[1] A 359–60.

claims is, at least in one peculiar instance, untenable? Why should it not still be possible to maintain that the noumenal, that upon which all the content of experience, inner and outer, depends, is completely unknown and in principle unknowable? The answer we must give to this question shows how inadequate is the answer we ventured to the previous one. When all is said and done, Kant's theory of the self is *not* exhausted by deploying, and supplementing, those features of it which are called upon in dispelling the illusions of rational psychology; nor is the thesis of transcendental idealism exhausted by that short statement of it in terms of dependence of existence which I have just given. The reason in both cases is the same. What Kant intends to express by the "I think" of apperception is not simply that connectedness of experiences, ensured by means of concepts of the objective, which is the fundamental condition of the possibility of empirical self-consciousness. For him the "I think" of apperception represents also the tangential point of contact between the field of noumena and the world of appearances. "In the consciousness of myself in mere thought I am the *being itself*, although nothing in myself is thereby given for thought."[1]

Of course transcendental idealism would scarcely merit its name unless some such point of contact were made. The title of "idealism" might indeed be justified by the recurrent suggestion that outer objects are reducible to "representations". The title of "transcendentalism" might indeed be justified by the doctrine that all that we know in experience, including our own states of mind, is dependent upon some unknown ground inaccessible to experience. But if that were all, there would be nothing particularly transcendental about the idealism and nothing particularly idealist about the transcendentalism. What makes the name "transcendental idealism" more than a mere conjunction is the language of extreme subjectivism in which the source of *all* the structural features of the world is declared to be in *our* subject, "the subject in which the representation of time has its original ground".[2] But what could we make of this language unless the "subject" of these slogans were *somehow* connected with what we ordinarily understand by ourselves?

The concept of a thinking being "in general" is supposed to supply the point of connexion. Each human being, though he can

[1] B 429. [2] B 422.

never be conscious of an object, himself, as merely a thinking being, but only as a being who thinks, feels or perceives, successively, now this, now that, yet *is* a thinking being, a seat of the categories, and to that extent a source, and not merely an outcome, of the conditions of experience. Kant goes much further, of course, in accordance with the demands of the disastrous model whose sources we have not yet fully explored. It is not merely *our* understanding which is the source of the categories, it is *our* sensibility to which the forms of space and time are due; and it is because the former must affect the latter in the generation of empirical self-knowledge that *we* appear to *ourselves* otherwise than *we* are in *ourselves*. The confident use of first personal pronouns is bewildering enough; but it is more than bewildering. It shows the model shaking itself to pieces. After all, it seems, a good deal can be known about the noumenal self, though not quite what the rational psychologist hoped. In a quite extraordinary clause Kant writes: "The being that thinks in us is under the impression that it knows itself through pure categories and precisely through those categories which (in each type of category) express absolute unity."[1] To that extent the "being that thinks in us" appears to be deluded. But if the being that thinks in us is under the impression that its understanding affects its sensibility in the production of a temporal succession of connected perceptions, feelings and thoughts (including this one), then, apparently, the being that thinks in us is not deluded at all, but absolutely right! I do not deny that all this, too, might be construed as a mere manner of speaking about the structural characteristics of phenomenal fact. So to construe it would be to treat the model *as* a model, an expository framework to be discarded when its purposes are served. But it seems, to say the least, unlikely that this is how Kant viewed the matter.[2]

[1] B 402.
[2] See further Part IV, especially Section 4.

III

COSMOS

My discussion of the "mathematical" antinomies will proceed as follows. First, I shall set out the arguments in which Kant claims to display the "conflicts of pure reason with itself", together with some standard, and some less standard, objections to those arguments. Then I shall re-present the issues in such a way as to show how one general form of "solution" is supposed to fit each of the "conflicts" concerned. Next, I shall distinguish and discuss three interpretations of this general form of solution, each corresponding to a different version of transcendental idealism. I shall mention a fourth version of transcendental idealism, only to show that it does not generate a fourth interpretation of the solution. Finally I shall consider the cosmological questions themselves which are supposed to give rise to the conflicts, together with some non-Kantian lines of thought about them.

Kant's regular procedure in the antinomies is to establish in turn each of two apparently exhaustive alternatives (the "thesis" and the "antithesis") by proving the falsity of its apparent contradictory. In the case of the mathematical antinomies, the existence of pairs of valid arguments which appear to have this character is claimed to be an indirect proof of the doctrines of transcendental idealism (viz. that space and time are mere forms of our sensibility and that all things in space and time are mere appearances). Obviously, if this proof is to be free from circularity Kant should not borrow from those doctrines in constructing the arguments. Except in the case of one subsidiary argument (for the second part of the antithesis of the second antinomy) Kant does not blatantly violate this rule. Yet we can scarcely understand the fact that the weak arguments he employs seemed good to him unless we suppose that, in his thinking, he unconsciously stiffened them with elements belonging to those doctrines which were to supply the "solution" to the "conflicts".

I. ARGUMENTS AND OBJECTIONS

The thesis of the first antinomy is that the world has (1) a beginning in time and (2) limits in space. Let us give Kant's argument, as regards the first part, a more concrete form with the help of the supposition that for as long as the world has existed, a clock has been ticking at regular intervals. Then the argument goes as follows. If we assume that the world has no beginning, but has existed for an infinite time, then it follows that up to the present moment, or up to any previous historical moment, an infinite number of ticks has occurred, an infinite series of ticks has been completed. But this, by the very nature of an infinite series, is impossible. "The infinity of a series . . . consists in the fact that it can never be completed through successive synthesis."[1] Therefore it is impossible that the world has existed for an infinite time. It must have had a beginning.

The argument seems plainly invalid. We can indeed validly argue that, since the series of ticks has a final member, it cannot be the case both: (*a*) that it has an infinite number of members and (*b*) that it has a first member. Either (*a*) or (*b*) must be rejected. But since the argument is supposed to be based on the hypothesis that (*b*) is false, it is clearly (*b*) that must be rejected and not (*a*).

How did Kant come to advance such an argument? I think it does no injustice to him to suppose that his central thought might be represented as follows: it would be impossible to complete the process of *counting*, as they occurred, an infinite number of ticks. And this may seem to us true. It seems true because we think of the process of counting as having to *start* at some time. But the fact that such a process of counting, which *started* at some time, could never at any subsequent time reach completion seems also either quite irrelevant to the question at issue or to beg it in favour of the assumption that the series of ticks also started at some time. The hypothesis to be disproved, however, is that there was no time at which the series of ticks started. We may assume that this is one of the points at which Kant is, perhaps unconsciously, reaching out to the doctrines which he is later to advance as a solution to the conflict he is ostensibly displaying.

The argument for the second part of the thesis, viz. that the world must have limits in space, appears still less satisfactory. It

[1] A 427/B 455.

incorporates what is deficient in the first argument and adds a further deficiency of its own. Kant maintains that the very thought of the infinite spatial extent of the world involves the thought of its being possible to *complete* a temporally infinite process of surveying successive finite parts of the world. We might make this thought more concrete in terms of the idea of observers travelling in space-vehicles through the universe and arriving from different directions at a given point on earth at a given time, each of them having traversed an infinite distance. This, says Kant, is impossible. Therefore the world in space must be enclosed within limits.

To this argument it can be objected, first, that the hypothesis of an infinite spatial extent of the world does not require the possibility of the completion of a temporally infinite process of spatial surveying of the world. For that possibility requires at least the further hypothesis that the world has existed for an infinite time. However fast an observer travelled, he could not cover an infinite distance through the world in a finite time. But the hypothesis that the world is infinitely extended in space does not appear to entail the hypothesis that it has existed, up to any given moment, for more than, say, ten million years, let alone the hypothesis that it has existed for an infinite number of years. Second, even if we waive this objection, it appears that in declaring the completion of an infinite temporal process to be impossible, Kant is repeating the mistake which we have found in his argument for the first part of the thesis. A temporal process both completed and infinite in duration appears to be impossible only on the assumption that it has a beginning. If, finally, it is urged that we cannot conceive of a process of *surveying* which does not have a beginning, then we must inquire with what relevance and by what right the notion of surveying is introduced into the discussion at all.

The arguments for the antithesis of the first antinomy are no stronger than those for the thesis. The first runs as follows. If the world had a beginning, then it began at some definite time, say *n* years ago, and before that time nothing existed at all. But when nothing existed at all, there would be nothing to distinguish one part of time from another and hence nothing to account for the world's beginning to exist at one time rather than at another. Hence the world cannot have had a beginning.

The most this argument even appears to show is that if the world had a beginning, then the question "Why did it begin when

M

it did rather than at some other time?" is in principle unanswerable. The conclusion that the world had no beginning would follow only if there were adequate reasons for believing that if the world had a beginning, then the question why it began when it did rather than at some other time must in principle be answerable. Kant produces no reason why we should accept this belief. Let us see if we can produce reasons for rejecting it. More precisely, we set ourselves the following task. We are to produce reasons for rejecting the belief that the question must be answerable if the hypothesis of a beginning of the world in time is true, for any interpretation of that question to which Kant's argument is relevant. This leaves open the possibility that there may be another interpretation of the question altogether, to which our reasons, and Kant's argument, are both irrelevant.

Let us consider the question, "Why did it begin when it did?", as asked of an ordinary process or series of events which forms a part of the history of the world. Such a question normally has, we may say, a doubly *external* character. First, in referring to *the time at which* the process in question began, it implicitly relates that process to a temporal framework of other events and processes. It is in relation to this external framework that the time at which the process in question began is determined. Second, it seeks to elicit the mention of some condition, also external to the process in question, which occurred or obtained at the time when the process began and which, occurring or obtaining then, is sufficient to account for the process's beginning then.

Now Kant's argument exploits the fact that, when our question is asked about the history of the world as a whole, it could not possibly elicit the mention of any external condition occurring or obtaining at the time when that history began, and hence could not elicit the mention of any external condition which might account for its beginning then. But we must also consider the implications of the fact that, when the question is asked about the history of the world as a whole, nothing could possibly answer to the first external reference normally implied by such a question. Doubtless, if the world had a beginning, there would (or might) be a true answer, whether we could know what it was or not, to the question "How long has it existed?" or "How long ago did it begin?" The phrase "the time at which the world began" would have a reference. But its reference could not possibly be such as to imply the existence of any temporal relations between the beginning of the world's history and other events or processes external to that history. Now it seems that we can sensibly ask questions such as "Why did the war between the North and South begin when it did?" just because we can sensibly suppose that the external time-relations of that conflict might have been different from what they actually were. In general, it seems that it is because of the existence of such external temporal relations that we are able to attach a meaning to the suppositions we express by means of hypothetical clauses, such as, "If he had been born a day earlier" or "If the war had started a week later", etc. We have noted, however, that if the world had a beginning, then there is nothing external to the history of the world to which its beginning can be temporally related. It is tempting to conclude at once that the supposition that it might have begun at some other time is as empty of meaning as the supposition that its external temporal relations might have been different; that it is, indeed, just the same as this empty supposition. This would indeed confirm the Kantian point that there can be no explanation of the world's beginning when it did and not at some other time. But it would confirm it by showing that there is nothing to explain; and thus deprive the point of any force it might seem to possess.

Is it possible, on the assumption that the world had a beginning, to interpret in any less empty way the supposition that it might have begun at some other time than the time at which it did begin? I shall consider two further suggestions of which one, I think, makes sense. It might be suggested that the supposition is to be interpreted not as that of a *shift* in time of the entire sequence of events actually making up the world's history, but as that of an earlier *addition* to that entire sequence of events. The thought is that the sequence of events which actually composed the first phase of the world's history might have been preceded by some other sequence of events which in fact did not occur at all. And I think that if the world did have a beginning in time, this must be admitted as a genuine logical possibility. But if we are to interpret the thought in this way, then the Kantian complaint that there can be no explanation of the world's beginning when it did rather than at some other time reduces to the complaint that there can be no (external) explanation of there *not* having occurred, earlier than anything which did occur, something additional to anything which did occur. It is not clear that this point has even the prima facie appearance of an objection to the thesis that the world had a beginning. It is not really a complaint, with regard to the actual sequence of events which constituted the first phase of the world, that we could not explain why that series of events began when it did. It is rather, now, a complaint that we could not explain the fact that nothing occurred before it. But the mere fact of the non-occurrence of something is never held to be in need of explanation unless it is something specific which, in given circumstances, might have been expected to occur.

The second suggestion can be introduced as follows. Is it not logically possible that we should all, at the present moment, be engaged in those activities which will as a matter of fact occupy us at this time tomorrow, and that we should now have memories of having been engaged yesterday in just those activities which are in fact occupying us at this moment, all the temporal relations of these activities to other events in the world's history remaining unchanged? And is it not equally logically possible that we should all at the present moment be engaged in those activities which in fact occupied us at this time yesterday, having at present no more than (at most) intentions and anticipations regarding such activities as those we are in fact at present engaged in, all the temporal relations of all these activities to other events in the world's history remaining unchanged? If so, then the supposition that the entire sequence of events belonging to the world's history might have begun a day earlier than it did is equivalent to the supposition that the first of these possibilities is fulfilled and the supposition that the sequence might have begun a day later than it did is equivalent to the supposition that the second of these possibilities is fulfilled.

The idea underlying this suggestion is clear. It is to make good the deficiency of external temporal relations for the entire sequence of events making up the world's history by an appeal to our sense of *the present moment*. It is in relation to *now*, to the present moment, that we are to conceive of the history of the world being differently positioned, shifted backwards or forwards, in time, with all the internal temporal relations of its parts intact. But this conception depends on the assumption that the identity of the present moment is, so to speak, wholly independent of the filling of time. "Well, isn't it?" one might think or say: "Now is *now*, whatever is happening now." But this thought or utterance helps not at all. Thoughts and utterances are included among the events which, in unchanged temporal relations with each other, we were to think of as possibly displaced in relation to the present moment. The notion of *everything* being differently positioned in time in relation to the present moment is really as empty as the thought of a change in the external temporal relations of the entire sequence of events in the universe.

What encourages the illusion is doubtless the fact that we can with perfect logical consistency tell stories in which particular sequences of events are displaced from their actual order relative to others. In this way it is indeed logically possible that anyone should be engaged now in activities in which he was in fact engaged yesterday or in which he will in fact be engaged to-morrow. But in the context of these limited suppositions the word "now" is not exerting, has no need to exert, its deceptive powers. It is only in the context of the supposition of total temporal displacement that those powers are called upon. Then the illusion is quite powerful; but is an illusion none the less.

It remains finally to consider whether a question of the form "Why did x begin when it did?" might not be understood in a quite different way, to which the whole of the previous discussion would be altogether irrelevant. Is it not just possible that such a question might be rightly construed as seeking an explanation in the internal nature of the process about which it was asked? It might, for example, be characteristic of a certain dance to be punctuated by hand-claps executed at intervals by the performers. Then the question "Why did it begin when it did?", asked after, say, the eleventh hand-clap, might be interpreted as having the force of "Why did it begin eleven hand-claps ago?"; and the answer might take the form of explaining how the internal structure of the dance would not have permitted the performers to reach their present positions except after precisely eleven hand-claps.

I do not wish to assert positively that the question about the beginning of the world could be construed as an internal question. My example, obviously, is but a poor analogy for any such question as that would be. I wish simply to point out that, if the question could be understood as internal, then any such argument as Kant's is powerless to show that the question, so construed, is unanswerable. For it is clearly an assumption of such an argument that the question is to be construed as seeking to elicit the mention of some condition extraneous to that process – the entire series of states of the world – regarding which it is asked why it began when it did. In order, therefore, to show that the question really is unanswerable, it must at least be shown that there is something illegitimate or absurd about the very idea of construing it as an internal question. I do not know how this could be shown. May it not be the aim of some physicist, now or in time to come, to show, on the contrary, that the question can be both construed and answered as an internal question?

Let us turn now to Kant's argument for the second part of the antithesis of the first antinomy. The argument seems to turn on an illegitimate play with the notion of a bound or limit. If the world were finite, or limited, in spatial extent, it would stand in a certain relation to empty space outside it, viz. that of being *limited* by empty space. But empty space is nothing at all, i.e. there would be nothing for the world to be limited by. Therefore it must be limitless or infinite in spatial extent.

The argument as it stands scarcely deserves comment. But an added footnote indicates that Kant has a better, though still unsuccessful, argument in mind. In general, if x is in y, then x has a definite spatial relation to y, and it makes sense to ask, for example, where exactly in y is x. But where x is the world and y is space, this question makes no sense. We may indeed say, with perfect propriety, that the world is in space; for by this we may mean no more than that all the things of the world are spatially related to each other. But the hypothesis that the world is finite in spatial extent would require us to say that the world is *in* space in the further and inadmissible sense of having some definite spatial relation *to* space – thereby licensing a question which is in fact senseless.

There is one valid, and one invalid, step in this argument. On the assumption that the geometry of physical space is Euclidean, the proposition that the world is finite in spatial extent would indeed entail the proposition that it is "in" infinite and otherwise empty space; and this is a different proposition from the proposition that all physical things are spatially related to each other. But this proposition would not license senseless questions about the spatial relations of the world to space. It would be equivalent to the proposition that there was nothing in logic, or in the physical geometry of space, to impose any limit on the spatial extent of the world. It would be equivalent to the admission that there was no *impossibility* in the idea of there being physical things at any number of units of distance beyond what are in fact the outermost parts of the universe. (Kant might have used, though he did not use, a similar argument against the possibility of the world's having a beginning in time. It would have been similarly answerable.)

Kant's second antinomy is concerned with composite, space-occupying material things or substances. He argues that such things both must be, and cannot be, made up of parts which are simple or non-composite. In the argument for the thesis he simply adopts the principle that from composite material substance, composition must be theoretically removable without prejudice to the existence of what the composite is wholly made up of. From this, of course, it follows at once that the composite must be wholly made up of non-composite or simple parts, the ultimate and elementary substances. On behalf of the antithesis he argues, in effect, that what is composite and space-occupying can be made up only of parts which are themselves space-occupying and that everything space-occupying is extended and therefore composite; hence that the composite cannot be made up of non-composite or simple parts.

Against the argument for the thesis it can be urged that Kant offers no proof of his principle regarding composite material substance. Nevertheless there are in fact quite good reasons for accepting the conclusion which he draws from it. For the only uses of the abstract notion of "compositeness" which it is relevant to consider in this context are the uses, if any, which are, or might be, made of it in physical theories of matter. The notion of composition has characteristically found a place in such theories in association with a correlative notion of non-composite constituents. The fact that one particular application of this latter notion may be displaced by another does not tell against the general association.

The argument for the antithesis is in a much worse case. It turns upon two propositions, both of which are challengeable: (1) that whatever is extended is not simple; (2) that whatever occupies a space is extended. As regards the first, there is no *a priori* reason to suppose that "composite", as used in physical theories, is implied by "extended", i.e. no *a priori* reason to suppose that "simple" implies "unextended". Elementary substances or particles might be conceived as having dimensions. On the other hand – and this brings us to the second proposition – they might be conceived as having position but no dimensions. But again there would be no contradiction or absurdity in a physical theory according to which a composite material body was made up of a finite number of simple and unextended point-particles each of which was the sole occupant of a part of the space occupied by the material body as a whole, the sum of these finite parts making up the whole of that space. Each point-particle would, presumably, on such a theory, be supposed to exert some causal power throughout the region of space of which it was the unique occupant. But one is no more obliged to suppose that a particle must fill the space which it uniquely occupies than one is obliged to suppose that the unique occupant of a railway carriage must fill the railway carriage – though one might suppose that his repellent aspect was what accounted for his unique occupation of it.

2. A PROBLEM IN ANY CASE?

Such are Kant's arguments for the thesis and antithesis of the two mathematical antinomies, and such are some of the objections that can be brought against them. If we accepted the arguments as valid, we should be faced with a serious philosophical problem indeed. We should be faced with the fact that to each of three apparently legitimate cosmological questions – concerning the extent of the universe, the duration of its history, and the constitution of matter – both of two apparently mutually contradictory answers could be proved to be true. Even if we do not regard the arguments as valid, we are still, on Kant's view, faced with a philosophical problem. We are still faced with the cosmological questions themselves, with an apparent choice between two mutually contradictory answers to each of them. We cannot, Kant points out, claim inevitable ignorance regarding the answers to these questions on the ground that they refer to supersensible objects.[1] They refer, if they refer to anything, to things in space

---

[1] A 478–9/B 506–7.

and time. On the other hand, he insists – and the point is central to the whole of the ensuing discussion – that "the solution of these problems can never be found in experience".[1] The philosopher cannot simply pass the problem on to the natural scientist. He must solve it himself. The concepts in terms of which the cosmological questions are framed are not such as we could ever have empirical grounds for applying.[2] The source of these concepts, and of the problems to which they give rise, is simply our own thought; and it is in our own thought that we must find the solution to those problems.

3. A RE-PRESENTING OF THE ALTERNATIVES

The two mathematical antinomies between them are held to embody three "conflicts of pure reason with itself". Each conflict is supposed to arise on the basis of our being presented with a pair of apparently exhaustive alternatives, one of the alternatives involving the notion of an infinite totality, the other involving the notion of a finite totality. Let us speak of these respectively as the infinite alternative and the finite alternative. It is clear enough how the finite – infinite antithesis enters into the first two conflicts. Either the duration of the world prior to any given moment in its history is finite or it is infinite. Either the spatial extent of the world is finite or it is infinite. Kant supposed it to be equally clear in the case of the third. Either a composite material substance is composed of an infinite number of non-simple parts or it is composed of a finite number of simple parts. He thought this because he was unaware of the mathematically admissible possibility that a body might consist both of an *infinite* number of extended parts and of an *infinite* number of unextended point-particles. For the sake of the argument, however, we will disregard this possibility. It is not one which would give Kant any reason for modifying the doctrines developed in his resolution of the conflicts.

Now to re-present the alternatives in such a way as to bring out clearly how Kant's general form of solution is supposed to fit all three conflicts. This must be done with the help of the notion of a *series*. In each case, to the idea of the finite alternative there corresponds the idea of a certain type of series as finite, i.e. as

[1] A 484/B 512.   [2] A 483/B 511.

having a finite number of members; and, in each case, to the idea of the infinite alternative there corresponds the idea of a certain series as infinite, i.e. as having an infinite number of members. We may say that in every case the idea of such a series, as either finite or infinite, will serve to *represent* for us the ideas of the finite and infinite alternatives, though they are not, in every case, just the same ideas as those they serve to represent. What, then, are these series?

In the case of the duration of the world, we might select as the first member of our series a class of events temporally co-terminous with the Napoleonic Wars. We might, in fact, select the Napoleonic Wars themselves. The second member of the series would be a class of events more or less closely preceding the Napoleonic Wars and with a finite temporal coverage not shorter than that of the first member. The third member would be another similar class of yet earlier events; and so on. This series must, it seems, be either finite or infinite.

The case of the extent of the world in space is rather more complicated. The discussion is, of course, to be conducted on the assumption that the geometry of physical space is Euclidean. But there seem to be all sorts of ways in which, as far as the *a priori* possibilities are concerned, the world might extend, finitely or infinitely, in Euclidean space. It might, for example, have a corkscrew shape; and this would be compatible with its having a limit at one end while being of infinite extent. Or it might have the shape of a ring; which would be compatible with its being finite in extent and yet such that a traveller, following a course of appropriate and constant curvature, would never reach a limit. Let us simplify the discussion by assuming that, if finite in extent, it has the shape of a sphere and, if infinite in extent, it extends infinitely in all directions from any sub-region of itself. Now we form the idea of a series of which the first member is some particular sub-region of the world, the second member another finite region external to the first, the third a similar region external to the second and more distant than the second from the first, and so on, every member of the series to lie on a three-dimensional path centred about a straight line, and no member to be of lesser extent in the direction of that line than its predecessor in the series. Of course there will be many possible series of this kind. But whichever series we select, if the finite alternative is the true one, the number of its members will be finite, and, if the infinite alternative is the true one, the number of its members will be infinite.

Every member of any of those series which represent for us the finite and infinite alternatives of the first antinomy is external to every other member of its own series. But any series which represents for us the alternatives of the second antinomy is of a different kind. Each member of such a series is included in the preceding member as a part of it. Any composite material substance might be the first member of such a series. The second member would be some part of that composite body, the third member some part of that part and so on. If composite substances are composed of simple parts, then any process of progressive decomposition by which successive members of such a series were successively isolated would come to an end in a finite number of steps; the series has a finite number of members. But if all the parts of composite substances are themselves composite, such a process would never reach an end by a finite number of steps; the series has an infinite number of members. (We have already remarked upon, and agreed to ignore, the point that these are not, mathematically speaking, truly exhaustive alternatives.) This type of series, like the others, is, then, either finite or infinite.

4. KANT'S SOLUTION: ITS GENERAL FORM; AND THREE INTERPRETATIONS

The general form of solution which Kant adopts for these problems is as follows. Since things in space and time are only appearances, none of those spatial or temporal series which represent the topics of the antinomies exists either as a limited or an infinite totality. Hence, with regard to each such series, we can consistently and correctly hold that, of the four following propositions, both of the first two are false and both of the last two are true:

(1) the series exists as a limited whole;

(2) the series exists as an infinite whole;

(3) if the series existed as a whole, it would exist as a limited whole;

(4) if the series existed as a whole, it would exist as an infinite whole.

The joint truth of all relevant propositions of the forms of (3) and (4), which is what is established by the arguments of the antinomies taken together, constitutes an indirect proof of the proposition that no such series exists as a whole, either limited or infinite; and this proposition is equivalent to the proposition that things in space and time are only appearances and not things in themselves. Thus the antinomies constitute a vindication of the thesis of transcendental idealism, and the thesis of transcendental idealism contains the solution of the apparent conflicts of reason with itself displayed in the antinomies.

So much by way of a formal statement of Kant's solution. The question is: what should it be taken to mean? At least three widely differing interpretations are candidates for consideration. Not that each of them can plausibly be represented as consistent with all that Kant says in the *Critique*. (That would be setting the standard for Kantian exegesis very high.) Perhaps only one of them can plausibly be represented as conforming to Kant's dominant intention in the chapter of the antinomies. Yet each of the three is worthy of consideration and none entirely lacks support in the text of the *Critique*. I have tried to frame my own short general statement of Kant's solution with an appropriate ambiguity, to formulate it in words which are close to some of Kant's own but which allow, with more or less strain, of any one of the three interpretations I shall consider. I shall refer to them, respectively, as the "strong", the "weak", and the "mixed" interpretation. To each, obviously, there corresponds a different version of transcendental idealism; and these versions might appropriately be named "strong transcendental idealism", "weak transcendental idealism", and "mixed transcendental idealism". The three interpretations are incompatible with one another, but this does not mean that there is no overlap between them. Some propositions may be common to different interpretations; in particular, the "weak" and the "mixed" interpretations share important features.

On the strong interpretation, the doctrine that things in space and time are only appearances is taken to mean that it only appears to be the case that there is anything in space or in time at all. It only appears to be the case that there is anything anywhere or that anything happens. Nothing is really anywhere, nothing really happens. Even its appearing to be the case that there are things in space and time cannot itself be something that happens or lasts, that occurs in, or takes, time. No spatial or temporal series of things exists as a whole, because no such series exists at all. There is nothing which could be a member of any such series. Doubtless if such a series did actually exist, it would necessarily exist either as a finite or as an infinite whole. But no question arises as to which alternative is actually realized in the case of any such series, for no such series exists. Nor does any comparable question arise regarding appearances. From the fact that it appears to be the case that there exist things spatially or temporally ordered in certain ways, it does not follow that either it appears to be the case that all such things exist as members of a limited series or it appears to be the case that all such things exist as members of an infinite series. In fact neither limb of this disjunction is true.

We need spend little time on this interpretation. It is far too difficult to reconcile with the presence in the text of almost everything that goes into the detailed working-out of the solution; and even if, by some feat of virtuosity, such a reconciliation could be achieved, it seems unlikely that the strong solution would emerge as anything but superfluous. Nevertheless this interpretation deserves a mention; for the corresponding version of transcendental idealism is not one that should be altogether overlooked in the discussion of that subject.

Let us turn to the other two interpretations. In the development of each of the three conflicts, whether it is the finite or the infinite alternative which is being presented, it is assumed that the series which represents the topic of the conflict exists as a whole. We are presented on the one hand with the idea of a finite series terminated by a limiting or final member, on the other hand with the idea of an infinite series with no terminating member. The development of the conflict presupposes that to one or the other of these ideas there must be an answering object. A proposition which Kant repeatedly affirms and which is central to both the interpretations of his solution which we are now to consider is the proposition that no possible experience could ever justify us in saying that we had met with an object answering to either of these two ideas. This proposition, I say, is central to both the weak and the mixed interpretations. But they diverge in the construction they put upon it.

First, the weak interpretation. To say that things in space and time are only appearances is not to say that there only appear to be things in space and time. There really are such things. The point of calling them "appearances only" is to rule out as senseless the whole conception of their having "in themselves" characteristics or relations quite distinct from any which they could possibly *appear* to us to have, i.e. such that it would be impossible for us ever to discover empirically that they have them. In no discussion or argument concerning things in space and time can there be any legitimate use for concepts such that no possible observations, no possible experience, could ever justify the application of those concepts. Now we are certainly justified in using the concepts of certain sorts of serial *ordering* of things in space and time. Thus memory and historical investigations justify the concept of a serial ordering of events starting from more recent events and proceeding backwards in time through more and more remote events, beyond the reach of memory. There is, in fact, a perfectly legitimate concept of a type of serial ordering corresponding to every one of the concepts of a type of series which form the topics of the antinomies. But it is an illusion, though a natural one, to suppose that for every such legitimate concept of a type of serial ordering there is an equally legitimate concept of the *whole series* of things ordered by the ordering relation in question.

The illusion is fostered in complex ways by many factors. The idea of a spatial or temporal series as a finite whole is the common core of many perfectly legitimate ideas which have empirical application. The entire regressive temporal series of Plantagenet kings, starting from Richard III; the complete spatial series of paving stones making up a path; the whole series of a set of nested boxes, starting from the outermost – all these are objects answering to such ideas. In every such series as these we know what counts as empirically discovering that such-and-such a member is the terminal member of the series. But then we are tempted to isolate the common core of all these ideas. We strip it of those descriptions which in fact enable us to know what would count as the empirical discovery of the terminal member of any such spatial or temporal series, and leave ourselves with, e.g., just the idea of the finite whole of the regressive temporal series of states of the world *in general*. But this idea is empty. Not only have we not the slightest conception of any experience which would justify us in claiming application for the words in which it is expressed; we can see that no such experience is possible.

Even the realization of this fact, so far from dispelling the illusion altogether, may simply encourage the complementary form of it. We may conclude that since nothing would justify us in claiming to have discovered that a certain region of the universe was the outermost or that a certain phase of its history was the first, then the entire series of regions or phases must exist as an infinite whole. Not only does no such conclusion follow, but the thought of the entire series as an infinite whole is just as empty as the thought of the entire series as a finite whole. The latter thought arises, or may arise, as we have seen, from depriving a perfectly legitimate class of empirically applicable ideas of all their empirical content. The former thought arises from trying to transplant an idea which flourishes in pure mathematics into the different soil of an empirical subject-matter. But the conditions of success in such transplanting cannot in this case be fulfilled. For the notion of any experience which would justify us in affirming that the serially orderable regions of the universe or the phases of its past history form, as a whole, an infinite series, is actually self-contradictory. Empirical inquiry into these matters must proceed by successive stages of discovery of ever remoter regions or phases, starting from some given phase or region, and could therefore never reach the point of proclaiming the series of regions or phases as infinite. We may say, if we like – more, we *should* say – that the task of investigating these serially ordered items is an endless task, in that nothing could justify us in saying that we have reached its end; we must always strive to find further members to add to those we have discovered already. But we must not think of the endless task of investigation as a task of investigating the endless.

To one who insists, then, that these serially ordered items must belong to a series which, as a whole, is either finite or infinite, we must reply that he is using words quite emptily, that "in its empirical meaning the term 'whole' is always only comparative"[1] and has no such unrestricted use as he is trying to make of it. It is really the emptiness of "the finite alternative" which, imperfectly understood, appears to force us to embrace "the infinite alternative" and, equally, it is the emptiness of "the infinite alternative"

[1] A 483/B 511.

which, imperfectly understood, appears to force us to embrace
"the finite alternative". The proper task is to withhold our embraces from both and keep them for our proper task of empirical
investigation of what falls within the scope of that activity.

This interpretation of Kant's solution of his problem has
obvious attractions. Evidently it obliges us to take a somewhat
oblique view of the arguments he uses in the development of the
"conflicts" and to adopt a somewhat sophisticated reading of the
position that all relevant propositions of the forms of (1) and
(2) above can be regarded as false, while the corresponding
propositions of the forms of (3) and (4) can be accepted as true.[1]
Strictly speaking, on this interpretation, the relevant propositions
of the forms (1) and (2) must be regarded as empty of content, or
of "cognitive meaning", rather than false. But perhaps we can
allow an extended use of "false" to cover this. The doctrine of
the joint truth of the corresponding propositions of the forms
(3) and (4) is slightly more troublesome. We can, on the view in
question, fairly readily understand the doctrine that if it were
correct to regard things in space and time as things in themselves,
then each of our series would exist either as a finite or as an
infinite whole. To think of things in space and time as things in
themselves is, on this interpretation, nothing other than to free
our thoughts about them from the restrictive condition imposed
by the principle of significance, the principle which forbids, as
empty, the employment of any concept for which no empirical
conditions of application could possibly be specified. Once that
condition is lifted, the thought of our serially orderable items as
belonging to a series which, as a whole, is either finite or infinite,
can reasonably be regarded as irresistible. The disjunction is one
which we can no longer refuse to accept. But what exactly are we
to make of the further claim of truth *both* for the proposition that
if things in space and time are things in themselves, then each of
our series exists as a finite whole *and* for the proposition that if
things in space and time are things in themselves, then each of our
series exists as an infinite whole? I do not think much can be done
for this except by a capricious use of the principle of significance.
We ostentatiously – or silently – waive it to secure the admission
of the disjunction and surreptitiously invoke it to rule out one of
the alternatives, thereby establishing the other. Kant's arguments

[1] See p. 187 above.

against the infinite alternatives in the first antinomy are not so very far removed from this; and the ghost of the same procedure can perhaps also be detected as animating the curiously unsatisfactory arguments of the antithesis.

This "weak" interpretation of Kant's solution has, as I have remarked, its attractions. It is, perhaps, the view we might wish had been his, and it certainly includes elements which must belong to any view which can plausibly be attributed to him. But, as it stands, it quite certainly is not his view. As it stands, it secures the relevance of transcendental idealism to the solution of the problem only by weakening that doctrine to the point of evanescence. As we shall see later, it would be possible to preserve the weak solution essentially intact, while re-invigorating the thesis of transcendental idealism; but this would only be at the cost of destroying the relevance of the latter to the former.

The strong solution denies the real existence of any spatial or temporal thing, be it inner state, objective alteration in outer object or outer object itself. The weak solution denies the existence of nothing: it simply proscribes certain expressions as mere empty pretenders to a place they do not possess in the language of natural science. The mixed solution falls between the two. It depends on that version of transcendental idealism, more prominent in the first than in the second edition, but dominant in both, which Kant's critics might with reason claim to show affinities with the idealism of Berkeley.

The central feature of this solution is that one type of essentially temporal series is accorded a real existence which belongs to no other temporal or spatial series whatever. This is the series of representations, or experiences, which "belong, in themselves, as determinations of the mind, to our inner states"[1] and really succeed each other in time. What are represented by us as the objects of these representations or experiences, whether we represent them "as extended beings or as series of alterations",[2] have no independent existence outside the series of our representations. This is a part of the meaning of the doctrine that the objects of experience, things in space and time, are mere appearances: "they have no existence outside experience."[3] (The other part of its meaning relates to their unknown noumenal cause which cannot be represented as in space and time, but must be taken to

[1] A 34/B 50.   [2] A 491/B 519.   [3] A 492/B 521.

N

have some sort of correspondence to the content of our perceptions, whence the latter may properly be called an *appearance* of the former.) "Nothing is really given us save perceptions."[1] These we "attain in themselves".[2] But these perceptions are not, strictly speaking, perceptions of objects independently existing in space and time. The objects are nothing over and above the perceptions themselves. We do indeed speak of the existence of particular objects in space and time even though we have had no actual experience which we can count as a perception of those objects. But here we speak simply under the guidance of those empirical laws concerning appearances which experience leads us to formulate and which, if there is to be such a thing as experience at all, it must be such as to enable us to formulate. Such laws are, fundamentally, nothing but rules regarding the connexions of perceptions; and assertions which invoke them do not really imply the existence of anything but perceptions themselves.

Now to apply this doctrine to our problem. The problem arises directly from the assumption that things in space and time exist independently of our perceptions of them. If they do, then certain series of such things must exist independently of our perceptions of them: series of phases of the world's history stretching backwards in time; series of remoter and remoter regions of the universe extending outwards in space; series of parts of parts of parts of material bodies occupying ever smaller volumes of the spaces occupied by those bodies themselves. If these series of items exist independently of our perceptions, then it must be admitted that they exist either as finite or as infinite totalities. We are necessarily faced with the finite and infinite alternatives in each case.

But, as the present doctrine holds, the items which make up these series, and hence the series themselves, do *not* exist independently of our representations, our perceptions. The relevant really existing series which we have to consider are the series of those successive perceptions which correspond to successive advances in our empirical investigations into ever remoter time past, ever more distant regions of the universe, ever more minute constitutents of matter. The essentially successive experiences which constitute the membership of the "exploring series" really exist; but the members of the "explored series" exist only in

[1] A 493/B 521.   [2] A 499/B 527.

so far as we "meet with them" at successive stages of the exploration. We could conclude that the members of the explored series really constituted a finite totality only if the exploring series came to an end in an actual experience which we could identify as having the character of an intuition of a limiting or terminal member of the explored series. We could say that the explored series existed as an infinite totality only if we had continued the exploring series infinitely far. Not only is it not necessary that one of these alternatives should obtain. It is impossible that either should. On the one hand, however far we prolong the exploring series, we can never reach the stage at which we can claim to have prolonged it infinitely far. On the other, we have no criterion which could entitle us to say that a given experience belonging to an exploring series was the last possible member of its series. On the contrary, we have always to strive to continue the advance of the series, e.g. through more refined or more powerful instruments.

There can be little doubt that this "mixed" solution corresponds the most closely to Kant's dominant intention in the Antinomies. It provides, as it were, a metaphysical stiffening or support for the principle of significance which the "weak" solution treats as autonomous. The reason why concepts which offer themselves as possibly applicable to things in space and time cannot legitimately be so employed unless there are possible experiential conditions for applying them lies in the metaphysical fact that – apart from the noumenal unknown to which spatio-temporal concepts are utterly irrelevant – nothing, after all, really exists but our representations and experiences, which in themselves are merely temporally successive inner determinations, though they admit, and necessarily admit, of being regarded as representations of outer things. If it were not for this metaphysical fact – an upholder of this view might maintain – we *should* have to allow that each of the temporal or spatial series which represent the topics of the antinomies did really exist either as a finite or as an infinite whole, even though it was in principle impossible for us empirically to determine which alternative actually obtained. But recognition of the metaphysical fact licenses, or rather requires, the plain denial that either alternative obtains, and enables us to see nothing but a confirmation of itself in the availability – if indeed they are available – of equally compelling proofs of the two propositions that any such independently existing series would be finite and that any such independently existing series would be infinite. (On this last point we may remark again, with perhaps even more justification, that it is only in the light of Kant's solution that we can begin to see why some of the "proofs" he offers in setting up the "conflicts" appeared to him to have the force he evidently ascribed to them. The claim to find confirmation of this version of idealism in the existence of the conflicts is correspondingly enfeebled.)

The mixed solution, though perhaps not formally irreconcilable with Kant's best thoughts,[1] as I have interpreted them in the study of the Analytic, has a prima facie lack of consonance with those thoughts. Moreover, it gives rise to problems of its own in the immediate context of the antinomies. Outside the unknown realm of the noumenal, nothing exists but temporally ordered perceptions, representations, experiences, inner determinations of the mind. But these really do exist in themselves. We "attain them in themselves". Are we not then obliged to raise with respect to them a question quite analogous to that considered in the first antinomy regarding the previous history of a supposed objective world? Has the series of perceptions a beginning or does it stretch infinitely backward in time? It is easy to begin discussing this question in a rather confused way. It may even seem, at first, to raise no particular difficulty. For it is not, as the corresponding question of the first antinomy seemed to be, a question concerning the previous phases of the history of the universe *in general*. It seems rather to be a question concerning a particular sub-class of events in that history, viz. the series of conscious experiences of beings capable of thought. Might we not have empirical grounds for assigning a beginning to that series? To this there are several immediate replies: e.g. that we could have no such ground unless experience could first warrant our claiming to have completed a survey of the whole extent of the universe in space, which has already been declared to be impossible.

There are profounder difficulties, however, in this whole way of discussing the matter. There can be no evidence of the existence of the perceptions of past generations which is not evidence of the existence, in an equally strong sense, of those past generations themselves. I can have no experience which warrants the declara-

[1] See Part IV, Section 6.

tion that certain representations occurred or existed in the conscious experience of some man in the past but which does not warrant the declaration that such a man existed (in no weaker sense than his experience) as an object in space and time. Indeed I can have no experience which warrants the declaration that there occurs or exists some experience similar to, and contemporary with, but other than, my own, which does not also warrant the declaration that, in a sense as strong as that in which that experience can be said to exist, there exists in space and time a man other than myself. Kant constantly talks in a collective style of "our" representations or experiences. Nothing, he says, is really given *us* save perceptions. (These we attain in themselves.) But your perceptions are not given to me nor mine to you. Here we have an acute dilemma for this version of transcendental idealism. Either it must turn into transcendental solipsism or it must be given up in favour of another version altogether, weak or strong. (A parallel dilemma confronts Berkeley.)

There is no evidence whatever in the *Critique* that Kant seriously considered embracing solipsism. The style in which he presents transcendental idealism is consistently the collective style. He speaks for us all and not for himself alone. "It is solely from the *human* standpoint that we can speak of space, of extended things, etc."[1] Yet the solipsistic tendency of mixed idealism, once noted, is too evidently irresistible to be ignored. It must strengthen us in the general resolve to find where we can in the *Critique* an interpretation of Kant's thinking which dispenses with the mixed version of transcendental idealism and accords equal reality to inner representations and their outer objects.

5. A FOURTH INTERPRETATION OF THE SOLUTION?

I have set out three possible interpretations of Kant's solution to the problem of the antinomies, each corresponding to a different version of transcendental idealism. I have not, however, exhausted the possible versions of the latter; and it is worth inquiring whether a fourth possible version of transcendental idealism may not give rise to a fourth interpretation of the solution. In the mixed version of transcendental idealism which we have just considered, the word "appearances" has really a double task to perform. It

[1] A 26/B 42.

serves to contrast what does not really exist at all, but only appears to, with what has real existence in time, viz. the succession of perceptions; and it serves also to contrast what has a real, but merely dependent, existence (viz. the succession of perceptions again) with the noumenal unknown which, in a way also unknown, gives rise to that temporal succession. Objects in space, objective occurrences in time, are appearances in that they do not really exist. What really exist are those experiences which succeed one another in time and are ranked as perceptions of such objects and alterations. But these perceptions depend for their existence and character upon the noumenal unknown which is neither spatial nor temporal. ("Inasmuch as it is *noumenon*, nothing *happens* in it.")[1] In this way perceptions, without prejudice to their real existence in time, can be counted as appearances too, appearances of the noumenal unknown on which, in an unknown way, they depend. Hence objects in space and objective alterations in time can be held to be appearances in a double sense: first, they have no real existence in themselves, being nothing but mental determinations or perceptions; and, second, *as* such, *as* mental determinations or perceptions, they are dependent for their existence and character upon the noumenal unknown.

If here, in the Antinomies, and elsewhere, in passages peculiar to the first edition or common to both, we seem to find an emphatic reduction of what appear to be objective things in space and time to mere representations or perceptions in temporal succession, we can, elsewhere, find an apparently no less emphatic repudiation of any such reduction. The existence of outer objects of which I am immediately conscious, but which are *distinct* from my representations of them, is held to be no less a condition of the possibility of experience than the successive occurrence of my representations themselves. No doubt this doctrine, most positively affirmed in the Refutation of Idealism, is itself subject to a variety of interpretations and could, in one of them, be reconciled with the reductive idealism we have just been considering. But we cannot ignore that reading of it which secures to objects in space, as distinct from representations, no worse a claim to real existence than a succession of representations in time. Now, of course, two equal claims may be equally good or equally bad. If we hold these two claims to be, in the final, i.e. the transcendental,

[1] A 541/B 569.

analysis, equally bad, then we return to the strong version of transcendental idealism, according to which it only appears to be the case (and only, really, non-temporally so appears) that there exists or occurs anything in space or in time at all, whether inner experience or outer object, perception or object of perception. But if we hold the two claims to be both, and equally, good, then we need another version of transcendental idealism.

It is not hard to see what this version will be. The doctrine that things in space and time are only appearances, not things-in-themselves, will amount to the doctrine that they are *dependent* existences, dependent both for their existence and their character upon the unknown constitution of things as they are in themselves, including ourselves as we are in ourselves (though we may remark, as always, that the constitution of the latter does not appear to be as unknown as it ought to be.) As soon as we have described this fourth version of transcendental idealism, however, it is obvious that from it, by itself, there follows no solution whatever to the problem of the antinomies. It is incompatible with both the strong and the mixed solutions; and though it could be held consistently with the adoption, in its essential features, of the weak solution, it neither entails that solution nor is entailed by it. It would obviously be highly unplausible to maintain that, of all the possibilities considered, a combination of the weak solution with this fourth version of transcendental idealism came closest to Kant's real intentions in this chapter.

6. THE COSMOLOGICAL QUESTIONS RE-CONSIDERED

Let us now consider the cosmological questions in their own right. Do they really raise any such problem as Kant supposed? If things in space and time exist "in themselves", then, Kant maintains, it follows, *first* and immediately, that all the members of each of three sets of disjunctive propositions having in common the form "Either the series of xs is finite or it is infinite" are true propositions and, *second*, by valid argument, that each of the mutually incompatible disjuncts of each disjunctive proposition is true. It is clear that Kant in fact fails to produce arguments, valid independently of his solution to his problem, to establish the second of these consequences; and hence that his problem, in its acute form, does not exist. This does not by itself entail that the doctrine he advances as a solution to his supposed problem is a false doctrine; only that it is false that it is a solution to any such problem.

One question we have to ask is whether the first of his consequences, by itself, gives rise to any philosophical problem at all. Kant himself, as we have seen, certainly thought that it did. He points out, correctly, that each disjunctive proposition gives rise to a cosmological question of the form "Is the series of *x*s finite or infinite?"; argues that these questions are, in principle, empirically undecidable; and – dismissing, again correctly, one plea of unavoidable ignorance – concludes that the fact of empirical undecidability is itself sufficient to show that the cosmological questions must, in one way or another, be dealt with, or disposed of, philosophically.

The shortest way of countering this brisk deduction is to deny that the cosmological questions are empirically undecidable. Certain mistaken beliefs about the nature of space and of matter, and a generally too narrow conception of the nature of empirical inquiry in these fields, blind Kant, it might be said, to the fact that the cosmological questions, or some of them, are fully as capable of being settled empirically as some others which incontestably belong to the sphere of natural science. Not that we can arrive, on these matters, at theories in principle unrevisable; but the revisability of theories is a general feature of scientific procedure. It is enough that we can frame theories, capable of being submitted to genuine empirical tests, which embody answers to these questions.

We will consider in a moment how far we can confidently go along this line. Meantime, there is another line to consider, opposed in a different way to Kant's own. Why, it might be asked, should we not accept it as a perfectly intelligible fact about a series of a certain kind both that the series is either finite or infinite and that it will never be possible to find out which it is? The fact certainly calls for philosophical acknowledgement and, perhaps for philosophical explanation. But the explanation is given when a clear description of the case is given. Consider, for example, on the assumption that physical space is Euclidean, the question of the spatial extent of the universe. We might discover, in our researches into outer space, that at some distance in any direction from the earth matter began to thin out and then seemed to cease altogether. We could not conclude that the universe was finite in extent. For we could not rule out the possibility that if we were to push our researches enormously further in some directions, we might come across matter again. If, on the other hand, with the help of enormously powerful instruments we did push our researches to the point of discovering other systems of galaxies at enormous distances from our own and yet others at enormous distances from those, we should still have no assurance that there was no outer limit to this system of systems. The question would remain open, whatever we discovered or failed to discover. But this does not mean that of the alternatives envisaged in the question one is not in fact true and the other in fact false. Since the systems of matter which make up the spatially extended universe exist independently of our observations of them, one or the other *must* be true.

The adoption of this view, we should notice, would not require us to give up altogether that cherished philosophical instrument, the principle of significance. It would require us only to exempt these particular questions from its application. They constitute, or belong to, after all, a quite distinctive kind of question; and it should not be too difficult to draft a subordinate principle which would cover their exemption from the general principle. One might appeal, for example, to the fact that the finite alternative is equivalent to an infinite disjunction of propositions each specifying, e.g., the actual extent of the universe as lying within certain limits. Though no member of this set of specifying propositions can be empirically verified, any member is in principle open to empirical falsification.

Both these non-Kantian lines of thought represent the cosmological alternatives as genuine alternatives, decidable or undecidable as the case may be. It would be consistent to take one line with respect to one (or two) of the cosmological questions and the other line with respect to the other two (or one). There is, however, yet a third non-Kantian line to be considered which, in common with Kant's own view, rejects the alternatives as non-genuine, but does so for somewhat different reasons from Kant's. This view may be summarized as follows. Each cosmological series presents, *a priori*, an infinite number of possibilities. If, for instance, we fix on some unit of distance or duration, then there is, as far as the *a priori* possibilities are concerned, an infinite number of possibly true answers to the question, "What is the spatial extent of the universe, expressed in terms of these units of distance?" and to the question, "What is the past duration of the world's history, expressed in terms of these units of duration?" But to say that there is an infinite number of possibly true answers to these questions is not to say that it is possible that the true answer is: an infinite number. This answer would be quite senseless; whereas any of the infinite number of answers which mentions a finite number of units is a perfectly meaningful and, as far as the *a priori* possibilities go, a possibly true answer.

This view has certain strengths. It does not question the legitimacy of the mathematical notion of infinity. Indeed it makes use of that notion. It only denies the significance of applying the notion of an infinite number to sets of which the members are empirically discriminable items. It does not represent as paradoxical any of the well-known properties peculiar to infinite numbers. It merely affirms that it would be paradoxical to the point of senselessness to affirm that any set whose members were empirically discriminable items might exhibit those properties. One who espouses the view can borrow from Kant any point the latter may make to show the emptiness of the infinite alternative. At the same time he can make, against Kant, the point that no member of the infinite set of possibly true answers to the cosmological question can possibly be empty of meaning; for any such answer is in principle empirically refutable and many have already been empirically refuted. The two-limbed finite–infinite disjunction disappears: the finite limb is as empty as the infinite limb, for no limit is set to the possibilities in declaring the cosmological series to be finite. In its place we have an infinite disjunction with no empty limbs at all. On the question whether an answer corresponding to one of its limbs might not be, in principle, empirically confirmable as well as empirically refutable, the upholder of this doctrine is not, as such, required to take up a position. He could consistently adopt either view.

It is perhaps worth labouring the point that this position secures to empirical investigation, or at least to the kind of step-by-step investigation envisaged by Kant, quite as unrestricted a scope as the infinite alternative seemed to do. To the objector who inquires: "Do you mean to say that it is *a priori* true that there is a certain number of members of the investigated series beyond which there are no further members to be found?" an upholder of this view can reply:

> Of any number of members it is true that there might be no further members of the series to be found beyond that number; but there is no number of members of which it is not true that there might be yet further members of the series to be found beyond that number. The investigator should not therefore invoke this philosophical position as a reason for throwing up his investigations at any point.

I have set out these three non-Kantian lines of thought in general terms. But we cannot hope to evaluate them without considering some of the cosmological questions individually in relation to actual developments in science.

Let us begin with the question which forms the topic of the second antinomy. A sub-atomic physicist could scarcely be expected to recognize himself in Kant's picture of an empirical investigator in this field, engaged in an endless task of successive division of ever smaller parts of matter. It is true enough that the series molecule-atom-electron has some analogy to the Kantian series. But it is not true at all that each theoretical advance in this field must be conceived in terms of the discovery of minute particles of which particles discovered at the previous stage are composed and which in their turn must be thought of as theoretically decomposable into still minuter particles, yet to be discovered. In so far as the particle model is held to be appropriate, it is indeed *open* to the theorist to take such a "decomposing" step as this, if a satisfactory theoretical explanation of the phenomena seems to demand it. But there is no necessity for theoretical advance to take this direction. The very conception of a fundamental "particle" has undergone a revolutionary change with the advent of quantum mechanics; and though, in recent sub-atomic physics, the number of recognized types of particle has indeed been added to, the new additions have been conceived as additional "elementary" particles rather than as constituents of particles previously regarded as elementary and now seen as composite. The endless open-ness to revision of physical theories promises, indeed, an endless task to the theorist; but theoretical revisions may be, in fact have been, of a quite different kind from any which Kant imagined. Kant, one might say, attributes to the theorist, as soon as he has evolved one theory, an obligation to ask, with respect to the material "elements" of his theory, the question, "What are these elements *composed of*?" But the theorist recognizes no such standard, simple obligation as this; only a much more general obligation to improve a theory, or devise a better one, to account for anything already known or newly discovered which, on the theory as it stands, appears arbitrary or unexplained. When he does make a theoretical change, it may be towards a complete re-conceptualization rather than towards a "decomposition" of his materials. Kant's conception of the "analysis of matter" as undertaken by the physicist, has a primitive simplicity which makes it at best only partially analogous to the changing conceptual structures which physicists actually produce.

What, now, of the second topic of the first antinomy, the extent of the universe in space? The situation here is in some respects analogous to that which we have just considered. Kant took it for granted that the geometry of physical space was Euclidean. But this assumption is precisely what is questioned in modern astrophysical theory. It seems that the empirical findings may turn out to be best accommodated by the theory that the geometry of physical space is of a certain non-Euclidean kind, of such a kind, in fact, that physical space itself is, if this theory is true, of finite extent; and if physical space itself is of finite extent, then, of course, so is the universe in physical space. If this theory succeeds in holding the field, then the cosmological question, as conceived by Kant, is simply side-tracked; for that question, as conceived by him, rests on an assumption which he held certainly true (however it was to be interpreted in transcendental idealist terms) and which turns out to be false, viz. that physical space is Euclidean.

It can be pointed out, of course, that even if the geometry of physical space is "discovered" to be of such a non-Euclidean kind, the fact that it is so is contingent; there is no necessity that the empirical findings should support such a theory. Since it is, if false, merely contingently false that physical space is Euclidean, we can neither simply dismiss nor regard as solved those philosophical problems, if any, which arise on the assumption that it is true. On the other hand, it seems impossible that our view of these problems should remain unaffected by the recognition that in this field, as in that of the investigation of the structure of matter, the development of theoretical thinking, the advance of inquiry, may take quite different forms and directions from any which Kant conceived of. The picture of the step-by-step, serial advance from the nearer to the farther object, from the larger to the smaller, loses its inevitability, seems quite inadequate, when we are confronted in either field by the actual process of evolving theory.

If we now turn back to those three non-Kantian lines of thought I described above and set alongside them that "weak" interpretation of Kant's own solution which would diminish transcendental idealism into an affirmation of the principle of significance, we see that no follower of any of these lines can claim unqualified support from the facts. Theories which embody *something like* a form of the finite alternative seem to be empirically grounded, even, at least provisionally, acceptable. Yet such theories can scarcely be represented as containing straightforward answers to the cosmological questions as conceived by Kant. It is hard to maintain that just those questions make perfectly good sense in relation to the kind of inquiry that Kant envisaged; yet it is hard to maintain that they are quite senseless when such theories are available as I have mentioned. Nor can we rule out *a priori* the possibility of empirically grounded theories which embody *something like* a form of the infinite alternative. In the case of the topic of the first half of the first antinomy such theories are already in the field. There is no *a priori* impossibility in the thought that they *might* have been in the field in the case of the topic of its second half also. Might not the movements of actually observable bodies have been such that, in the context of a Euclidean physical geometry, the maximum simplification of laws fitting those movements could be obtained with the help of the assumption that bodies extended infinitely in a certain distribution in all directions from the point of observation?

Perhaps we should say that the cosmological questions, as framed by Kant, neither have a clear meaning nor are clearly devoid of meaning. They serve to hold open the field of empirical inquiry, though not, or not only, in the way in which Kant supposed they did. They leave it open for the framing of testable theories of kinds unforeseen by him, which might in a sense be said to embody answers to the questions, but only by quite transforming the look of them. Kant offers, one might say, complementary impossible tasks to the imagination and draws far-reaching metaphysical conclusions from their impossibility. Yet physical theory may transformingly occupy, take possession of, the field of those impossible tasks. From the point of view of a philosophical critic, one thing at least is clear: Kant was mistaken in his belief that it was a field on which a decisive battle could be fought, and a decisive victory won, for the doctrines of transcendental idealism.

IV

GOD

It is with very moderate enthusiasm that a twentieth-century philosopher enters the field of philosophical theology, even to follow Kant's exposure of its illusions. The quality of Kant's presentation of his own doctrines seems to suffer some deterioration as he approaches this subject. His dismissive analysis of the three "proofs" of God's existence – the only possible three, according to him – has, at least superficially, an admirable crispness and clarity. But the approach to this bright triptych of argument is shadowed in confusion.

The subject of "absolutely necessary being" makes its first appearance in the fourth antinomy; but I shall begin by considering the two "dynamical" antinomies together. Though I am not here directly concerned with Kant's doctrine of freedom – the topic introduced by way of the third antinomy – there are revealing parallels and divergencies in Kant's presentation and treatment of these two "conflicts".

I. THE DYNAMICAL ANTINOMIES: THE CONVENTIONAL CRITICAL SOLUTION PASSED OVER

I have already expounded and discussed Kant's doctrine that, in the first two antinomies, thesis and antithesis, in so far as they are to be understood as truly incompatible with each other, are both false; for they share the false presupposition that the cosmological series in question exist as wholes, whether finite or infinite. When we turn to the third and fourth antinomies, we find a quite different situation. Whereas the *thesis* of each of the third and fourth antinomies embodies a precisely parallel "false" presupposition to that embodied by both thesis and antithesis in the first and second antinomies, no such presupposition at all is embodied in the *antithesis* of either. The fact that Kant never makes this difference quite explicit is surely connected with a striking anomaly in his "solution" to the later antinomies. Noticing the difference, we might reasonably expect the following resolution of the conflict between thesis and antithesis, viz. that in so far as they are properly understood as incompatible with each other, the thesis is false and the antithesis is true. At no point, however, does Kant offer this conclusion as a solution to either of these two conflicts. Instead, he suggests that the solution is found only when it is recognized that the "demand of reason" expressed in each thesis may, in a sense, be satisfied, that the dialectical assertions expressed on either side of each antinomy, when correctly interpreted, "may *both* alike be *true*".[1] Let us look at this situation in more detail. The anomaly just noticed is not the only one we shall encounter.

The type of series which represents the topic of the third antinomy is a series of *causes*. The argument of the thesis is that the truly sufficient or complete causal determination of any state of the world requires that at some point in the backward series of preceding causes of causes there should be an instance of causality which is itself uncaused, which initiates a forward causal series *spontaneously* or *freely*. We cannot, indeed, insist on the necessity of a spontaneous beginning of a causal series except as regards the initial state of the world and in order "to make an origin of the world conceivable"; for "all the later following states can be taken as resulting according to purely natural laws".[2] But once causality through freedom is admitted, it is permissible to entertain the thought that other causal series, occurring within the course of the world's history, may be similarly initiated through freedom.

The argument, as is correctly noted in the antithesis and acknowledged in the observations on the thesis, derives what force it has solely from the assumption of a beginning of the world. Deprived of this prop, it would reduce to the following false principle: for some state, x, to be a truly causally sufficient condition of some state, y, it is necessary either that there should be no antecedent causally sufficient conditions of x or that the backward series of antecedent causally sufficient conditions starting from x should terminate in a member with no antecedent causally necessary conditions of its own.

The antithesis is a simple denial of freedom, and it is supported, consistently with the conclusion of the argument of the second

[1] A 532/B 560.   [2] A 449/B 477.

Analogy, by an appeal to the universal application of the principle of causality.

It seems obvious what the correct "critical" solution of this conflict should be. Since things in space and time are appearances, the series of ever remoter causes should no more be regarded as existing as a whole than the series of ever remoter temporal states of the world or the series of ever remoter spatial regions of the world. Since the series does not exist as a whole, there is no question of its existing either as an infinite whole or, as is asserted in the thesis, as a finite whole with a first, uncaused member. Every member of the series which is actually "met with" in experience, however, may, and must, be taken to have an antecedent cause. The thesis, then, is false, the antithesis true.

Kant, as I have said, passes over in silence the possibility of this "conventional" critical solution. Before we consider what he offers in its place, let us turn to the fourth antinomy.

The thesis of the fourth antinomy reads curiously like a confused variation on that of the third, modified by a change in wording and the admission of the infinite alternative. A simple and prima facie plausible way of making sense of the distinction between them is to suppose that while the third antinomy is primarily concerned with antecedent sufficient conditions, the fourth is primarily concerned with antecedent necessary conditions. The argument begins with the assertion that the world "contains a series of alterations". Every such alteration, it seems, is "conditioned", i.e. it "stands under" an antecedent causal condition which "renders it necessary".[1] The emphasis here seems to be on sufficient or determining conditions; but I think a more reliable clue to Kant's intentions is given by the remark, in the observation on the thesis, that "alteration proves empirical contingency; that is, that the new state, in the absence of a cause which belongs to the preceding time, could never of itself have taken place",[2] i.e. is dependent upon an antecedent necessary condition. The argument continues as follows. If we consider the series of "conditioned alterations" as a whole, it is obvious that we must admit something in the world which is not thus conditioned. This may be something which is necessary and sufficient to start the whole series off, but which is not itself dependent upon anything antecedent to it, or, alternatively, it may be nothing else

---

[1] A 452/B 480. [2] A 460/B 488.

than the whole series itself which we are to regard as independent of any extraneous necessary condition. Roughly speaking, the series either owes its existence as a whole to nothing at all or to something in particular which owes *its* existence to nothing at all. In the former case (the infinite alternative) the thing which is unconditioned is the series as a whole, in the latter (the finite alternative) it is the starting cause.

Kant says that the unconditioned thing is an "absolutely necessary" being. In the context of the argument this expression appears both curious and confusing. The essential point about the unconditioned thing is the negative one that it does not owe its existence to any antecedent or extraneous necessary condition of itself. If we are to domesticate Kant's use of the expression "necessary" in this context, the safest way is to paraphrase it, in the light of his use of the notion of "empirical contingency", as "not contingent upon anything".

The antithesis, in its first part, is a denial that the world contains any necessary being. Kant once more appeals to the principle of universal causality to dispose of the hypothesis of an uncaused starting cause. Against the alternative hypothesis that the series of alterations as a whole is necessary (unconditioned) he argues that the existence of a series cannot be necessary if no single member of it is necessary. What a poor argument this is, and how it defeats the general purpose of argument for the antithesis, we see when we translate out the reference to necessary existence, and obtain the equivalent argument that if every member of a series owes its existence to (is contingent upon) an antecedent causal condition, then the same must be true of the series as a whole!

Some explanation of the confused presentation of issues in the fourth antinomy emerges as the *Critique* proceeds. In the meantime we must emphatically make the parallel point to that already made regarding the third antinomy. The argument of the thesis rests clearly on the assumption that the relevant series (the series of ever remoter alterations extending backward in time) exists as a whole, either with or without a first member, and concludes by presenting us with a choice between the consequences of each alternative. If this assumption is rejected, the consequences of its exhaustively alternative forms may also both be rejected, as is done in the antithesis. Surely, then, the critical doctrine requires that the antinomy should be resolved by adopting just this course.

the sufficient or necessary conditions of change in the sensible world, we may (Kant suggests) allow at least for the possibility that an unconditioned condition of what belongs to the sensible – a freely acting cause, an existence which depends on no extraneous necessary condition – may exist outside the sphere of the sensible altogether. Thus the demand for the unconditioned expressed in the thesis of the dynamical antinomies is at least not incompatible with the insistence in the antithesis on the thoroughly conditioned character of all that belongs to the sensible.

Kant explicitly claims on behalf of this suggestion that it represents the *only* possible means of resolving the conflicts presented in the dynamical antinomies.[1] The claim seems, on the face of it, preposterous, the suggested solution both redundant and irrelevant. The argument for the thesis in each of the two antinomies rests squarely, as we have already seen, on the false presupposition that the relevant series of "conditioned" items exists as a whole, and a solution on critical lines follows immediately from the falsity of this presupposition. Long ago, at the beginning of the Dialectic, Kant made it clear that we are to understand the role of reason, in its theoretical employment, as that of striving to secure completeness and unity for empirical knowledge, the knowledge obtained by the understanding. The thought of this aim as actually achievable is precisely the thought of the objects of any progressive inquiry as forming together a *complete* set or series.[2] So it is by no means a peculiarity of the mathematical antinomies that they rest on the assumption that the relevant series exists as a whole, and by no means an aberration that the same assumption underlies the argument of the thesis of the third and fourth antinomies. From the point of view of the demands of theoretical reason, we can no more relevantly step outside the sphere of the sensible in search of limiting causes or existences than we can in search of limiting members of any other temporal or spatial series. In Kant's language of faculties, theoretical *reason* can have no interest in any employment of the concepts of "cause" and "necessary existence" except such as is also permitted to *understanding* when the latter faculty is about its business in the acquisition of empirical knowledge. The nature of this employment has already been made clear enough in the Principles. "Cause" is indissolubly bound up with time, in this employment, so that any

[1] A 558/B 586 and A 564/B 592.   [2] A 307–8/B 364.

application of the concept to the noumenal (in which "nothing happens") is irrelevant to the interests of theoretical reason. On "necessary existence" the doctrine of the Postulates of Empirical Thought is clear and unequivocal. We must distinguish between "formal and logical necessity in the connection of concepts" and "material necessity in existence". The application of the latter notion is solely to that which is causally determined in accordance with empirical laws. "Necessity of existence can . . . be known . . . only from connection with that which is perceived, in accordance with universal laws of experience".[1]

What underlies Kant's deviation from the "true" critical solution of the third and fourth antinomies? The factors are many and complex. But it is obvious enough what, in the case of *Freedom* v. *Universal Causality*, is the chief of them. It has nothing to do with the interests of theoretical reason. It has to do with the interests of "pure practical reason", i.e. of morality. Kant is anxious to show that the causal determination of every event by temporally antecedent conditions is not incompatible with the idea of certain events having another kind of cause which, as belonging to the noumenal sphere, is exempt from the condition of time and may be thought of as "acting" freely. Though we cannot understand this possibility, we cannot rule it out on the ground of determinism in Nature; and it is something which morality seems to demand, though we cannot claim theoretical knowledge of it on that account.

Here the rationale of the "new" solution is clear: it is the solution to a new conflict – a conflict not presented in the arguments of the third antinomy at all.

Can we find a parallel to this in the case of the fourth antinomy? We can, at the end of the section which claims to present the solution to that antinomy, find the shadow of a parallel. For there it is implied that where pure reason is employed *"in reference to ends"* (i.e. once more, practically), it may have an interest – of a different kind from that safeguarded by the new solution to the third antinomy – in the existence of an *intelligible cause* outside the series of the empirically conditioned.[2] The "solution" then consists in pointing out again that the thoroughly conditioned character of appearances is not incompatible with the existence of such a "purely intelligible being". The exact character of *this*

[1] A 227/B 279. [2] A 564/B 592.

interest of pure reason, when employed "in reference to ends", is not here disclosed. Later it will be revealed as an interest in the possession by a supersensible being of properties which we analogically conceive in terms of omnipotence and benevolence. Perhaps it is natural enough that the exact character of *this* demand of reason should not be disclosed at this stage. The transition from a theoretical to a moral interest in the idea of a freely acting cause is a relatively smooth transition. But the distinctive attributes required of divinity by morality have no connexion with the ostensible topic of the fourth antinomy. Once more, but this time only through the thickest of veils, the new solution appears as a solution to an entirely new conflict in which, this time, the identity of one of the antagonists is barely glimpsed.

It seems that Kant has allowed his presentation of issues and of doctrines to get out of order at this point. Let us try to re-order them a little. (The disentanglement of doctrines is not, of course, to be confused with their espousal or defence. Even the re-ordering is only provisional: not all the factors involved are before us yet.)

First, antinomies arising from the theoretical interests of reason, having the general character of the third and fourth antinomies and concerned, therefore, with series of causally sufficient and causally necessary conditions of alterations in the world, may properly be developed; but, having been developed, they should be resolved on the conventional critical lines I have already indicated.

Second, it may properly be pointed out that the doctrine of transcendental idealism, invoked in the critical solution of all the antinomies, involves the thesis that all appearances whatever are dependent on a noumenal ground which, as being non-sensible, is empirically unconditioned. One purpose of this reminder, at this stage, should be precisely that of warning us against being misled by any apparent analogy between the notion of a noumenal ground and that of an empirical causal condition into supposing that the interests of theoretical reason, as manifested in the theses of the dynamical antinomies, could be in any way met by reference to the non-sensible ground of appearances.

Third, Kant could then proceed, without danger of confusing the issues, to exploit this reminder for a second and, for him, perhaps, more important purpose. In accordance with general critical principles, theoretical knowledge is necessarily confined to the empirical, so that the "inherent constitution" of the non-sensible ground of appearances necessarily remains completely unknown to us.[1] But this confinement of reason in its theoretical employment, this necessary ignorance of the non-sensible, turns out to be a positive advantage to the "interests of reason in its pure practical employment", i.e. to the demands of morality. For it means that there is no theoretical impediment to a faith, based on morality, that the noumenal ground provides, though in a way we cannot understand, both for human freedom and divine omnipotence.

Finally – though this is to anticipate the outcome of Kant's discussion of philosophical theology – it may be argued that the interests of theoretical reason, too, entitle or even require us to think of the non-sensible ground of appearances *as if* it were the repository of certain attributes analogically conceived in terms of freedom, purpose, and supreme intelligence. But this interest of theoretical reason, if it exists, is not manifested in the theses of the dynamical antinomies; for these are concerned solely with temporally regressive series of causal conditions.

This re-ordering of themes is, as I remarked, provisional. To one complication of considerable interest, which it omits, I turn now. Others will emerge later.

3. EMPIRICALLY UNCONDITIONED EXISTENCE: EMBARRASSMENT ABOUT SUBSTANCE

What, after all, *is* the topic of the fourth antinomy? The presentation in the argument and observations from B 480 to B 488, though clouded in places, seems tolerably clear. The empirical series we are concerned with is, it appears, a past series of temporally successive states of the world and/or of alterations involved in the transition from one state to another. To speak of its members as "empirically conditioned" or "contingent" is to refer to the fact that any member owes its existence to some antecedent member, the latter being a causally necessary condition of the former. The "demand of reason for the unconditioned", then, appears to be a demand that would be satisfied *either* by the existence of a "beginning in the series of alterations",[2] a "highest

---

[1] A 681/B 709.   [2] A 453/B 481.

member of the cosmical series",[1] which did not depend for its existence on any causally necessary antecedent condition *or* by the finding that the series as a whole was free of any such dependence. Both these alternatives should, one supposes, be ruled out as involving a false or empty presupposition; and any inclination that might be felt to divert the search away from the empirical series altogether towards a transcendental or intelligible ground should be checked as involving an illegitimate and irrelevant employment of the categories concerned.

When we turn, however, to the section on the solution of this antinomy,[2] we find that its topic seems to have changed. We are concerned, it seems, "with the unconditioned existence of substance itself"[3] or with "the derivation of the contingent existence of substance itself from necessary existence".[4] The series of alterations, or of successive states of things, is not really the series which represents our topic. It is another series altogether which we have in view, a series of "dependent existences",[3] of "*things in the world*" which "have only an empirically conditioned existence".[4] It was relevant to refer to the series of alterations just to remind us that "since everything in the sum-total of appearances is alterable, and therefore conditioned in its existence, there cannot be in the whole series of dependent existence any unconditioned member".[3]

Let us note, first, the invalid transition in the last quoted sentence, the transition from "*x* is alterable" to "*x* is (empirically) conditioned in its existence". Kant is indeed committed to the validity of the different step from "*x* is an alteration" to "*x* is empirically conditioned in its existence, i.e. owes its occurrence to some antecedent necessary condition of that occurrence". But there is no principle which he has adopted or argued for which sanctions the transition from "*x* *undergoes* alteration" to "*x* is dependent for its existence on some empirically necessary condition of that existence". Not only does he lack a principle which sanctions that transition; he is, prima facie, committed to a principle which forbids it. For he has argued in the Analytic that the existence of substance, or matter, as something *permanent* in the field of appearances, is a necessary condition of the possibility of experience in general. The empirically contingent is that which

[1] A 458/B 486.   [2] A 559/B 587 et seq.
[3] A 559/B 587.   [4] A 560/B 588.

would not have existed in the absence of some other empirically discoverable condition which is temporally antecedent to, or at least simultaneous with, it and which is causally necessary to its existence.[1] But permanent substances can neither go out of, nor come into, existence in the field of appearances: there can be no question of empirically establishing their causal dependence on anything. For once, it seems, reason's demand for the empirically unconditioned in the field of appearances is satisfiable; for substance, or matter, is empirically unconditioned in its existence, though not, of course, in its states or in the alterations which it undergoes.

Does Kant, or should he, accept this conclusion? The issue seems to cause him some embarrassment, an embarrassment which pursues him through the chapter on philosophical theology which follows. At one point in that chapter he seems clearly to allow that no argument could possibly establish the empirical contingency of matter.[2] At another he seems to attempt to provide just such an argument: all the real properties of matter are effects which must have causes, and are therefore derivative in character, are conditioned and "so allow of being removed – wherewith the whole existence of matter would be removed".[3] This bad argument is presumably intended to make a different point from the one made on the previous page, viz. that the existence of matter is not logically necessary[4] – a point which goes no way at all towards showing that its existence is dependent on any empirical condition.

It might be said that, at least as far as the interests of empirical inquiry are concerned, the question need cause Kant no embarrassment at all: that he can perfectly consistently admit that matter in general – the permanent in the field of appearances – is empirically unconditioned in its existence, while at the same time insisting that this empirically unconditioned existence does not constitute a terminal member of any of those series of conditioned and conditioning items into which it is the business of theoretical reason to conduct a never-ending empirical investigation. No assurance of the empirically unconditioned existence of matter in general attempts us from the task, for example, of endeavouring to explain its particular observable properties. It would, doubtless, be an exaggeration to insist, as Kant presumably

[1] A 460/B 488.   [2] A 635–6/B 663–4.
[3] A 618/B 646.   [4] A 617/B 645.

would, that every level of explanation automatically sets us a further task of explanation at a yet deeper level; yet it is certainly reasonable to deny that we could ever quite confidently claim to have reached the last limit of theory, to have finally uncovered the fundamental laws and elements of material nature. The empirically unconditioned existence of matter in general, then, leaves us precisely where we were in regard to any empirical inquiries we may undertake into the properties or constitution of matter.

I do not wish to suggest that it is just the sort of explanatory series involved in this type of investigation – more reminiscent, after all, of the second than of the third antinomy – which Kant has in mind in his section on the solution of the fourth. Though Kant constantly uses the word "series" in this section, it really remains unclear exactly what series he is talking about. Perhaps we come nearest to his sense if we suppose that his dominant thought is that of the empirical contingency of all individual or particular existences – be they things or happening or states – which we encounter in experience *and which fall under ordinary empirical concepts*. The field of experience of such particular existences is the field of contingency – of what would not have been, or would not have been as it is, but for some other condition, itself similarly contingent. Here, again, the reign of universal empirical contingency is in no way limited by the principle that the existence of matter in general is not empirically contingent.

Yet we should still ask what exactly is meant by the existence of "matter in general" or "substance" as something "permanent in the field of appearance". Kant's official view of the argument of the first Analogy is that it establishes, as a necessary condition of the possibility of experience, the existence in the field of appearances of a permanent framework of substance, or of substances, which retain their identity through all those alterations of their "determinations" which constitute or underlie the changing states of the world. These are presumably particular existences, though not such as fall under ordinary empirical concepts. We must remember, however, that whatever merits this doctrine may have, or may have had, as a presupposition of physical science, the actual course of argument in the Analogies proved inadequate to establish it. What, if anything, was there established was, rather, the necessity of an abiding framework of spatial things, of which no individual member or constituent need be conceived of as permanent. So, by a pleasing irony, we can arrive, by way of criticism of Kant's argument concerning substance in the Analytic, at sympathy with his position concerning substance in the Dialectic. For if it is only the "abiding framework" of spatial things which is permanent, and if, by the relevant part of the doctrine of transcendental idealism, however interpreted, it is false that the set or series of individuals which constitute that framework exists *as a whole*, then we may conclude that neither the set as a whole (for there is no such thing) nor any of its members has non-contingent existence. Thus we reconcile the doctrine that the existence of matter in general is non-contingent with the doctrine that nothing in the field of appearances has unconditioned existence. But we must remember that this feat is made possible only by the repudiation of the official view of substance set out in the Analogies.

4. THE TRANSITION FROM "COSMOLOGICAL" TO "TRANSCENDENT" IDEAS

If we set aside the interests of morality, as Kant conceived them, how, finally, are we to understand his claim that the solution to the third and fourth antinomies lies in a reference to the non-sensible as a possible source of satisfaction of the "demand of reason for the unconditioned"? We must at least think that he has expressed his thought imperfectly. But what is the thought thus imperfectly expressed? The thought cannot be that of a possible reconciliation of the claims made in thesis and antithesis, as they there stand. The thought is, rather, of a possible *diversion* of the demand expressed in the thesis, so that it no longer conflicts with the truth of the antithesis. Kant is careful to point out that he is not saying that the diverted demand can actually be met. He is indeed committed, on general critical grounds, to saying that the diverted demand involves at least an invitation to an illegitimate employment of the categories. No object of a possible experience can answer to the ideas of an uncaused cause or a non-contingent particular existence (on which others causally depend but which itself is not causally dependent on any other) even when they are construed as cosmological ideas, i.e. as relating to things in space and time. How much graver, then, is the risk of offence against critical principles when they are metamorphosed into transcendent ideas. We are left with the minimally reconciling point that the diverted demand, even though it cannot be met, even though it involves an empty use of concepts which have their only proper employment in the sphere of experience, yet, for these same reasons, involves no conflict with the truth of the antithesis, with the thoroughgoing application of the law of universal causality to appearances, with the thoroughgoing contingency of all particular existence in that sphere.

Even when the claim to have produced a solution is thus whittled down, an urgent and yet unanswered question remains; viz. how does this diversion of the demand of reason for the unconditioned come about? We might be tempted, and by Kant's own exposition, to turn for an answer to the doctrines of transcendental idealism. One part of that doctrine, as we have seen, can be invoked to provide the "true" critical solution to the third and fourth antinomies. Yet another part provides for the dependence of all appearances whatever, empirically caused alterations or empirically contingent particular existences, on a transcendental ground which, as being non-sensible, is certainly neither empirically contingent nor empirically caused. Here, we might say, is the source of the temptation to divert the dynamical demand for the unconditioned to the sphere of the non-sensible. But this explanation is hardly consistent with the general spirit of the Dialectic. The doctrine of transcendental idealism is not supposed, as it were, to put Ideas into reason's head. The ideas of reason are supposed to arise naturally, without assistance from the critical philosophy. The metamorphosis, then, of the dynamical ideas of the unconditioned into transcendent ideas must be supposed to be a metamorphosis which they somehow naturally undergo when the search for an object corresponding to them in their more respectable form as cosmological ideas encounters the insuperable obstacles set up by the arguments for the antitheses of the antinomies.

We need not, however, rest the whole burden of explanation on this theory of natural metamorphosis. In the next chapter, entitled The Ideal of Pure Reason, Kant introduces, with variations, yet another idea of reason which, in so far as it is an idea of an object, is certainly an idea of a non-sensible object and which has a kind of affinity with the dynamical ideas of uncaused cause and non-dependent existence, encouraging their metamorphosis into transcendent ideas and drawing strength from them in their new form. So it is with a complex equipment of ideas that theoretical reason undertakes the most ambitious of all its ventures beyond the limits of experience.

5. THE IDEAL OF PURE REASON

It is an essential characteristic of an idea of reason that it arises inevitably in the course of empirical inquiry. Such an idea, in fact, is supposed to be nothing but a projection of the aim of achieving final unity and completeness in some very general type of such inquiry. That aim it is proper to hold before ourselves, even though it is unattainable, as an incentive to continued investigation. Illusion is generated only when – as we inevitably do – we mistake the thought of this aim for the thought of an actually existing object of which we may hope to gain knowledge, but only, since it lies beyond the reach of experience, by purely rational methods.

Kant makes two attempts, substantially independent of each other, to show how there arises that idea of reason which, with the assistance of the transformed dynamical ideas, gives impetus to the attempt at extra-empirical knowledge of God. He argues, first, that the idea of a supremely real being is an idea we are inevitably led to entertain by the commonplace thought of every particular object of experience as having a thoroughly determinate character and, second, that the idea of a supremely wise Author of Nature is a presupposition of natural science.

The course of argument in which Kant presents the first suggestion is far from compelling. It goes somewhat as follows. Suppose we knew, of some particular existing object, that it belonged to the class of animals. This characterization leaves open a wide range of mutually exclusive possibilities as to what species of animal it belongs to; and we obtain fuller information about the particular object in question in so far as we are able to "limit" those possibilities by eliminating all except one. There still remain open, of course, all sorts of further possibilities regarding its history and characteristics; and increase of information concerning this individual goes with a further "limitation" of these possibilities. We must necessarily think of each actual individual as being essentially determinate in respect of all the possibilities which, in relation to any given state of information, might seem open concerning it. The world, then, is full of determinate individuals, each, as it were, a locus of limitation of all the possibilities which apply to an individual of its kind. The notion of the sum-total of all such possibilities is, therefore, necessarily given with the notion of the actual world of determinate individuals. Kant's suggestion is that we are inevitably led to form the idea of a wholly unlimited super-reality corresponding to the sum of all the possibilities which are limited in the case of actual individuals, a reality which we think of as the source or ground of those possibilities, as containing in itself "the whole store of material from which all possible predicates of things are taken".[1] This idea, Kant says, is not that of a mere aggregate or collection. It is that of a single, pre-eminently real individual, its individuality corresponding to the unity of the world of things in space and time, its pre-eminent reality being what makes it the source or ground of all the possibilities presupposed by the determinate characters of actual things. Kant does not, in this passage, refer to Leibniz; but the echoes are unmistakable. It is hard, however, to feel any sympathy with the suggestion that the idea of a supremely real being arises naturally in this way.

Though Kant represents his second suggestion as a natural extension of the first,[2] it seems in fact to be independent of it. The aims of natural science, Kant says, are served by thinking of the world as if it owed its existence to a "supreme intelligence" outside the world, which, "in originating the world, acts in accordance with wise purposes".[3] Properly employed, this conception is not a claim to knowledge, but an aid to the acquisition of knowledge. The proper aim of theoretical reason is to maximize the systematic unity of our knowledge of Nature. We must think of Nature as so constituted as to lend itself to the pursuit of this aim and yet our thought must not be such as to impose any limit on our incessant striving towards a greater degree of systematic unity in physical theory. Both requirements are satisfied at once by the thought of a supreme governing intelligence outside the world. Kant at times seems to write as if to aim at maximizing systematic unity in knowledge of Nature and to think of all natural connexions "*as if* they were the ordinances of a supreme reason of which our

[1] A 575/B 603.   [2] A 583/B 611, footnote.   [3] A 697/B 725.

reason is but a faint copy"[1] were one and the same thing. If so, if those working scientists who honestly disavow the thought of any such analogy are really in the same case as those who acknowledge entertaining the idea of God as, say, a "supreme mathematician", then one must conclude that Kant's claim of regulative utility for this idea of reason is really a minimal claim.

This claim, however weakly or strongly it is to be interpreted, is accompanied, of course, by reiterated denials of the possibility of *knowledge* of any object answering to the idea. It is a purely analogical conception of which the whole significance has already been described in setting out its regulative use.

> We misapprehend the meaning of this idea if we regard it as the assertion or even the assumption of a real being to which we may proceed to ascribe the ground of the systematic order of the world. On the contrary what this ground which eludes our concepts may be in its own inherent constitution is left entirely undetermined.[2]

For the purpose of acquiring knowledge of such an object there simply "are no concepts available; even the concepts of reality, substance, causality, nay, even that of necessity in existence, lose all meaning and are empty titles for concepts, themselves entirely without content, when we thus venture with them outside the field of the senses".[3]

6. THE ILLUSIONS OF PHILOSOPHICAL THEOLOGY

Now we are to see how the idea of a supreme being and the dynamical ideas in their transcendent form combine to generate the illusions of philosophical theology. Kant makes it very clear that he regards the idea of a non-contingent ground of contingent existence as providing the main motive power behind the exorbitant claim to knowledge of God's existence. He pictures us as almost irresistibly driven to seek an escape from the endless chain of causal dependence of one empirical existence on another by assuming that there exists something upon which all that contingently exists depends finally for its existence but which is itself free from causal dependence on anything else and therefore does not belong to the sensible world at all. To the truth of this

[1] A 678/B 706.   [2] A 681/B 709.   [3] A 678-9/B 706-7.

conclusion, taken in the sense of transcendental idealism, Kant is, of course, himself committed on other grounds. But to its correctness *as a conclusion* of such a process of thought as the above he is, and can consistently be, utterly opposed. Such a process of thought involves a double misapplication of the universal causal dependence of every particular existence or occurrence, first in using the principle "to advance beyond the sensible world", second in using it to infer a first or uncaused cause.[1]

To follow the further progress of the illusions of reason, Kant invites us to suppose nevertheless that this conclusion to a non-contingent ground of contingent existences is validly drawn. He points out that we still have no definite conception of the nature of this non-contingent existence upon which any contingent existence is to be thought of as directly or indirectly depending. Lacking any such conception, we are really as far as ever both from the final satisfaction of theoretical reason, which demands a complete explanation of everything, and from the achievement of the philosophical theologian's aim of proving the existence of God.

At this stage, Kant suggests, looking around for a definite conception of something which owes its existence to nothing else, we naturally fasten on reason's idea of an unlimited or perfect being which contains in itself the maximum of reality. Such a being, if it exists, cannot depend for its existence on anything other than itself. It must be a non-contingent existence. Since we have taken ourselves to have proved that a non-contingent being exists, we conclude that a being of unlimited reality exists.

The inference, however, is invalid. We cannot non-fallaciously convert the proposition that if a being of unlimited reality exists, it exists non-contingently to yield the proposition that if anything exists non-contingently, it is a being of unlimited reality. The notion of unconditioned or non-contingent existence carries with it no such definite conception. The cosmological proof, even if we allow its first, illegitimate step, still falls short of its aim.

This proof, the First Cause argument, however mistaken, embodies a natural illusion of human reason. It is otherwise, Kant suggests, with the ontological proof on which a sophisticated ingenuity falls back to repair the deficiencies of the cosmological argument. The contrast between contingent and non-contingent

[1] A 609–10/B 637–8.

existence, as it figures in the cosmological proof, is the contrast between the existence of something which depends for its existence on something else and the existence of something which does not depend for its existence on anything else. In the ontological proof this is replaced by a quite different contrast between the logical modalities of existential propositions; anything of which the existence could be denied without self-contradiction exists contingently, only that of which the existence cannot be denied without self-contradiction exists non-contingently, i.e. with absolute necessity. It is then suggested that the concept of the supremely real being includes the concept of existence, so that the proposition that such a being exists is analytically necessary. Kant's scornful refutation of this suggestion, though its form might be improved, is really conclusive. To form a concept, however rich, is one thing; to declare it instantiated is another. Logical or analytical necessity relates solely to the connexion of concepts with one another. No concept can logically guarantee its own instantiation in something not itself a concept. In the sense of "necessary" employed in the ontological argument, the notion of an absolutely necessary being is a mere confusion.

If proof from concepts, and proof from the fact of contingent existence in general, alike fail of their aim, there remains but one possibility of success in the enterprise of theoretical theology. That is the attempt to prove the existence of God from the character of our actual experience of things in the world. Kant shows a certain tenderness towards the Argument from Design, or physico-theological proof; but he is firm about its limitations. A propounder of the argument is exposed to a dilemma. Either he may represent it as depending on none but purely empirical principles of analogical argument, in which case he escapes, perhaps, the critical strictures to which the two previous types of argument are exposed, but necessarily falls short of his theological aim; or he may strive to make good this deficiency by having recourse once more to non-empirical or transcendental modes of argument, in which case he, too, is exposed to those criticisms. To follow the first alternative is to rest the argument solely on a supposed analogy between an order and mutual adaptation of part to part to be found in Nature and the admittedly purposive order and mutual adaptation of part to part to be found in the products of human art. Whether the case for the existence of any such

P

analogy can be truly made out is, Kant hints, itself highly questionable. But if it could, the utmost that we could conclude would be that a being of high intelligence and power disposes *given* materials, subject to *given* laws, in such a way as to produce the notable effects we observe. The argument, so understood, is not an argument for a divine creator at all, but for an "architect of the world"[1] doing his best with material for which he is not responsible, subject to laws he did not make. If we seek to remedy the inadequacy of this conclusion, we can do so only by abandoning what has been represented as a purely empirical mode of argument. We must fall back on the argument from the empirical contingency of all empirical existence; and when this fails once more, our only recourse is to the argument from mere concepts, the ontological proof.

The case against a theology based on the theoretical employment of reason is concluded. Neither by *a priori* nor by empirical arguments can the existence of a divine being be established. "The only theology of reason which is possible is that which is based upon moral laws or seeks guidance from them."[2] Nevertheless a thorough understanding of the necessary incompetence of theoretical reason in this sphere is not without a twofold negative utility to theology itself. If we are inhibited from asserting, we are also inhibited from denying, on theoretical grounds, what we may have other, perhaps moral, grounds for accepting; and we are restrained from importing empirical impurities into any conception of an ideal being in which a moral theology may give us grounds for belief.

7. FINAL OBSERVATIONS

Let us now look back over the whole course of discussion from the fourth antinomy to the end of the Dialectic, detaching ourselves from the detail of argument and trying to aim at a clear view of the essential features of Kant's position. Once again we shall disregard the interests of morality and the possibility of a moral theology. It is the interests of theoretical reason which concern us. With this restriction we can see the discussion as centring upon five main ideas. Our question is to be how far Kant's account of the inter-relations of these ideas is satisfactory

[1] A 627/B 655.   [2] A 636/B 664.

in itself and how successfully it harmonizes with the general demands of his system. The ideas in question are the following.

[1] *The ideal of completeness and systematic unity in scientific explanation.* The ideal is set before us as a governing but ever-receding aim of research and theory-construction, as something we may hope constantly to be approaching rather than finally to achieve. Kant's dual emphasis, on the aim of systematic unity on the one hand, on the perpetual openness to revision of actual theories on the other, gives his picture of the enterprise of natural science a profound authenticity. How far the picture is marred by the teleological note – sounded in this *Critique*, it must be added, less emphatically than in later writings – will perhaps be a matter of debate.

[2] *The concept of empirically unconditioned or non-contingent existence.* This is the concept of something of which the existence is not causally dependent on the existence of something else, i.e. the concept of something such that there is nothing extraneous to it which is temporally prior to or simultaneous with it and is a causally necessary condition of its existence. Kant uses the expression "necessary existence" interchangeably with "unconditioned or empirically non-contingent existence" and by doing so seems to invite confusion with the quite different notion of necessity in existence treated of in the Postulates of Empirical Thought or with the notion of formal or logical necessity in existence – (5) below – which he himself rejects as a malformed concept.

[3] *The conception of a transcendental, non-sensible ground of all sensible appearances.* To this conception Kant is committed by the doctrines of transcendental idealism.

[4] *The idea of unitary divine purposive intelligence and power.*

[5] *The idea of "absolutely necessary" existence,* i.e. of something, not itself a concept, of which the existence is logically guaranteed by the concept under which it falls.

Very summarily, Kant represents the demand for something answering to (2) as a facet or expression of (1) and represents

(1, 2) as entitling or requiring us to think analogically of the object of (3) in terms of (4) without, however, making any presumptuous and empty claims to knowledge of anything answering to (3, 4). (5) is eliminated as a perversion of reason into which we may be led in the empty hope of establishing just such a claim.

From the point of view of the requirements of the system this solution is not without elegance. No inferences forbidden on critical principles are sanctioned, an idea of reason plays its ordained part, transcendental idealism is accommodated, knowledge is restricted to its proper sphere, room is left for faith.

In other respects the solution is less satisfactory. We have already noted the weakness of the link between (1) and (4) taken by themselves. It is certainly not absurd to suggest that the link may exist, and be fruitful, in some minds; but it is false that the link exists in all minds to which major scientific advance is due. The situation cannot be saved by erecting the pursuit of systematic unity in science into a logically sufficient condition of thinking of the natural order as if it were ordained by a divine intelligence outside the world. This would be to sacrifice the doctrine under the pretence of defending it – a procedure adopted by some modern theologians, but not one which enhances the credit of their subject. If this step were taken, however, and held to be an elucidation of the doctrine, we should then lose nothing by eliminating any further reference to (4).

What of the absorption of (2) by (1)? Kant must be taken to think that (2) cannot be adequately dealt with in accordance with what I described as the conventional critical solution to the fourth antinomy. On the other hand he properly refuses to allow "reason's demand" for something corresponding to (2) to be the basis of a legitimate inference to something answering to (3), which, as being non-sensible, would certainly be empirically unconditioned. Still less does he regard this demand as the basis for a legitimate inference to something answering to (4). The absorption of (2) by (1) has at least the merit of resolving these tensions. From Kant's point of view it may have a greater merit. For perhaps it is just the conflation of the ideas of the non-dependently existent and of the finally explanatory which gives what plausibility it possesses to the doctrine that the pursuit of (1) is necessarily bound up with the thought of some extra-mundane intelligent source of the order of the world. This is, in the present context, the importance of the absorption of (2) by (1).

Suppose we resist this conflation. As I have already pointed out, Kant's official doctrine of substance provides internal reason for doing so. The notion of the finally explanatory is a regulative idea only, something it is richly worth while pursuing, though recognized as unattainable. But on Kant's official view the notion of empirically unconditioned existence seems to be nothing of the kind. The existence of permanent substances in the field of appearances has been argued in the Analytic to possess a necessity quite distinct from the spurious formal or logical necessity of existence dismissed in the refutation of the ontological argument, namely the kind of necessity which, in Kant's view, attaches to the causal principle; and what is in question in the case of substance is the necessary permanence of particular items (substances) which can neither come into, nor go out of, existence. Surely such items must possess a strong claim to the status of non-contingent existents. In so far as Kant considers the claims of these claimants (i.e. of permanent substances) to the status of empirically non-dependent existents, he gives bad reasons for rejecting them. One, which can scarcely be seriously intended, consists in pointing out that the non-existence of matter is thinkable without contradiction; but this would answer only a claim made in the name of that very notion of conceptually or logically guaranteed existence which he rightly condemns as a perversion of reason. The other is that if we accepted the existence of matter as non-contingent, the free operation of the regulative principle of never-ending pursuit of explanation would receive a check. This is not so, since these non-contingent existents must be supposed to supply not the answers to our questions but their topic, the very matter of our inquiry. If this point itself is made a reason for rejecting the claimants' claim to answer to (2), then the disputed conflation of the two ideas of the non-dependently existent and the finally explanatory is simply being re-affirmed.

The above is an internal criticism, framed in Kant's own terms, and perfectly compatible with the acceptance of transcendental idealism. It could be met either by simply separating the conflated ideas and acknowledging the claimants' claim or by modifying the doctrine of the necessary permanence of substance in the way

I have already indicated, i.e. by admitting that the only "permanent" of which the necessary existence is established in the Analogies is the abiding spatial framework of which none of the individual constituents need be supposed to enjoy any but a contingent existence. Neither decision need involve any sacrifice of transcendental idealism. But the first involves some sacrifice. The link between (1) and (4) would have to stand on its own, without any such strengthening as it owes to the absorption of (2) by (1). (As Kant realizes, the link between (1) and (4) cannot properly be maintained to owe anything to (3) alone, in so far as (3) simply forms part of the doctrine of transcendental idealism.)

Suppose, now, we step outside the framework of transcendental idealism altogether, abandoning (3). What, then, of the relations between (1) and (2)? If the abandonment of transcendental idealism carries with it a freedom from restraints on speaking of the world *as a whole*, then we can give a new turn to the distinction between (1) and (2). Every particular existent in the world may be empirically contingent, and yet the world as a whole cannot be, for there is nothing for it to be dependent upon. Once more the empirically non-contingent existence provides no term to investigation, but only its topic.

Now, oddly enough, with our five main ideas reduced to two – (1) and (2) – and their separateness maintained, we can still find in the philosophical tradition a conception which has some analogies with Kant's scheme, though it contains nothing of the extramundane. If some such attitude as (4) provides for is thought desirable or necessary, room can be found for it. Once transcendental idealism has been laid aside, there is no obstacle to accepting Nature or the world-whole itself – empirically unconditioned existence, all-embracing reality – as the object of such an attitude. How could inquiring human reason find a more appropriate object for its admiring and humbly emulative devotion than that which is at once the inexhaustible topic of its questions and the source of its endlessly provisional answers? For human reason itself is part of Nature. In a few paragraphs towards the end of the Dialectic[1] Kant seems even to show some sympathy with this conception, or with a part of it; though any fully developed view of this kind, such as Spinoza's, would certainly be alien to his thought and perhaps morally repulsive to

[1] A 699–701/B 727–9.

him. If only in respect of economy, such a conception may perhaps be judged superior to Kant's *"as if* theology"; but the saving (of the super-sensible) is not, of course, one that an upholder of transcendental idealism can make.

It must finally be said, setting aside transcendental idealism, that it is hard, from the point of view of the interests of reason, to see anything in the thought of an extra-mundane world-directing intelligence which contains the "therefore for every wherefore" but the pardonable indulgence of a kind of *fatigue of reason*, a temporary reversion to a primitive and comforting model. There is, after all, no good reason why (1) should not be recognized as an autonomous ideal and (2) as an idea which, if it has any employment at all in application to particular existents, has only such as the advance of empirical discovery may, at least provisionally, confer upon it.

PART FOUR

The Metaphysics of Transcendental Idealism

THE METAPHYSICS OF
TRANSCENDENTAL IDEALISM

Under this heading are to be grouped together a number of inter-connected doctrines all of which have already made their appearance at one point or another in the exposition, but which have not yet been systematically marshalled and displayed in the full extravagance of their mutual dependency. This must be done; partly because to Kant himself they seemed the indispensable framework of his thought, partly because my own reports of them so far have echoed without too much question a persistent note in Kant's exposition which, strangely enough, seems to have the effect of domesticating his doctrine, of disguising to some degree its phantasmagoric quality. Kant constantly speaks of "our" sensibility, of "our" understanding, says that this and that are "in us", that "we ourselves" are responsible for this or that; and it may seem surprising that the assured use of these personal pronouns and possessives – seeming to embrace Kant and his readers and the rest of humanity – should have any power to diminish the sense of the strangeness of doctrines which themselves show how very far from the ordinary this use of these words must be. Yet that Kant's use of these words does have something of this effect becomes clear, I think, when we expel them, as I shall try to do, from the statement of the doctrines.

After stating the doctrine, I shall try to answer what seem to me the main outstanding questions about it. But before we have the questions, we must have the statement.

I. THE DOCTRINES

These I shall set out in short numbered sections, with the minimum of qualification. In particular, I shall ignore those deviant interpretations which I have previously referred to as seeming momentarily attractive, or at least worth consideration, in connexion with this or that division of the *Critique*, but which cannot for long be held to represent Kant's views.

[1]   *The supersensible: things as they are in themselves.* There exists the sphere of supersensible reality, of things, neither spatial nor temporal, as they are in themselves.

Within this sphere there obtains a certain complex relation (or a class of cases of this relation) which we can speak of, on the model of a causal relation, in terms of "affecting" and "being affected by". Let us call it the A-relation. We may speak of the affecting (active) thing (or things) and the affected (passive) thing (or things) which enter into this relation, without prejudice to the possible partial or complete identity of these terms, without prejudice to the possibility of the relation's being partly or wholly self-reflexive.

There is indeed an at least partial identity between the terms in (or in any case of) the A-relation. For there belongs to the affected thing in any such case a feature called "sensibility" in respect of which that thing is affected. But there also belongs to the same thing a feature called "understanding" in respect of which that thing is active, affecting itself in respect of its sensibility.

There are other affecting elements or features which enter into (or into any case of) the A-relation. But whether these belong to the same thing as the (relevant) sensibility and understanding is unknown. If we call sensibility a form-yielding element (to mark its passivity) and understanding a form-producing element (to mark its activity), we may call the residual factors entering into the A-relation matter-producing elements. The reason for the "form-matter" antithesis in these descriptions will appear in the next section.

[2]   *Experience.* Experience is the outcome of this complex quasi-causal relation holding in the sphere of things in themselves; and the co-operation of all the elements so far mentioned is essential to its production. The matter-producing element and the form-producing element must both affect the form-yielding element in the generation of experience.

Experience consists of temporally ordered intuitions so conceptualized and connected that: (1) many such intuitions have the character of perceptions of a law-governed world of objects (bodies in space and time) enjoying their own states and relations irrespective of the occurrence of any particular states of awareness of them; and (2) there exists for all such intuitions at least the potentiality of their being ascribed by a self-conscious subject to himself as his own states of awareness.

The *temporal* character of experience in general and the possession by some intuitions of the character of *spatiality* which allows of their being ordered in such a way as to confer upon them the character of perceptions of objects *in space* are both alike due to the passive element in the affected thing (the former to "inner", the latter to "outer" sense). That is why the passive element, or sensibility, may be called a *form*-yielding element.

The conceptual connexions in virtue of which intuitions possess the character of perceptions of a *law-governed world of objects* are due, though in their most general character only, to the active or affecting element in the same thing. This is why the active element (understanding) in that thing may be called a *form*-producing element.

The residual characteristics of experience are due to the residual factors entering into the A-relation (the matter-producing elements).

[3] *The physical world nothing apart from perceptions.* What actually exists as the outcome of the quasi-causal A-relation is nothing but experience itself, the temporally ordered series of conceptualized and connected intuitions. Although, given the character of the form-yielding and form-producing elements of the affected (and at least partially self-affecting) term, it is necessary that these should include at least some having the character of perceptions of law-governed objects (bodies in space and time) enjoying their own states and relations irrespective of the occurrence of any particular states of awareness of them, yet bodies in space do not actually exist, enjoying their own states and relations independently of the occurrence of *any* states of awareness of them. Apart from perceptions, they are really nothing at all.

[4] *Empirical knowledge.* What emerges from the A-relation, viz. experience, may be said to include empirical knowledge of physical nature and empirical self-consciousness or knowledge of states of oneself. This reflects the fact that experience involves the

employment of concepts of the objective, hence a commitment to the distinction between experiences themselves and an experienced physical world.

Nothing that emerges from the A-relation can be said to be knowledge or consciousness of things as they are in themselves.

[5]   *Appearances of things as they are in themselves.* The contents of empirical self-consciousness, being the temporally ordered outcome of the A-relation, are not knowledge or awareness of anything as it is in itself. Yet they may be said to be *appearances* of that thing to which sensibility and understanding both belong. For the conceptualizing power or power of thought is temporally manifested in all empirical recognition or classification; and this power, though its manifestation in experience must be temporal, is really identical with, or has its source in, the form-producing feature (understanding) of that non-temporal thing in itself to which the form-yielding feature (sensibility) also belongs.

The physical or spatial world, though in a different sense, may also be called an appearance of things as they are in themselves. In a different sense, for it is not simply, like the temporally ordered series of experiences, a *dependent* existence, the outcome of the A-relation. It only *appears* to exist, is really nothing apart from perceptions. Nevertheless there is further point in speaking of the natural world as an appearance of things as they are in themselves, besides the point that is made by speaking of the contents of consciousness, as such, as appearances of that thing to which both sensibility and understanding belong. And this is the point that matter-producing as well as form-producing and form-yielding factors must enter into the A-relation which holds among things in themselves and of which the outcome is experience. The contents of experience in general may be said to be an appearance of the matter-producing factors under the conditions imposed by the form-yielding and form-producing factors.

[6]   *Creative awareness (intellectual intuition).* Nothing which emerges from *any* affecting relation can count as knowledge or awareness of the affecting thing as it is in itself. Therefore there can be no knowledge or awareness of things which exist *independently* of that knowledge or awareness and of which that knowledge or awareness is consequently an effect. More exactly,

there can be no knowledge of such things as they are in themselves, but only as they appear – only of their appearances.

Hence either there is no such thing as knowledge of the supersensibly real as it is in itself or the supersensibly real is created by that very awareness and does not exist independently of it. In so far as the supersensibly real is thought of as a possible object of such a non-sensible awareness (intellectual intuition), it is entitled "noumenon".

[7] *Non-empirical knowledge of appearances.* Empirical knowledge is the outcome of the action both of the matter-producing elements (in the supersensibly real) and of the form-producing element on the form-yielding element. But some knowledge of appearances (of natural objects in space and time) is also attainable which is independent of the action of the matter-producing elements and hence may be called non-empirical knowledge of appearances. For the form-yielding and form-producing elements together determine the character of experience in certain respects, whatever the contribution of the matter-producing elements may be. What these respects are may be ascertained (in time, but independently of the actual course of experience) in two ways: (1) the form-yielding elements can be activated, independently of the matter-producing elements (in "constructions in pure intuition"), to yield, e.g. geometrical knowledge of space and of bodies in space; (2) the implications of the understanding's requirement of the conceptualizability-in-general of the temporal data of experience can be brought out by critical reflection (as in the Analytic).

[8] *Non-empirical knowledge only of appearances.* Non-empirical knowledge, so arrived at, is no more than what it is described as, namely knowledge of certain features the presence of which in experience is independent of the actual content of experience, i.e. independent of the particular contributions made by the matter-producing elements. Such non-empirical knowledge, arrived at in experience though independently of its actual course, is therefore knowledge of appearances only. Apart from knowledge of such truths as are certified by logic alone, there is no other possible source of non-empirical knowledge, arrived at in experience.

2. SOME QUESTIONS

Many questions arise about these doctrines. What claims does Kant make on their behalf and how should those claims be evaluated? To what extent can the doctrines be shown to be mutually inconsistent, or otherwise incoherent, or to be inconsistent with more acceptable parts of his theory of knowledge? To what extent can they be explained as perversions of more intelligible principles? What is the exact significance, not merely in the context of transcendental idealism, but in that of Kant's theory of human experience as a whole, of the relatively familiar kind of phenomenalistic idealism outlined at paragraph 5 above, and how, if at all, is it reconcilable with Kant's assertion that his transcendental idealism is an empirical realism? Is there anything at all in these doctrines which should be preserved, or should it be our task to show that they can be completely detached from what is of value in Kant's analysis of the structure of experience and thereupon discarded without loss?

Some answers to these questions will emerge in the course of the following sections.

3. THE CLAIMS

In several connected but distinguishable ways the doctrines of transcendental idealism appear to Kant to make vital contributions to the rest of his system. I shall first consider briefly, under four heads, the claims which he makes on behalf of these doctrines; and then proceed, in the following sections, to examine in more detail the doctrines themselves.

[1]   *The demands of morality.* The briefest possible résumé of his views concerning human knowledge must include at least two points: that we can have some non-empirical knowledge (knowledge which does not rest on the actual course of experience) of objects of possible experience in space and time, and that we can have no other non-empirical knowledge, and hence no knowledge at all of anything else. The negative part of this thesis is important to him not only in a negative way, as discrediting, once for all, the pretensions of transcendent metaphysics. It has a different kind of importance as leaving room for certain morally based

convictions, not amounting to knowledge. If the natural world were all there was, Kant holds, human freedom would be an illusion and the ideal of moral justice would be a dream perpetually mocked by the facts. But the sphere denied to knowledge is thereby left open to a morally certified, though uncomprehending, faith that the reality of human freedom is somehow secured in that sphere and moral justice is really there attained.

Clearly the belief in the supersensible reality is essential to this part of Kant's doctrine; and the form of that belief seems to be conditioned by the doctrine in a way with which I shall be concerned in the next section. But there will be found few, I think, to regard the ideal of moral justice as an adequate basis for such a belief, or to view the problem of human freedom as demanding, or allowing of, solution with its help. Moreover, it would be entirely foreign to Kant's thinking to rest the case for the doctrines of transcendental idealism on such considerations. Although he claims it as a merit in those doctrines that they make room for faith in human freedom and moral justice, he does not, and he could not consistently, use this claim as a premise from which to argue to their truth.

[2] *The principle of significance; the mathematical antinomies.* In his critique of transcendent metaphysics, the elaboration, in its purely negative aspect, of the doctrine that we can have no non-empirical knowledge, and hence no knowledge at all, of anything which is not an object of possible sensible experience, Kant frequently invokes what I have called his principle of significance, the principle that we can make no significant use of concepts in propositions claiming to express knowledge unless we have empirical criteria for the application of those concepts; and he seems to regard this principle as a consequence of certain of the doctrines of transcendental idealism. We must inquire more closely from just which of these doctrines Kant thinks of the principle as deriving its force.

Let us consider, first, the chapter on the antinomies, in which a free and fruitful use of the principle of significance appears, at first glance, to be directly associated with doctrines of transcendental idealism. If things in space and time were things in themselves, Kant says, a certain disjunction framed in terms of concepts of limited or unlimited wholes would necessarily apply

Q

to them. Since they are not things in themselves, but only appearances, it follows that it is only if we could specify a possible experience which would justify the application of such a concept of a limited, or of an unlimited, whole that such notions would, in this connexion, have any significance. Since we can specify no such possible experience, the concepts are empty of meaning.

Here we must ask what is meant by the denial that things in space and time are things in themselves. It is not, of course, the otiose denial that they are supersensible things, things *not* in space and time. It is, rather, the denial that they have any existence apart from our temporally ordered representations or perceptions. If the use of the principle of significance is here made to rest on any aspect of transcendental idealism, it is made to rest on this phenomenalistic idealism regarding the physical world, a doctrine which can be, and has been, maintained, or entertained, by philosophers quite independently of the belief in a supersensible reality or of the thesis that the temporal series of experiences is the outcome of quasi-causal transactions in the sphere of the supersensible. As I have already remarked in discussing this chapter, the only plausible alternative interpretation which confronts us is one which grants autonomy to the principle of significance and leaves none but an ironical meaning to the phrase "things as they are in themselves".

Elsewhere, where Kant appears to relate the principle of significance to the doctrines of transcendental idealism, it is mainly in connexion with the categories, or pure concepts of the understanding, in general, that he does so. When he writes of them as merely rules for an understanding which is powerless to make use of them in knowledge unless material for their application is given to it, through sensibility, from elsewhere, it is indeed possible to read this warning in terms of the model of the affecting relation between supersensible terms and hence to connect the warning with the whole structure of the metaphysics of transcendental idealism. It is possible. But it is also quite unnecessary. Even if we choose to preserve, in this warning, the psychological idiom of an active understanding, the source of concepts, and a passive sensibility, yielding intuitions, we can perfectly well do so without thinking of "understanding" and "sensibility" as attributes of anything more unfamiliar than human beings, creatures who have a history (are in time) and a bulk (are in space); so that the principle of significance, even when expressed in the idiom of faculties, appears as something quite independent of the structure of transcendental idealism.

We may conclude that the principle of significance is either effectively independent of the doctrines of transcendental idealism or at most it depends, for Kant – in some cases of its application – only on that relatively familiar phenomenalistic idealism which transcendental idealism appears to include.

[3]   *Non-empirical knowledge of appearances.* What, now, of the non-empirical knowledge of objects of experience which Kant declares to be available to us and of which he claims to explain the nature and the possibility? It is here, surely, at least from the epistemological, if not from the ethical, point of view, that the heart of the system lies, and here that the Copernican Revolution is held to yield its large rewards. This non-empirical knowledge is said by Kant to be of two kinds. On the one hand, it embraces mathematical knowledge in general; on the other, it consists of knowledge of certain principles which constitute both the necessary foundation of natural science and the conditions of the possibility of experience in general. As regards the first, it is only in respect of geometry, the "mathematics of space", that Kant makes any serious effort to show that the fact of mathematical knowledge requires the theory of transcendental idealism for its explanation. We have yet to examine his theory of geometry; but it may be said in advance that, though we strain to the limit our sympathy with Kant's insight in this field, the reach of that straining falls infinitely short of his conclusions.

There remain those principles of which the proofs are variant forms of the thesis that they embody conditions of the possibility of experience. Let us waive the thought that those principles which Kant actually advances do not have the status which he claims for them, and assume, for the present purpose, that some at least of those proofs are valid. It must be noted, as Kant himself notes, that we do not, strictly speaking, have *knowledge* of the principles in question – even though we take them for granted in our empirical inquiries – until the critical inquiry undertaken in the Transcendental Analytic is successfully carried to its conclusion. These principles need proof[1] and no other kind of proof

---

[1] Cf. A 737/B 765.

is possible than this. Until it has been supplied, scepticism, such as Hume's, regarding such principles is legitimate, and even welcome, as providing a stimulus to the critical inquiry by which it is finally dispelled.

Non-empirical knowledge of the principles is obtained, then, only by following the course of argument pursued in the Analytic; and it is there obtained solely by reflection on the implications of what "understanding" requires of a possible experience in time. The requirement of "understanding", at its barest minimum, is that experience should be conceptualized, that it should issue in judgement or recognition; and it is this requirement, traced through the necessary self-reflexiveness of experience ("transcendental apperception") and its necessary objective reference, which leads ultimately to the proof of the principles. But the premise of this course of argument, since it does no more than define that of which the conditions of the possibility are to be investigated, in no way depends for its acceptability on the doctrines of transcendental idealism. If the premise does not, then neither does the proof; and if the proof does not, then neither does our non-empirical knowledge of the principles established by the proof.

In this too short demonstration, it might be objected, certain features of the course of argument actually followed in the Analogies are overlooked. For Kant there remarks that if things in space were things in themselves, if they existed independently of our representations (perceptions), we could have no knowledge of them at all. There would be no such thing as knowledge of objects. Yet our perceptions must yield knowledge of objects if experience is to be possible. Hence the objective reference of our perceptions must consist in nothing but their subjection to rules of connexion, such as are provided for by the principle of causality.[1]

On this we may make two comments. One is an echo of a comment made earlier during the discussion of the Transcendental Deduction.[2] If the conception of the objective is to obtain any employment in experience, experience must indeed contain a ground for it in that connectedness of perceptions which is inseparable from the employment of concepts of the objective. But

[1] Cf. A 190–1/B 235–6.
[2] Cf. above "Objectivity and Unity", Section 5.

in order to make this point, it is not necessary to invoke the doctrine that what we ordinarily conceive of as objects existing independently of our perceptions of them are really no such things. Of course, this latter view may be independently held on the ground (see 6 of Section 1 above) that if objects in space did really enjoy an existence independent of what we count as perceptions of them, then those perceptions could not constitute awareness or knowledge of those objects as they are in themselves; since those perceptions would be the outcome of an affecting relation and nothing which is the outcome of such a relation can be knowledge of the affecting thing as it is in itself. But then this view, thus independently advanced, plays no essential role in the explanation of the possibility of such non-empirical knowledge of objects of experience as is here in question.

The second comment is an obvious, and a recurrent, one. It is that the aspect of transcendental idealism here most prominent is once more that phenomenalistic idealism which it includes, according to which physical things are nothing apart from our perceptions.

It is worth adding that here, as elsewhere, we may be subject to that disconcerting "change of aspect" on the part of some of the doctrines of transcendental idealism. They may seem to change, before our eyes, into blandly ironical reminders that questions we may be tempted to ask about the nature of things in space and time, *as they are in themselves* – apart from anything we could find out about them empirically, through perception, and the construction and testing of perceptually based theories – are senseless questions, empty of content. It would, indeed, be hard to understand how Kant could hold to the doctrines but for this ambiguity of aspect. But, as I have repeatedly remarked, we delude ourselves if we persist in viewing them under their acceptable aspect alone.

Behind all the argument and analysis concerned with our supposed non-empirical knowledge of objects in space and of the natural world in general there lies, we must finally admit, a crude and incoherent model of the mind as it timelessly is in itself, and of things as they timelessly are in themselves, the former, affected by the latter and self-affecting, being responsible for certain features of experience of which the mathematician and the critical philosopher, by special exercises of self-analysis, conducted in

time, can obtain knowledge, without reference to the actual course
of sensible experience.

[4] *The fourth Paralogism (first edition)*. There is one more point to
be mentioned at which Kant explicitly invokes the doctrines of
transcendental idealism. In the first edition's version of the discussion of the fourth paralogism, Kant claims, by their help, to
show the way of escape from the predicament of problematic
idealism and to dissolve the problem alleged to be posed by the
action of body upon mind. How can we be confident of the existence of external objects in space when the only ground for this
belief must be an inference from inner perceptions? How can
the motions of bodies in space produce effects so utterly different
in kind as mental states? Both these questions, Kant says, pre-
suppose what is false, viz. that bodies exist independently of our
perceptions. Hence both problems disappear when the falsity of
the presupposition is recognized. That is *is* false is a part of the
thesis of transcendental idealism.

Once more we must recognize that, as in the case of the
problems posed by the mathematical antinomies, Kant's solution
rests on an appeal to a part only of the doctrines of transcendental
idealism, namely to the phenomenalistic idealism which it includes. Though the passages in question were omitted in the
second edition, they were omitted not because Kant thought
them mistaken, but because he thought them misunderstood.[1]

What is the outcome of this brief review of the claims made by
Kant on behalf of the doctrines of transcendental idealism? In
asking this question, I am not concerned with the validity of his
arguments or solutions but with their structures; and it must
surely strike us that, with certain reservations, the only element in
transcendental idealism which has any significant part to play in
those structures is the phenomenalistic idealism according to
which the physical world is nothing apart from perceptions. The
reservations concern, first, the crude model alluded to above,
which, however, does not feature prominently in any of the
detailed structures of argument in the book; second, more
specifically, the argument from geometry, which has yet to be
considered; and, third, the supposed demands of the moral con-

[1] The significance of these passages is discussed more fully in Section 6
below.

sciousness which, Kant thinks, can only, and incomprehensibly, be met in the sphere of the supersensible. Of course, we must not assume that Kant would for a moment have regarded the included phenomenalistic idealism as tenable apart from the rest of the metaphysics of transcendental idealism. It is time to seek further enlightenment by examining in greater detail some of the particular doctrines which belong to that metaphysics. I begin with one of the obscurest points of all, a point which is of the greatest importance to Kant if the demands of the moral consciousness are, however incomprehensibly, to be satisfied.

4. THE THING-IN-ITSELF AND APPEARANCES IN INNER SENSE

I have remarked already on Kant's confident use of the first personal pronouns and possessives in stating, or alluding to, the doctrines of transcendental idealism. It is, manifestly, of importance to him to ensure that there is a point of connexion, in the way of identity, between the supersensible world and the world of human beings, between things as they are in themselves on the one hand and Kant and his readers, the ordinary referents of personal pronouns and possessives, on the other. Without such a point of connexion, in the way of identity, the claim that freedom is at least possible (though to us incomprehensible) as a property of supersensible beings, would be without relevance to the moral nature or situation of human beings. Without such a point of connexion, in the way of identity, between that thing which is, in itself, the seat of space, time and the categories, and the human student of geometry or of the critical philosophy, it would be impossible to assemble, let alone to work, that crude model of imposed necessities available, through self-analysis or self-inspection, to our non-empirical knowledge. The mere use of the personal pronouns and possessives does nothing, however, to show where the point of connexion lies. We have to ask what *we* human beings, Kant's readers, can unambiguously understand by "us" and "we" and "our" when these expressions are so easily and loftily used to convey the doctrines of transcendental idealism.

The answer is indicated at various points in the book. There is an incautious statement of it in the Antinomies, at a point where the supposed interests of morality are uppermost in Kant's mind:

> Man, however, who knows all the rest of nature through the senses, knows himself also through pure apperception; and this, indeed, in acts and inner determinations which he cannot regard as impressions of the senses. He is thus to himself, on the one hand phenomenon, and on the other hand, in respect of certain faculties which cannot be ascribed to sensibility, a purely intelligible object. We entitle these faculties understanding and reason.[1]

The point of contact, in the way of identity, between a man as a natural being and himself as a supersensible being is to be found, then, in the man's consciousness of his own possession and exercise of the power of thought, of the faculties of understanding and reason. There immediately arise, on Kant's own principles, the objections, first, that anything which can be ascribed to a man as a case or instance of such self-consciousness must be something which occurs in time and, second, that it must be consciousness *of* himself as reasoning or recognizing or thinking something, as intellectually engaged at some point, or over some stretch, of time. Any such self-consciousness must, it seems, belong to the history of, and must be consciousness of some episode belonging to the history of, a being which *has* a history and hence is not a supersensible being, not "the subject in which the representation of time has its original ground".[2]

Kant faces these difficulties again and again in more cautious passages in the Aesthetic, in the Deduction, in the Paralogisms. He distinguishes between "original" self-consciousness and empirical self-consciousness. In the former, which is not really knowledge of myself at all, I am conscious of myself not as I appear to myself nor as I am in myself but only that I am. "This representation is a thought, not an intuition."[3] In the latter, which yields the only knowledge of myself available to me, I am conscious of myself only as I appear to myself, not as I am in myself.

Repeated like spells, these pronominal incantations are as inefficacious as spells. In the dictum regarding knowledge of oneself (empirical self-consciousness) the identity which has to be explained – the identity of the empirically self-conscious subject

---

[1] A 546–7/B 574–5.   [2] B 422.   [3] B 157.

and the real or supersensible subject – is simply assumed without being made a whit more intelligible. If the appearances of x to x occur in time, they cannot be assigned to the history of the transcendental, supersensible subject, for that being has no history. That is to say, they cannot justifiably be described as appearances *to* myself as I (supersensibly) am in myself, nor – since what they are appearances *to* they are also appearances *of* – as appearances *of* myself as I (supersensibly) am in myself. The reference to myself as I (supersensibly) am in myself drops out as superfluous and unjustified; and with it goes all ground for saying that, in empirical self-consciousness, I appear to myself as other than I really am. If, on the other hand, we are not to put a temporal construction on the verb *to appear*, how are we to understand it? Are we to say that it non-temporally appears to be the case, to the transcendental subject, that it enjoys a series of temporally ordered states? The limits of intelligibility are here traversed, on any standard. And if they were not, we should still be as far as ever from making good the identity which is in question. What has the non-history of the transcendental subject to do with us?

Kant fails to overcome the difficulties concerning identity because they cannot be overcome. There is no refuge but incoherence from the question how the connexion is to be made, in the way of identity, between the natural being, the man, with a mental history of thoughts, perceptions, and feelings and the supersensible being, with no history at all, "in which the representation of time has its original ground". It is, indeed, an old belief that reason is something essentially out of time and yet in us. Doubtless it has its ground in the fact that the propositions of logic and mathematics, certified by reason alone, appear to owe nothing to, and to fear nothing from, the accidents of time. And we grasp these timeless truths. But it is too late, now, in the day to think that who grasps timeless truths must himself be timeless.

5. THE THING-IN-ITSELF AND APPEARANCES IN OUTER SENSE

From one aspect of incoherence in the theory of transcendental idealism we turn to another. The aim is not solely to exhibit incoherence as such, but to observe, if we can, by what distortions and perversions it arises.

Knowledge through perception of things existing independently of perception, as they are in themselves, is impossible.
For the only perceptions which could yield us any knowledge at
all of such things must be the outcome of our being affected by
those things; and for this reason such knowledge can be knowledge only of those things as they appear – of the appearances of
those things – and not of those things as they really are or are in
themselves.

The above is a fundamental and unargued complex premise of
the *Critique*. To it is added the premise that all our "outer" perceptions are caused by things which exist independently of our
perceptions and which affect us to produce those perceptions.
From this conjunction of premises there follows the conclusion
that outer perceptions yield no knowledge of the things which
cause them as those things really are, but only of the appearances
of those things.

Let us consider, as far as outer perception is concerned, this
contrast between appearance and reality in connexion with the
thesis of the causal dependence of perceptions on independently
existing things which affect us to produce them.

First, as to the contrast between appearance and reality in
general. These concepts are not always set in opposition to each
other. For we may, and do, say, sometimes, that things are as they
appear. But in the present case they clearly are set in opposition
to each other. We perceive the things which, by affecting us,
cause our outer perceptions, not as they really are, but only as they
appear. What, then, we must ask, are the general conditions of the
significant application of the contrast, or opposition, between
appearance and reality, and are they satisfied in Kant's application
of the contrast to the case of outer perception?

Two concepts which seem inseparable from any significant
application of this contrast are the concept of identity of reference and what might be called the concept of the corrected
view. When it is said that a thing appears to be thus-and-so, but
really is not, it seems to be implied that there are two different
standpoints from which it would be natural to make different and
incompatible judgements about the *same* thing, and that the
judgement naturally made from one of these standpoints would
be, in some sense, a *correction* of the judgement naturally made
from the other. The standpoints, it seems, must have something

in common, so that there is some way, neutral as between them, of securing identity of reference to the thing which is judged. This is as general a statement as I can find of the conditions for the employment of the contrast; and it is easy, without a tedious multiplication of examples, to see how both conditions are normally satisfied. The corrected view may be that of an unusually well-placed or well-informed observer *vis-à-vis* that of the generality; it may be that of a normal observer *vis-à-vis* someone suffering from special defects or limitations; it may be that which would result from the removal of some distorting factor in the environment; and so on. In many of the commonplace cases that come readily to mind, the condition of securing identity of reference is satisfied in ways that turn on what might loosely be called the spatio-temporal location of the object judged.

It would be irrelevant to linger on commonplace applications of the contrast. But there is one familiar *philosophical* application of it which seems far from irrelevant; for it turns, precisely, on the fact that our sensible experience is the causal outcome of our being affected by the objects we say we perceive. It seems both intelligible and true to say that the appearances which things present to us are causally dependent upon the character both of the things themselves and of our physiological make-up, that they are the joint effect of both. Common sense and common observation can tell us something about the causal mechanisms involved, and science can tell us a great deal more. We are not logically compelled to draw from these facts the conclusion that things, as they really are, are different from things as they appear to us under normal conditions of perception. But equally we are not logically debarred from doing so, provided the general conditions I set out for the application of the contrast between appearance and reality are observed, provided, that is to say, that the possibility of identity of reference is secured and that some standard is adopted for the corrected view. It is important that the adoption of this standard should be made quite explicit; otherwise people will become confused and suffer irrelevant emotional reactions, the result of the fact that the use of habitual standards for the corrected view continues at the same time as the intermittent and perhaps provocative use of the new ones.

Though there is no logical compulsion to take such a step, the evident fact is that many philosophers (e.g. Locke and Russell) have felt a strong compulsion of some kind to take it. Objects *as they really are* are credited with the properties ascribed to them in the physical and physiological theories in terms of which the explanation of the causal mechanisms of perception is given; whereas those other features which we normally ascribe to them on the strength of our perceptions are eliminated from the description of objects as they really are. Their apparent possession of these properties is explained as simply the effect of a causal process which can be fully described without mentioning such properties, viz. the action of physical things upon our sensory and nervous equipment. Were that equipment different, the apparent properties of things would be different; but things would not differ in their real constitution.

In this operation the general conditions for a significant application of the contrast between appearance and reality are satisfied. The standpoint of the corrected view is successfully indicated without prejudice to securing identity of reference. Things, as they really are, are not removed from the spatio-temporal framework of reference. They are simply things as science speaks of them rather than as we perceive them. The corrected view is the view of science; it is a different view, but it is a view of the same things as our ordinary uncorrected view is a view of.

Only there is one thing to be added: namely that, in one sense, it is not a *view* at all. That is to say, one element present in ordinary applications of the contrast between appearance and reality to physical objects is sacrificed in this philosophical application of it. In ordinary applications, the standpoint of the corrected view is very often such that from that standpoint things actually (sensibly) *appear* as they are. In this philosophical application, on the other hand, the standpoint of the corrected view is not one from which things *appear* as they are; it is merely one from which things are spoken of, or thought of, in an abstract style in which they could not sensibly appear at all. Berkeley grew indignant over this; but we may merely note it without indignation. (It should be noted, also, that the antithesis I here make between the ordinary and this philosophical application of the contrast between appearance and reality is a fairly crude one which cannot be pressed in detail and all along the line.)

Now it is quite clear that Kant's intention, in making *his* application of the contrast between appearance and reality, was quite different from that of the scientifically minded philosophers who take the step I have just described. He himself stresses the difference, taking pains to put us on our guard against supposing that their view – which he regards, indeed, as far as it goes, with sympathy – is equivalent to that which he espouses in his doctrine of transcendental ideality.[1] Yet it is impossible to ignore the parallels between their view and his. Kant constantly affirms that the fundamental reason why we are aware of things only as they appear and not as they are in themselves is just that the mode of intuition or awareness which we have is one in which the object *affects* our faculties of awareness so that object and faculty thereby jointly produce the representations, the "sensations" or particular experiences of awareness, which we in fact have. He as constantly equates this fact about our mode of awareness or intuition with the fact which he expresses by saying that our mode of intuition is *sensible* intuition. It is just because these remarks, taken by themselves, are reminiscent of the doctrines of the scientifically minded philosophers that they seem in themselves unextraordinary. It is only when we join these remarks with the doctrine that space and time themselves and everything in them fall on the side of appearances, that the reminiscence seems suddenly irrelevant, that the comparison with the doctrine of the scientifically minded philosopher seems nothing but misleading; for the Locke-like doctrine, based upon the causal scientific account of the effects of objects upon our sensory and nervous equipment, turns on regarding the objects as they are in themselves (and indeed our receptive equipment as well) as spatio-temporal things.

Yet, if it seems that the comparison must be misleading, it seems also that it is inescapable. For when we read that, in speaking of space and time in general, all we are really to understand by this is a capacity or liability of ours to be affected in a certain way by things not in themselves in space and time, we have no clue to the meaning of this remark but the analogy with what a scientifically minded philosopher might mean when he says that in speaking of the colouredness of things, all we are really to understand by this is our own liability to be affected in a certain way by objects not in themselves coloured. All the terms used, the talk of objects affecting the receptive faculties of

[1] A 29–30/B 45, A 45–6/B 62–3.

sensibility, seem to belong to a doctrine – that of the scientifically minded philosopher – which is rejected as wholly inadequate in the application made of those terms. And this rejection seems to leave us, so far, with no clue at all as to how the general requirements of any significant application of the contrast between appearance and reality are to be satisfied. How, given this rejection, is it possible to specify the standpoint of the corrected view and to specify it in such a way that identity of reference to objects as they appear and as they really are is intelligibly secured?

This question, or the first part of it, is not left by Kant entirely unanswered. He does undertake, with reservations, to specify the standpoint of the corrected view. Indeed, such a specification is implicit for him in the *generality* of the reason why we can be aware, in perception, only of objects as they appear and not as they are in themselves. The reason for this is that our perceptions are the outcome of our being *affected* by the object; and this reason would hold good for any mode of perception which depended on the independent existence of the object. ("Our mode of intuition is dependent on the existence of the object and is *therefore* possible only if the subject's faculty of representation is affected by the object."[1]) Hence the corrected view would be the view available to a "non-sensible intuition", an intuition not passive or receptive, but active, spontaneous, original; a mode of awareness in which the faculty of awareness was not affected by the object because it created its own object. Of such a mode of awareness Kant frequently remarks that we are unable to comprehend its possibility:[2] an important reservation. The specification of the standpoint of the corrected view is given in terms which, it is admitted, we cannot really understand; and the task of making it intelligible how identity of reference is secured is, *a fortiori*, impossible of performance.

That Kant fails to satisfy the conditions for a significant application of the contrast between things as they really are and things as they appear – that, indeed, he violates his own principle of significance both in his application of this contrast and in the associated use of the concept of cause – is, perhaps, a point evident enough. We are left with the task of trying to explain, if

[1] B 72.

[2] He says, once, that "as far as we can judge", it could belong only to God, the primordial being (B 72).

we can, the striking parallel which we have noted and the even more striking failure of that parallel, the extraordinary transposition of the whole terminology of things affecting faculties which takes that terminology entirely outside the range of its intelligible employment, viz. the spatio-temporal range. Perhaps we cannot do more than recall Kant's early and old attachment to the notion of "the intelligible world" and record that he thought he had found the uniquely correct method of connecting it with, and yet sealing it off from, the world of phenomena, in such a way that the interests of morality, of empirical science, of mathematics, and of a reformed metaphysics were simultaneously satisfied. But perhaps a little more, a little more immediately germane to the topic, can be said.

The extraordinary generality of Kant's thinking is constantly straining against what he himself recognized as the limits of intelligibility. He remarks that we cannot comprehend the possibility of any form of intuition other than the sensible. He is not talking about "the senses", as we might enumeratively, or even generally, understand the term. He means that, as far as our comprehension of possibilities goes, the thought, at its most general, of becoming aware of objectively existing things includes the thought of those things as existing independently of our becoming aware of them and hence the thought of our awareness of them as dependent on a relation between those things and whatever powers of awareness we possess. They must *affect* us in respect of our powers of awareness. This general principle of sensible intuition is independent of any empirical discoveries we may make regarding causal mechanisms of sense-perception. Experience is simply what emerges from the affecting relation, and all the distinctions we draw within experience are drawn within the sphere of what emerges from this relation. Yet sensibility *in general*, the power of awareness *in general*, must have a "true correlate", the thing as it is in itself, regarding which, in experience no question is ever asked, or could be answered if it were.[1] But, again, because all the distinctions we draw, all the concepts we employ must, if they are to be significantly employed, find an empirical use, have empirical criteria for their application, the very concepts employed in the general principle of sensible intuition must find a surrogate application in experience. So we

[1] Cf. A 30/B 45.

must have our own usable concepts of the objective, treating certain appearances as if they were independently existing things, making our own picture – the scientific picture – of the causal dependence of subjective impressions on things and our faculties together.

I have tried to make evident here how the drive towards unlimited generality of principle encounters the limiting requirement of intelligibility in application and how perverse, in spite of its brilliance, is Kant's treatment of their impact. For of course the general principle that any perceptual awareness we may have of independently existing things is causally dependent on those things affecting whatever powers of awareness we possess, is acceptable; and the empirical content we give it is acceptable too. The latter is nothing but the specific form, increasingly filled in as knowledge advances, which, as things are, the general truth assumes. But Kant perversely and inconsistently pays the general principle the excessive honour of regarding it as stating a truth on its own, a truth such that no empirical content which might, in any world, be given to the principle could possibly be a specific instance or case of just that truth; so that the truth must have its own, non-empirical field of application, while we, for our part, must be content with representing it, in experience, with what is really only its shadow.

As to why Kant is tempted by such a perversion, we must refer once more to his old attachments, and to the interests, as he conceived them, of ethics, metaphysics, and science.

6. TRANSCENDENTAL IDEALISM AND EMPIRICAL REALISM

The topic of the last section and the topic of this interpenetrate each other. We are to discuss Kant's claim that his transcendental idealism is an "empirical realism".

Kant's analysis of experience drives steadily to the conclusion that the experience of a conceptualizing and potentially self-conscious being must include awareness of objects conceived of as existing and enjoying their own states and relations independently of the occurrence of any particular states of awareness of them. For us, these objects are spatial objects, material bodies in space. So far from its being necessary to make a problematic inference from our inner perceptions to the existence of spatial objects as their causes, the very consciousness of inner perceptions as ours is possible only through an immediate consciousness of the existence of objects in space, distinct from our perceptions of them.

Here, surely, is a dualistic realism of some kind. Kant qualifies the titles. It is only an "empirical" dualism, an "empirical" realism he is propounding. The qualification goes with the denial that bodies in space exist as things in themselves. We may be tempted, at times, to think that there is no more to the qualification and the denial than a re-affirmation of the principle of significance in relation to the material world, an insistence, with no further metaphysical implications, that we should be raising a question without meaning if we inquired into the nature of "the objects of our senses as they are in themselves, that is, out of all relation to the senses".[1] We have seen already how difficult it is to hold to any such interpretation. In the assertions of the Aesthetic, in the arguments of the Deduction and the Analogies, in the solutions of problems offered in the Dialectic, we find repeatedly the refrain that bodies in space, being appearances only, have no existence distinct from our representations or perceptions, that they are but a species of the latter, that, apart from our perceptions, they are nothing at all. It is true that in the arguments concerned with objectivity, in the Deduction and the Analogies, we were able to exhibit this doctrine as superfluous to the essential structure of reasoning, as an extra wheel, zealously but idly turning. But this was not how Kant saw it. And in the discussion of the mathematical antinomies it became quite clear that in Kant's understanding of his own solution this doctrine played an indispensable part, though a part which, it also became clear, brought starkly into question that collective "our" which Kant so freely employs.

Is the proclaimed dualism of bodies in space and states of consciousness really reconcilable with the phenomenalistic idealism which the transcendental variety seems to include? Before we attempt to answer this question, it is worth noting in slightly more detail how, in the first edition version of the discussion of the fourth paralogism, Kant uses this included phenomenalistic idealism to solve two problems. The passages in question, in

[1] A 380.

R

summarizing which I shall attempt no refinement of statement, contain strikingly bold affirmations of the included phenomenalistic idealism. If the doctrine were affirmed nowhere else, we might simply disregard these passages on the ground that Kant discarded them in the second edition, in favour of the Refutation of Idealism, with which they are by no means obviously compatible. But the doctrine is affirmed too often elsewhere for us to have any reason to disbelieve Kant's declaration that he discarded the passages because he thought them misinterpreted by his critics, not because he thought them false.

Scepticism concerning the existence of body constitutes the first of these two problems. The grounds of such scepticism are given in the following short argument. Only what is in ourselves can be perceived immediately, i.e. is an object of non-inferential awareness. Therefore the belief in the existence of bodies, external objects, has no more justification than it receives as the conclusion of a doubtful inference from the occurrence of perceptions within us which we take to be the effects of body as an outer cause.[1] Kant's solution is stated as follows. Bodies are simply a species of our representations or perceptions, viz. those which we distinguish as belonging to outer sense, i.e. as being spatially orderable. Therefore we may admit the existence of matter, not as inferred but as immediately perceived, without going outside the contents of consciousness.[2] Of course there are illusions, i.e. representations, apparently of outer sense, which are not connected with other representations according to appropriate empirical laws. But this does not mean that we are not immediately aware of bodies. For to say that we are immediately aware of bodies is simply to say that we have representations of outer sense which *are* connected according to appropriate empirical laws.[3]

The second and related problem concerns the action of body on mind. How, it is asked, can matter, which is essentially spatial and extended, produce by its action (which is nothing but movement) such utterly heterogeneous effects as states of consciousness, representations, thoughts, feelings and perceptions which are not themselves in space?[4] Kant answers that the question is entirely misconceived. For bodies are not distinct in kind from

[1] A 367–8.   [2] A 370–2.
[3] A 376.   [4] A 386–7, 390.

representations. They are nothing but representations of a certain kind. We have manufactured for ourselves a difficulty which does not exist. To say that bodies cause our representations of bodies can really, at best, be only a misleading way of saying that "the representations of our sensibility are so interconnected that those which are entitled outer intuitions can be represented according to empirical laws as objects outside us" – a truth which "is not in any way bound up with the supposed difficulty of explaining the origin of our representations from quite heterogeneous efficient causes outside us".[1] Other questions about the action of body on mind present no greater difficulty. For, once more, bodies are simply one kind of representations or contents of consciousness; and there is nothing strange about the law-like association of different kinds of representations, different kinds of contents of consciousness. "As long as we take inner and outer appearances together as mere representations in experience, we find nothing absurd and strange in the association of the two kinds of sense."[2]

How, then, is the doctrine that bodies are but a *species of representations* to be reconciled with the doctrine that we are immediately conscious of the existence of objects in space, *distinct from our perceptions*? There is but one way which can at all plausibly be represented as Kant's way of even seeming to effect this reconciliation. What is needed is a distinction between the import of the question, "Do bodies exist independently of perceptions?", as raised within the conceptual scheme to which we are committed in experience, and the import of that question, as raised within the context of the entire critical philosophy. One of the results of the critical philosophy – of that part of it which is concerned with the analysis of experience – is to show that we *must* connect our intuitions with the aid of concepts of objective things, existing independently of our perceptions, which we take those intuitions to be perceptions of. Nothing would count as a possible experience, as a kind of experience which we could make intelligible to ourselves, for which this necessity did not hold. So long as our questions and replies are raised and given within the framework of the scheme of ideas to which we are necessarily committed in experience, the answer to our question must be affirmative – and a trivial enough affirmative at that.

But the critical philosopher, Kant must hold, achieves a certain

[1] A 387.   [2] A 386.

detachment from the scheme to which, as a being concerned with empirical questions and answers, he is wholeheartedly committed. The detached point of view from which the necessities of that scheme can be appreciated is also a point of view from which our question assumes a quite different import and demands, not an affirmative, but a negative, answer. From this point of view, we have a quite different standard for what really exists from the standard to which we are empirically committed. Judged by this critical standard there really exist only, on the one hand, the transcendental and to us unknown causes of our perceptions or representations and, on the other, the effects of those causes, the representations themselves. The former we do not, the latter we do, "attain in themselves". There is no place in this scheme for bodies as real existents, though there is a place, and that a necessary one, for the operation with that conceptual scheme which includes the *conception* of our awareness of bodies distinct from our experiences of them.

As it is with the question "Do bodies exist independently of perceptions?", so it must be with the question, "Do bodies cause our perceptions of them?" From the point of view of the scheme to which we are empirically committed, the answer again must be "Yes". We investigate empirically the physical and physiological mechanisms of this causation. But from the point of view of the critical scheme, the answer must be that bodies are nothing apart from perceptions and that the real cause of the latter is the unknown transcendental object.

It is unnecessary for me to repeat the criticisms of this doctrine which have already been set out in previous sections. The fact that within the framework of the theory of transcendental idealism a form of reconciliation is possible between the thesis that we are aware of bodies in space as objects distinct from our perceptions and the thesis that bodies in space have no existence apart from our perceptions has no power to restore to the theory of transcendental idealism the coherence and intelligibility it has been shown to lack. But one or two comments of a different order may be made.

First, it might seem that Kant had, after all, a more substantial reason than the risk of misinterpretation for omitting from the second edition those problem-solving exercises which he undertook in the earlier discussion of the fourth paralogism.

Was it not disingenuous to represent the supposed heterogeneity of outer causes and inner effects as constituting even the appearance of a problem when his own thesis commits him to no smaller a degree of heterogeneity of causes and effects – transcendental causes, outside space and time, and temporal effects, representations in time? Again, was it not disingenuous to represent his solution to the problem posed by sceptical idealism as a real solution to a real problem when he holds us necessarily committed to a conceptual scheme of which one of the governing principles is that we are *immediately* aware of bodies in space distinct from our perceptions of them? Or, if he is not, in this second respect, disingenuous, must he not hold the awkward view that, if experience is to be possible, we must be empirically committed to a conceptual scheme which is itself incoherent?

This last consequence Kant might be ready to accept; and he might point to his treatment of the mathematical antinomies in support of his readiness. But I think, in the present connexion at least, he is in a position to reject this alternative and to rebut both charges of disingenuousness. For he is committed, as we have seen, to the overriding principle that no perceptions dependent, as ours are, on independently existing objects as their real causes can possibly yield knowledge of those objects as they really are. He could hold that the arguments of the sceptical idealist and of those who cannot stomach "physical influence" represent a confused apprehension of this truth: an apprehension of it in so far as they both involve rejecting the thought that we could ever *know* the real causes of our perceptions to be independently existing objects in space and time; a confused apprehension in so far as they envisage no other status for bodies in space and time except that of really existing independently of our perceptions. The arguments, on this view, do not merely pose pseudo-problems. They embody, rather, a confounding of the two conceptual schemes, the critical and the empirical. This natural confusion itself constitutes a real problem, which is solved by separating the schemes and acknowledging that each has its own validity.

Next, and more importantly, we must ask how the situation stands regarding "empirical realism" when we discard the doctrines of transcendental idealism. Of course the situation is transformed. The analytical argument to conclusions about the necessary structure of experience must be evaluated on its own merits. If we accept the conclusion that experience necessarily involves awareness of objects conceived of as existing in time independently of any particular states of awareness of them, then we must accept it without reservation. We have no extraneous standard or scheme in terms of which we can give an esoteric sense to the question whether such objects *really* exist, as we must empirically conceive of them as existing, independently of our perceptions. The question can be understood only in the sense of the scheme itself to which we are committed and in that sense it admits of but one commonplace answer. The philosophical achievement consists in showing that the answer is not merely a commonplace, though it is that. It consists in showing the place of this commonplace in any intelligible conception of experience we can form, in showing that it holds such a place even if we take the conception of experience to the last point of abstraction it can reach before disintegrating.

It might be pointed out that if we discard the doctrines of transcendental idealism, we not only discard the incoherences associated with the conception of the supersensible reality – which has to be at once linked with and sealed off from the natural world – but also deprive ourselves of the problem-solving and analytical argument-aiding powers ascribed by Kant to the enclosed phenomenalistic idealism. But to lose these is to lose nothing. We have already noted the ultimate disutility of the doctrine in connexion with the problems of the Antinomies; we have repeatedly seen it to be superfluous to the analytical argument; and that argument itself deprives the pseudo-problems of the fourth paralogism of any force unborrowed from principles belonging to the theory of transcendental idealism.

Finally, I must mention the possibility of its being disputed that what I have called Kant's way of reconciling the denial with the affirmation of the distinct existence of bodies is really his way of effecting this reconciliation. It might be urged that when Kant declares bodies to be in us as a species of representations, he does not mean by this to deny that, even in terms of the scheme of transcendental idealism, they really enjoy an existence in space distinct from the existence of our perceptions of them. He merely means to affirm that their existence in space is the outcome of the transcendental subject's being affected by things in themselves.

It seems almost too obvious for argument that this is not his view. None of the problem-solving powers he ascribes to the thesis that bodies are not things in themselves would even seem to belong to that thesis on this interpretation. Moreover, the thesis would generate problems of its own. For example, we should have to answer the question whether our perceptions of bodies in space were the direct outcome of our being affected by things in themselves or were the outcome of our being affected, in our empirical constitution, by bodies in space. The former answer would require a thesis of pre-established harmony such as Kant explicitly rejects; the latter would require us to have knowledge of the real causes of our perceptions, a thesis which he also explicitly rejects.

7. FORMAL CONCEPTS AND SIGNIFICANCE: EXPERIENCE AND REALITY

Among the doctrines which together form the metaphysics of transcendental idealism we have not yet found, nor shall we find, any which there is a case for preserving as well as explaining. But there are one or two truths which can perhaps be seen in faint analogy with some of those doctrines, can be heard, perhaps, as their muted echoes. They can best be so seen or heard in relation to the themes of the chapter entitled Phenomena and Noumena.

The structure of the chapter is fairly simple. It begins with an emphatic statement of the principle of significance. The employment of concepts in judgements involves essentially the thought of their possible application to objects – ultimately to objects not themselves concepts. The general conditions of the applicability of concepts to objects essentially involve the general conditions of our becoming aware of objects, i.e. involve our modes of intuition. Our mode of intuition is sensible and spatio-temporal. We are aware of objects, in experience, under the conditions of space and time. We cannot detach our concepts from these conditions of their application to objects and hope at the same time to preserve any significant employment for them in recording, or advancing, knowledge of objects. It is only in application to objects of possible experience that concepts have any such use. We must remember above all that this truth holds for the categories, those pure concepts of the understanding which secure to the contents of experience that unity without which the objective reference of experience would be impossible.[1]

For in respect of the categories, Kant goes on, "we are subject to an illusion which it is difficult to escape".[2] The categories in a sense do "extend further than sensible intuition, since they think objects in general without regard to the special mode in which they may be given".[3] Now by the whole structure of the metaphysics of transcendental idealism we are committed to the conception of objects in general, objects as they are in themselves, independently of our modes of sensible intuition. Hence we are subject to the temptation, to the illusion, of supposing that the categories supply us with the conceptual resources for arriving, by pure thought, at valid conclusions about objects as they are in themselves.

The corrective to this illusion is to remind ourselves that we cannot divorce the significant use of concepts from the conditions of awareness of the objects to which they are applied. But no kind of awareness involving sensibility, i.e. no kind of awareness which depended on the faculties being affected by an independently existing object, could possibly be awareness of things as they are in themselves. We can indeed say to ourselves that there might be a kind of awareness in which sensibility played no part, in which understanding gave itself its own object; and we can introduce the name of "noumena" for the objects of such a purely intellectual intuition. But we cannot in the least understand what we are talking about when we say this. We can form no conception of such a kind intuition, or of an understanding capable of such a kind of intuition. The pure concepts of *our* understanding, the categories, remain useless and inoperative unless material for their application is given them from elsewhere, through sensibility, through our being affected by things as they are in themselves, of which, since we are aware of them only in being affected by them, we continue to know nothing as they are in themselves.

It would be unprofitable to pursue the struggle with Kant's thinking deep into the mysterious terrain here hinted at. We may remember the anxiety which Kant displays, when the interests of morality and religion are uppermost in his mind, to qualify the doctrine that we can have no *knowledge* of supersensible objects through the categories with the contention that we may never-

[1] B 294–305.   [2] B 305.   [3] B 309.

theless legitimately *think* of such objects in terms of the categories; and we may wonder how this contention is to be reconciled with the doctrine of the present chapter, and of the Note which follows it, that the objects of a non-sensible intuition would not be known through categories at all,[1] that the categories would not be "appropriate to",[2] or "valid in respect of",[3] such objects. Kant claims that though we cannot comprehend the possibility of non-sensible intuition, the idea of such an intuition, and of its non-sensible, noumenal objects, is free from contradiction.[4] About this contention we may wonder, too, when we read his critique of Leibniz, an exercise which he conducts, with some brilliance and, as usual, some forcing of points, in that concluding Note. Leibniz was supremely one who committed what Kant regarded as the original sin of dogmatic metaphysics. He undertook to affirm truths about objects in abstraction from the spatio-temporal conditions of sensible intuition which in fact alone give sense to our talk of objects. This attempt to speak of objects of a purely intelligible and wholly non-sensible character had, as Kant points out, the natural enough consequence that much of what Leibniz says is coherent only on the assumption that he is not really talking about objects, as opposed to concepts, but about concepts themselves. Kant once more affirms that for any knowledge of purely intelligible objects – as opposed to concepts – we should require that of which we cannot comprehend the possibility, viz. a non-sensible, purely intellectual intuition. We may wonder whether it is not, instead, something of which we can comprehend the impossibility. Can the words mean anything but that the objects of such an intuition would both have to have, and have not to have, the abstract character which belongs to general concepts or to such abstract individuals as numbers?

It is better to turn from these fruitless calculations to try to catch those faint echoes I spoke of. The categories are said to "extend further than sensible intuition, since they think objects in general without regard to the special mode in which they may be given".[5] We are reminded of many features of the critical apparatus: of the so seriously held duality of faculties; of the metaphysical deduction of the pure categories from the forms of

[1] A 256/B311–12.   [2] A 287/B 343.
[3] A 286/B 342.   [4] A 254/B 310.
[5] B 309.

logic; of the further limiting step taken in the Schematism, where the categories acquire empirical use and life through a temporal interpretation. We have seen how much there is in this to invite doubt. But there is also something to be preserved. There are a number of concepts which we might call "formal concepts" and which share certain features at least analogous to some of the features ascribed by Kant to pure categories. They include such concepts as the following: identity, existence, class and class-membership, property, relation, individual, unity, totality.

Perfectly general deductive connexions belonging to formal logic can be asserted as holding in the region of formal concepts: e.g. from any assertion to the effect that a certain individual has a certain property there follows an assertion of the existence of something having that property. Such concepts are also *applied* or *exemplified* in empirical propositions which do not belong to logic. The concept of identity is *applied* in any straightforward statement of identity; the concepts of individual and property are *exemplified* in any statement to the effect that a certain specified individual has a certain property. Of course the application or exemplification of the formal concepts in empirical propositions turns on the existence of *empirical* criteria for the application of other, non-formal, empirical concepts, of, e.g., properties or kinds of individual. But we cannot specify in advance what empirical criteria are permissible in the application or exemplification of the formal concepts in non-logical statements. We cannot impose any limitations in advance on the possible formal analogies which may permit the use or exemplification of the formal concepts in ways antecedently undreamt of by us. There must be conditions, directly or indirectly related to what Kant calls intuition (i.e. awareness of objects not themselves concepts) for any employment or exemplification of the formal concepts in non-logical statements. But those conditions are not limited in advance by the scope of our actual knowledge and experience.

Kant remarks of the categories that their meaning is not restricted by sensible intuition, since "they think objects in general without regard to the special mode in which they may be given". Of the formal concepts we may make the parallel remark that their meaning is not restricted by any empirical criteria we in fact employ in their application or exemplification. Kant accompanies his remark with the warning that we must not therefore suppose that we can significantly employ the categories in assertions about objects without regard to the conditions of sensible awareness of objects. We may issue a parallel warning: formal concepts cannot be significantly employed in making non-logical assertions without the employment of empirical criteria for the application of other concepts, giving body to the particular applications or exemplifications of the formal concepts involved in such assertions. Kant's warning derives its urgency from his belief in things as they are in themselves which, if objects of awareness (as they are in themselves) at all, would be objects of a special kind of intellectual intuition. The bounds of sensibility are not co-extensive with the real. The point of the warning is that we must not think we can cross those bounds and gain knowledge of non-sensible objects with the help of the categories.

At this point the echo grows fainter; but it does not entirely disappear. The bounds of the real, we may say, are indeed not co-extensive with the types of sensible experience we in fact enjoy. We must not suppose that the nature of reality is exhausted by the kinds of knowledge which we have of it. To suppose this would be a kind of restrictive dogmatism as unjustified in its way as the inflated dogmatism which pretends to a knowledge transcending experience. The latter makes an unjustifiable *a priori* claim to expand knowledge beyond experience. The former would make an equally unjustifiable *a priori* claim to restrict reality within the bounds of the kind of experience we in fact have.

Of course, in resisting this kind of restrictive dogmatism, in allowing the concept of objective reality to extend beyond the types of sensible experience which we enjoy, we make no such divorce as Kant made between objective reality as it is in itself, things as they are in themselves, and objective reality as we know it, things as we experience them. In refusing to commit ourselves to the dogmatic position that, though we do not know everything, we know at least every kind of thing there is to know about every kind of thing there really is, we do not have to deny that we know things of some kinds about some kinds of things there really are. What we do, for example, is modestly to recognize that just as it would be folly for the blind to deny that things of which they have experience have a kind of property of which they have no experience, so it would be folly for the sighted to deny the possibility that with a richer equipment of sense organs they too might discover in objects properties of which, as things are, they can form no conception. Again, it is a familiar truth that, in the advance of science, the existence of both new types of property and new types of individual entity is acknowledged. (We some-times, though not always, express such results in terms of dis-coveries about the composition and make-up of more common-place individuals.) It would again evidently be folly to suggest that there can be no further discoveries of this kind just because we can at present form no conception of them. Nor is it only in these two rather specific directions, suggested by ordinary ex-perience and theory-making, that this rejection of restrictive dogmatism is supposed to leave the way open. We have, and can have, no reason to deny *a priori* the possibility of different kinds of revelation of objective reality for which we have no easy analogy like that of a new sense-organ or a new scientific theory. (And of course no reason to affirm it either.) The only thing we can insist on is that any further aspect of reality must stand in some sort of systematic connexion with those aspects we know already.

To admit *this* concept of objective reality as thus limiting the claims of actual sensible experience (and of actual theory based upon it) to be "co-extensive with the real" is, as I have remarked, very different from adopting the Kantian conception of things as they are in themselves. The disanalogy extends to the conception of the role of formal concepts and categories respectively in relation to these different limiting ideas of "the real". Kant appears, as we have seen, to deny that categories would be applicable to the noumenal, to the real as object of a non-sensible intuition. It is quite otherwise with the relation of formal con-cepts to the modestly conceived substitute for the noumenal. To admit this modest conception is simply to reject the dogmatic denial of the possibility of knowledge of new types of *individual*, *property*, and *relation*, new applications of the concept of *identity*. It is precisely to see such formal concepts as possibly admitting of new types of employment or exemplification in non-logical propositions.

There remains a point of analogy. Kant's main concern in this chapter is to insist that the necessary admission of a reality transcending sensible experience altogether does not disclose a field for transcendent metaphysics, though the open character of the pure concepts may delude us into the belief that it does. Similarly the admission that the conception of reality is not bounded by the types of sensible experience we actually enjoy discloses no field beyond that of empirically based theory (or purely formal science) for the fruitful employment of formal concepts. The modest concept we substitute for that of the noumenal really has the negative character which Kant claims for the concept of the noumenal. It simply means: those aspects of reality, if any, of which we have not, as things are, any conception.

In the place of Kant's reflections on the nature of "pure understanding", we may find it more realistic, and certainly less perilous, to see the formal concepts as emerging, in all their unlimited generality, as a result of progressive analogy and extension from their basic paradigms in experience. Nevertheless, in the recognition of the unlimited generality of the formal concepts; in the complementary recognition that the concept of reality must be allowed an extension beyond the limits of our actual sensible experience; in the warnings against supposing that both recognitions together open a field for metaphysics; in these we may, if we choose, see some uncontentious and unpretentious parallels to some theses belonging to the metaphysics of transcendental idealism.

It must be added, finally, that Kant's formulation of the principle which underlies the warning, his description of the conditions of making significant assertions about objects, or aspects of reality, is crude and narrow. That description is always framed in terms of the necessity of a mode of *intuition* of the object or aspect, a way in which it is *given* to us. The phrases suggest difficulties about, e.g., "unobservable" entities of science. A partial answer, on Kantian lines, might be that in so far as such entities are conceived as spatio-temporal, they thereby fall within the scope of what Kant refers to as our modes of sensible intuition. This is an issue which Kant scarcely refers to in the *Critique*, and in so far as he does, his words suggest a different answer. On the subject of the "magnetic matter" which we know to "pervade all bodies" he sounds a little like Locke deploring our lack of microscopical eyes: "were our senses more refined, we should come also in experience upon the immediate empirical intuition of it".[1]

---

[1] A 226/B 273.

That is to say, the items in question are taken to be in principle directly observable. Neither type of answer seems particularly satisfactory. The concept of spatial location, for example, seems to have little relation to the entities of depth psychology; and as far as direct observation is concerned, the questions of what is to count as such or whether anything is, seem often somewhat arbitrarily decidable or of little moment.

A fuller answer, then, than any which Kant gives is called for to the question how we should describe that condition of the significant employment of concepts which is loosely expressed by saying that they must be so employed as to have application in a possible experience. I shall not attempt to answer the question. But the main conditions which a fuller description would have to provide for can be indicated. We should begin by noting that there is little difficulty in explaining what we mean by observational criteria for the application of many kinds of established, unproblematic concepts. Then we may remark that in order for a newly introduced or problematic concept (or concept-extension) to have significant employment, it is necessary that it should be possible to state or indicate types of observable situation in which it has application – which is not to say that its *objects* must be observable. It is further necessary that its application in such a situation should have consequences or implications which do not merely duplicate those of other, established, non-problematic concepts. The temptation here is to say "testable consequences or implications"; and that addition, though calling for further elucidation, is no doubt on the right lines in so far as we are concerned with the concepts we call scientific. But perhaps we can also be said to extend our knowledge of the world by learning to see it afresh, to extend or modify our classifications and descriptions, in ways and directions with which natural science has little to do. And then the consequences will relate more to the nature of our experience itself and to the connexions we make in it than to the possibility of confirmatory or disconfirmatory tests which we might undertake.

8. CONCLUSION: THE STRUCTURE OF EXPERIENCE

Interwoven with, and dependent upon, the other doctrines of transcendental idealism is that strand of theory which seemed to

Kant to constitute a revolution in philosophical thinking analogous to the Copernican revolution in astronomy. On behalf of the doctrine that appearances conform to our modes of representation, to the forms of sensibility and understanding, he claimed that it alone explained both the possibility of geometry and of pure mathematics in general and the feasibility of the entire programme, carried out in the Analytic, of establishing the necessary structure of experience.

The latter part of this claim has already been briefly discussed and dismissed. But it may be felt that its dismissal leaves us at least with an unanswered question. How is it, after all, possible to establish that experience must exhibit such-and-such general features? We may reply that this is just an abbreviated way of saying that we can form no coherent or intelligible conception of a type of experience which does not exhibit those features. But the more careful formulation merely leads to further questions. If we cannot, what is the explanation of the fact that we cannot? And by what kind of argument is it shown that any particular feature has this character of being an indispensable element in any coherent conception of experience we can form? What are the tests for this kind of indispensability?

Now if someone should ask *in general* why there should be any limits at all to what could be conceived of as constituting a possible experience, we should think his question absurd. For this would be like asking how it should be possible to say "Experience might be like this . . ." and then go on to put words together in incoherent ways. So any question which asks why there are limits to any coherent conception of experience we can form must be asking why there is *this* or *that* limit. And now we can see that such a question cannot be asking for anything wholly different in kind from what is asked for in the questions about arguments and tests. For it is quite clear that there is no sense in the idea that we might look to facts altogether outside our experience in order to find an explanation of there being this or that limit. (This is why – apart from the fact that his arguments do not rest on it – we can simply dismiss Kant's "model".)

There remains the question concerning the kind of argument, or test, by which certain features are shown to be indispensable in any coherent conception of experience we can form. Here we may remark to begin with that we are concerned with the temporally extended experience of conceptualizing or thinking beings. This conception is filled out, given content, by reference to general features of our actual experience which are exhibited in relations of progressive or mutual dependence. Thus we proceed from the necessity of conceptualization to the self-reflexiveness of experience – to objectivity and the potentiality of self-consciousness – to the distinction between objective time-relations and time-relations between subjective experiences – to the idea of a persisting framework within which objective time-relations hold – to the idea of re-identifiable particular objects – to that of causal law or regularity – to that of law-governed objects in space. The governing principle is that any element already admitted as necessary to the general conception must be provided with some basis in experience, must reflect, e.g. some distinction which could actually be drawn within experience. If the governing principle is accepted and some particular feature is admitted as providing a basis of the sort admitted to be generally necessary, then the necessity of that particular feature can be effectively challenged only by making us able to understand the possibility of an alternative. The possibility of effective challenge is minimized by maximizing the *generality* of the statement of conditions and at the same time introducing into that statement a looseness, or vagueness, which is in marked contrast with the strict *universality* of some of Kant's principles. Nevertheless, as has been sufficiently indicated, challenge might effectively be offered at certain points, notably as regards spatiality as we ordinarily understand it, and as regards the singleness of the persisting framework of the objective.

It might be asked: could not the enterprise be carried farther than it is here carried? and: was not Kant in error to separate so sharply the cognitive, or "speculative", from the active, or "practical", side of our natures? Perhaps it could and no doubt he was. My aim has been to show what he achieved and how his arguments and conclusions might be so modified as to be made more acceptable. That he conducted the operation under self-imposed handicaps – though not in itself a matter for congratulation – makes it the more remarkable that he achieved so much.

But surely, it might finally be objected, we have a much wider and less restrictive conception of a possible experience *in general* – even of a temporally extended experience of a conceptualizing being – than is here allowed for. Surely it is absurd to claim that the ideas listed as entering into any coherent conception of experience that we can form really, even though only implicitly, enter into all experience. Surely infants and non-human animals have experience! – This is not denied. But we must think of how we think, of how we must think, of the experience of such creatures. We have no way of doing so except on a simplified analogy with our own. Any specific ascription of experience to animals we may make involves thinking of them as perceiving this or that kind of thing, recognizing this or that individual, pursuing this or that purpose in relation to such things. Any description we can give, any thought we can entertain, of *their* experience must be in terms of concepts derived from ours. We can say, if we like, that such ascriptions must, in these thoughts, bear some confused or attenuated or diminished sense. But we must admit that we cannot say what that sense is. At best we can draw on cooler recollections of confused states of our own; and the inadequacy of this resource becomes clear when we reflect that it is absurd to say that a healthy animal is, in normal circumstances, confused.

We must, in this matter, be content with knowing ourselves. We lack words to say what it is to be without them.

PART FIVE

Kant's Theory of Geometry

KANT'S THEORY OF GEOMETRY

The great issues with which the previous parts of this essay have been concerned will not be raised again in this concluding part. It is really an appendix to the rest. Its purpose is to redeem a promise made in Part II – to evaluate Kant's theory of "pure intuition" as the source of geometrical knowledge and to exhibit its connexion with the doctrine of transcendental idealism as regards space. We saw that, as far as the Transcendental Aesthetic is concerned, the doctrine of the transcendental subjectivity of space rests on no other discernible support that that provided by the argument from geometry.

I. THE THEORY AND ITS CRITICS

Kant's argument from geometry is easier to state than it is to understand. Geometry, he says, offers us a body of propositions which combine some of the features of empirical propositions with some of the features of analytic propositions, but which are not themselves either analytic or empirical. Experience, ordinary empirical intuition, can provide a basis for propositions connecting characteristics not analytically connected, i.e. for synthetic propositions. But such propositions, so based, will not have the character of necessary propositions. By asserting, on the other hand, only what cannot be denied without self-contradiction we can obtain necessary propositions; but only necessary propositions asserting analytic connexions, i.e. only propositions which are not synthetic. Geometrical propositions combine the character of being synthetic with that of being necessary; hence are neither analytic nor based on empirical intuition. Might they not owe their synthetic character to their being based upon *some* kind of sensible intuition, and their necessary character to this kind of intuition's being non-empirical? Kant claims that if we accept the doctrine of the subjectivity of space as a mere form of intuition belonging to our cognitive constitution, then there is no difficulty in seeing how such a kind of spatial intuition can exist, and how the synthetic propositions which it yields can be known to apply with absolute necessity to the ordinary spatial objects of empirical intuition.

So we have the words "non-empirical intuition"; and we have the picture of the mind inspecting in itself the medium in which objects must appear before it and determining from that inspection, independently of the actual appearance of objects, truths which must hold of objects *when* they appear. But neither to these words nor to this picture is it easy to attach any clear meaning.

Most modern critics of Kant would probably say that it was wasted labour to try to attach a clear meaning to either the phrase or the picture. Phrase and picture alike, they would say, are invoked to supply a solution to a problem which does not really exist: the problem of the synthetic necessary character of geometrical propositions. The problem does not exist, on this view, because in so far as there are necessary geometrical propositions, they are really truths of logic, only incidentally geometrical; while those propositions which are both synthetic and essentially geometrical are not necessary truths at all, but empirical hypotheses concerning the structure of physical space, subject to empirical confirmation or disconfirmation.

There seems no doubt that these views are, at least to a very great extent, correct. It is not clear, however, that they warrant quite so abrupt and total a dismissal of Kant's theory of geometry.

For the sake of brevity I shall speak of the anti-Kantian view I have just summarized as "the positivist view". I have referred to one way in which this view allows that propositions which may be called "geometrical" may also be regarded as necessary. It turns on the fact that in a rigorously formalized geometrical system the theorems are deduced by pure logic from the axioms or postulates. This point Kant himself makes in his own not wholly satisfactory way when he says that all mathematical *inferences* proceed in accordance with the principle of non-contradiction. It has the consequence that the hypothetical propositions corresponding to all steps in such deductions are absolutely necessary propositions and indeed, in so far as their necessity is concerned, propositions of pure logic. The fact that the protases and apodoses of these hypotheticals are geometrical propositions has nothing to do with their necessity. What, then, of the status of the axioms and theorems themselves, as distinct from the hypotheticals connecting them? There are two ways, according to the positivist view, of regarding the axioms and theorems. In the first place we can regard them as formulae in an uninterpreted calculus, i.e. one in which no meaning has been assigned to the non-logical expressions. In this case the question as to their status as propositions does not arise, because they are not propositions. Alternatively we can take it that a physical interpretation has been assigned to the non-logical expressions. For example, a standard physical interpretation of "straight line" is the path of a light ray in a homogeneous medium. But once such a physical interpretation is assigned to the non-logical expressions of a geometrical system, the question whether its axioms and theorems are true becomes an empirical, factual question to be settled by experiment, measurement and observation. The axioms and theorems are synthetic, but not necessary, propositions.

One variant of the positivist view allows, indeed, of a way in which, if we are sufficiently determined, we can secure to the axioms and theorems the status of necessary propositions. If any observation appears to contradict any theorem of our geometry, we can always find the fault somewhere else than in the theorem. We can say, for example, that our measuring instruments are defective or our use of them inaccurate, so that the recalcitrant observation must be discounted; or we can say that, contrary to our assumption when we made the observations, what we took to be, say, straight lines were not really straight, but bent by some deforming influence, so that our observations do not really contradict the theorem; and so on. If we adopt this course without being ready to envisage any circumstances at all in which we should depart from it, then indeed we do secure the necessity of our axioms and theorems; but only by qualifying our announced physical interpretation of the non-logical expressions of the theory by the rule that nothing whatever is to count as a falsification of the axioms or theorems. This way of guaranteeing the necessity of geometrical propositions is also, some would say, a way of rendering them analytic. Whether or not we choose to apply the word "analytic" in this way or to call this rather a conventionalist necessity, it is clear that necessity so guaranteed does not call for any special kind of intuition: merely for determination, coupled with fertility in the invention of alternative descriptions of awkward cases.

To accept the positivist account of geometry is to deny the existence of Kant's problem and so to remove the main theoretical support for his theory of *a priori* intuition. We should distinguish, as is not always done, between accepting this account and merely drawing attention to the existence of consistent non-Euclidean geometries. Since Kant holds that no self-contradiction is involved in negating the axioms or theorems of Euclidean geometry, a Kantian can consistently admit the existence of consistent non-Euclidean geometries. What he cannot admit is that there is any possibility of a non-Euclidean geometry fitting the actual structure of physical space. For, being a Kantian, he holds that the structure of physical space is necessarily Euclidean; and that there is any necessity about this (except at most a conventionalist necessity) is precisely what the positivist view denies. No doubt the *determined* Kantian may refuse to be impressed by a merely philosophical view which contradicts his own. But when we turn from philosophy to physics, even the most determined Kantian is presumably shaken. For it appears that according to modern physics the possibility that the structure of space is non-Euclidean is at least something more than a bare possibility. Given a certain agreed physical interpretation for the non-logical expressions of geometry, it appears that the findings of astro-physics are more easily accommodated by the use of a geometrical theory of space incompatible with the Euclidean set of axioms and theorems than they are by a determined adherence to the Euclidean theory; a result, of course, quite consistent with the fact that Euclidean geometry provides an accurate enough account of the structure of physical space over distances less than those with which astrophysics is concerned.

What is the point of mentioning the determined Kantian and the facts which might shake his determination? Apart from any such facts, the positivist view may well appear to us both intelligible and plausible, whereas we may doubt whether the Kantian view has even the first of these characteristics; without which it can scarcely qualify for the second. Yet it is worth mentioning the determined Kantian, because the positivist view neglects certain features of the situation which Kant takes account of. It is these features which explain the existence of the determined Kantian, though they do not show him to be right in his major claims. These features I shall try to set out; at first without much qualification and in a way certainly exposed to criticism. Then I shall mention some of these criticisms and indicate how they might be dealt with.

2. PHYSICAL AND PHENOMENAL GEOMETRY

Leaving aside conventionalism as I have described it – it is certainly quite alien to Kant's thinking on the matter – let us consider once more the two ways permitted by the positivist view of looking at the axioms and theorems of a geometry. We can, on this view, see them either as uninterpreted formulae in a pure calculus which express no propositions at all about anything; or, given a physical interpretation, as propositions about what may in a broad sense be called physical objects in space. If we ask in which of these two ways Kant looked at the propositions of Euclidean geometry, the answer is quite clearly that neither is adequate to his view of the matter. He certainly never considered seeing such propositions as uninterpreted formulae which had nothing in particular to do with space. From the start he saw them as having spatial significance. But equally clearly he did not think that the only way in which they could have spatial significance was by having a physical interpretation, i.e. by the meaning of the fundamental expressions being explained in terms of physical objects of *empirical* intuition, such observable or determinable objects as a taut string or the path of a light ray or, for that matter, a line drawn on paper with a ruler and a sharp pencil. He thought indeed that the propositions of Euclidean geometry were true of physical objects of empirical intuition. But he was quite firm in the belief that there was no need to have recourse to, or even to consider, such physical objects of empirical intuition, in order to ascertain the truth of the nevertheless spatially significant propositions of Euclidean geometry. Certainly we might, with great advantage, draw lines on paper (with or without a ruler) in the course of a geometrical demonstration. But the objects of empirical intuition thus provided were not the essential objects of this activity; they were there simply to provide assistance to the essential activity of *pure* intuition of which the objects were not physical objects at all. What then *are* the spatial, but not physical (nor physically determinable) objects of pure outer intuition?

One way of approaching the answer to this question is to remember that Kant said that it did not matter whether "construction of a [spatial] concept in pure intuition" took place with the aid of a figure drawn on paper *or simply in the imagination*. Now the visual imagination cannot supply us with physical figures. But it can supply us with what, for want of a better word, I will call *phenomenal* figures. (It is important to note here that I am not using this word "phenomenal" as Kant uses it in the *Critique*, where it would apply also to physical objects.) The straight lines which are the objects of pure intuition are not physical straight lines. They are, perhaps, phenomenal straight lines. They are not physical objects, or physical edges, which, when we see them, look straight. They are rather just the looks themselves which physical things have when, and in so far as, they look straight. An arrangement of physical lines or edges may look triangular. But it is not the physical lines, so arranged, which constitute the triangle which is the object of pure intuition; it is, rather, the triangular look which they have, the phenomenal triangle which they present, which is the object of pure intuition. If there can be such a thing as a system which is neither an uninterpreted calculus nor a physical geometry, but a phenomenal geometry, then it would be reasonable to say that it is, in a sense, independent of *empirical* intuition. So long as we can imagine spatially, we do not need, for phenomenal geometry, to check our results by reference to sense-given spatial objects. On the other hand, such a geometry will not be without relation to sense-given spatial objects; for the appropriate exercise of imagination produces just such phenomenal figures as *can* be presented by physical objects in ordinary sensible intuition. (Indeed there would be no reason to suppose that imagination would be capable of producing such phenomenal figures unless physical objects of empirical intuition could, and sometimes did, present them.) If there is such a thing as phenomenal geometry, then we could reasonably say that it would be primarily the geometry of the spatial *appearances* of physical things and only secondarily, if at all, the geometry of the physical things themselves. (Here again it must be noted that I use the word "appearances", like the word "phenomenal", in a different way from Kant, for whom physical objects themselves are appearances.)

If we can make sense of this notion of a phenomenal interpre-

tation for Euclidian geometry, then perhaps Kant's theory of
pure intuition and of the construction of concepts in pure intuition can be seen, at least up to a point, as a perfectly reasonable
philosophical account of it. To bring out the status of the propositions of such a geometry, it is best to take an example. Consider
the proposition that not more than one straight line can be drawn
between any two points. The natural way to satisfy ourselves of
the truth of this axiom of phenomenal geometry is to consider
an actual or imagined figure. When we do this, it becomes evident
that we cannot, either in imagination or on paper, give ourselves
a picture such that we are prepared to say of it both that it shows
two distinct straight lines and that it shows both these lines as
drawn through the same two points. Such an impossibility used
to be expressed by saying that such axioms are necessarily true
because self-evident. This left the character of the necessity, or the
impossibility, insufficiently explained. We can explain it by saying
that the axioms are true solely in virtue of the meanings attached
to the expressions they contain, but these meanings are essentially
phenomenal, visual meanings, are essentially picturable meanings.
Any picture we are prepared to give ourselves of the meaning of
"two straight lines" is different from any picture we are prepared
to give ourselves of the meaning of "two distinct lines both of
which are drawn through the same two points" in a way which
we count essential to our having pictured what these expressions
mean. Such pictures, so far from being inessential features of
geometry, are quite essential features of Euclidean geometry in
its phenomenal interpretation.

Kant's phrase, "the construction of concepts in pure (i.e. non-
empirical) intuition", does not seem at all a bad description of
this essential method of exhibiting and elaborating the meanings
of the expressions of phenomenal geometry. Moreover, attending
to the phenomenal interpretation helps us to see how it was
possible to develop Euclidean geometry so satisfactorily in spite
of the fact, pointed out by later and more rigorous mathematicians,
that, as it used to be expounded, not all its theorems can be
rigorously deduced by pure logic from the stated axioms and
definitions. Where the rigorous mathematician would complain
that a premise necessary to the logical strictness of a demonstration or construction has been omitted, the fact is presumably that
the pictured meanings of the relevant expressions really rule out

any alternative to the truth of the missing premise. For example, in the first problem in Euclid's Elements it is assumed that a circle which has its radius equal to a given straight line, and its centre the point terminating that line at one end, *intersects* with the circle with the same radius whose centre is the point terminating the given straight line at its other end. This assumption is not justified by any appeal to an explicitly stated postulate, definition, or axiom. But we cannot picture to ourselves any figure which we should be prepared to count as adequate to the sense of the rest of the above description, for which this assumption does not hold. The picture of the sense of the description rules out any alternative to this assumption.

How, then, should we assess Kant's general theory of geometry, pure intuition and the subjectivity of space in the light of these considerations? He thought that Euclidean geometry applied to physical objects, to sense-given things in space. He was aware that the truth of its theorems was not simply guaranteed by logic and by explicit verbal definition. These two considerations led him to say that it was a body of true synthetic propositions. On the other hand he attributed to the axioms and theorems a necessity inconsistent with their being merely empirical propositions. Here, then, we appear to have the problem of their synthetic necessary status. But the problem has two separate parts which Kant does not distinguish. For a purely phenomenal interpretation of the geometry, the problem of a necessity which is not the result merely of verbal definitions is solved by the theory of construction in pure intuition, which shows how necessity may be secured by a phenomenal exhibition of meanings. This is intuitive self-evidence with the sting drawn. The word "synthetic", if we agree to tolerate it here as qualifying "necessity", signifies no more than that we could not do without this phenomenal exhibition of meanings in developing *this* geometry. Perhaps it would be preferable to use the phrase "phenomenally analytic", where the adverbial qualification "phenomenally" serves just the same purpose. In any case, it seems not too much to say that Kant's theory of pure intuition can be construed as a reasonable account of the nature of geometry in its phenomenal interpretation.

But, of course, the theory is not presented as a theory of Euclidean geometry in its phenomenal interpretation. Here we come up against the second part of the problem. Kant attempts to use his insight into the necessities of *phenomenal* geometry to resolve the other and greater difficulty, the difficulty created by the apparently necessary application of Euclidean geometry to physical space. *This* difficulty, *this* necessity, are indeed illusory. Kant's fundamental error, for which, at that stage in the history of science, he can scarcely be reproached, lay in not distinguishing between Euclidean geometry in its phenomenal interpretation and Euclidean geometry in its physical interpretations, i.e. in interpretations in which it serves still for many purposes, and in which it was first used, and then laid aside, in astro-physics. Because he did not make this distinction, he supposed that the necessity which truly belongs to Euclidean geometry in its phenomenal interpretation also belongs to it in its physical interpretation. He thought that the geometry of physical space *had* to be identical with the geometry of phenomenal space. And this mystery does invite the suggestion that the geometry of phenomenal space embodies, as it were, conditions under which alone things can count as things in space, as physical objects, for us. Especially does it invite this suggestion if we think of something's counting as a physical body for us in terms of its *appearing* to us, presenting to us a phenomenal figure, a figure of the kind which phenomenal geometry treats of. If we add to this the fact that phenomenal geometry is *in a sense* independent of sense-given physical objects – imagined constructions will do as well as the looks of pencilled lines for the purposes of phenomenal geometry – then I think it just begins to be intelligible (though only just) that Kant should think of the source of space in its phenomenal character, and hence also of space in its physical character, as being subjective, as being in the constitution of our minds or, as he put it, our faculty of sensibility. But to say that it begins to be intelligible that he should think this is not to say that what he thinks begins to be intelligible.

I said earlier that the positivist view, though in a sense correct, neglects certain features of the situation which Kant takes account of. To repeat the central points. The positivist view offers us two ways of looking at the propositions of Euclidean geometry: as formulae in an uninterpreted calculus; or as the body of logically connected empirical propositions which result from the adoption of a physical interpretation for the fundamental expressions of the formulae. In the latter case the testing of Euclidean geometry by observation and measurement shows its theorems to be verified with an acceptable degree of accuracy for extents of physical space less than those with which astro-physics is concerned; but for astro-physics itself, a different physical geometry, incompatible with the Euclidean, is found to accommodate observations and measurements more simply. Both these ways of looking at Euclidean geometry are correct. What we have had to notice is that there is a third way, different from either of these, which is also possible, and which the positivist view neglects. With certain reservations and qualifications, to be considered later, it seems that Euclidean geometry may also be interpreted as a body of un-falsifiable propositions about phenomenal straight lines, triangles, circles, etc.; as a body of *a priori* propositions about spatial appearances of these kinds and hence, of course, as a theory whose application is restricted to such appearances. In the course of the development of pure mathematics on the one hand (in respect of rigour), and of physics on the other, this aspect of Euclidean geometry has come to seem unimportant. For, on the one hand, rigour in mathematics turns on logic, not on looks – which is why Russell said that the development of mathematics showed Kant's *Anschauung* to be superfluous; and, on the other hand, the physical applications of geometry turn on physical tests and measurements of many kinds, and not on the mere contemplation of phenomenal appearances. Hence the positivist neglect of the phenomenal aspect of Euclidean geometry.

Though this aspect of geometry may have become unimportant in the later development of mathematics and physics, it can scarcely be said with confidence to be unimportant for the original development of systematic geometry. Nor can it be said now to be unimportant in the initial stages of *learning* geometry. Anyone who remembers his schooldays must acknowledge that he learnt geometry neither as an uninterpreted logical calculus nor as an axiomatic physical theory, but as a body of self-evident truths about spatial figures and the logical consequences of these truths. Individual learning aside, it seems very plausible to suppose that what underlies the systematic development of geometry as a mathematical discipline is the curious facility with which phenomenal figure-patterns can be elaborated to exhibit an extensive system of relations between phenomenal spatial concepts. This is not to suggest that in such elaboration lay the very first historical sources of geometry. No doubt geometry owes its beginnings of existence to human concern with problems of terrestrial measurement, and the discovery of metrical techniques with little or no systematic connexion between them. Something encountered in Nature was needed to stimulate the human imagination originally in a Euclidean sense; and though this *might* have been, say, the appearance of designs against the sky like an enormous blackboard, it of course was not. It was rather the fact, of importance in solving practical problems, that there are physical things for which certain relationships are actually found to hold when checked by physical standards. But, whatever its natural source, it remains important to recognize the place which phenomenal geometry can be seen as having in Kant's theorizing and which it is plausible to suppose that it has in the systematic development of geometry in general.

3. OBJECTIONS AND QUALIFICATIONS

Now we come to some objections. This account of phenomenal geometry has been very cursory, and exception might be taken to it on a number of grounds.

First, it might be objected that the terminology of looks and of phenomenal figures is highly suspicious. One may draw a figure on the blackboard, and the figure may appear to exhibit certain characteristics for which we have geometrical names. But it is at best obfuscating to speak as if, in addition to the physical figure which we see, there is something else which we see, or quasi-see, namely the look of the figure. It is unsatisfactory to explain Euclidean geometry, even in one comparatively unimportant interpretation, as being *about* such objects as these; for it is simply too unclear what these objects are, or whether there are such objects at all. The appeal to visual imagination does not improve matters. Certainly it would be odd to speak of a visualized figure only appearing to have certain characteristics in a way that it is not odd to speak of a physical figure only appearing to have certain characteristics. But to use this fact to suggest that what visual imagination gives one is, as it were, just the kind of *look* which a physical figure has, but without the physical figure itself, is to try to illuminate one dubious notion by making a dubious use of another already sufficiently obscure notion viz. that of the visual image.

I think this objection has to be taken seriously. But I would prefer not to meet it head-on, but to side-step it – by admitting that some of the vocabulary I have used is not particularly happy, and is meant to be suggestive rather than precise. The problem is whether the nature of phenomenal geometry can be described without a dangerous reliance on the possibly dubious concept of the phenomenal figure – a concept which, though dubious, is satisfying to one's simple-minded wish for a set of *objects* to be the peculiar subject-matter of the study. I think it can be so described, and that I have already in part so described it. But before I enlarge on this, let me mention another objection.

This is that the whole conception of phenomenal geometry, as so far outlined, makes the geometer's role too passively contemplative. It represents the geometer as one who merely looks at the figures he has drawn to see relationships between the concepts whose sense he pictures. But Euclid's geometer is called upon to solve problems of *construction*. The very first problem in the *Elements* is: to describe an equilateral triangle on a given finite straight line. How does construction fit into the notion of phenomenal geometry? Is not construction anyway essentially a physical operation, to be conducted, e.g., with straight edge and compass?

To consider first the point about construction's being a physical operation. Suppose we are just given the figure appropriate to some construction, e.g. the figure which accompanies the text in the solution of the problem I just mentioned, that of constructing an equilateral triangle on a given finite straight line. We might suppose that someone surprisingly produces it by absent-minded doodling or that it just appears step by step against the sky. Would it matter if our own subsequent attempts to produce it with a ruler and compasses, following the steps of the solution, kept on going wrong in one way or another, or went wrong as often as not? Would such practical failures make us inclined to suspect that something was wrong with the solution? Certainly not. So far as phenomenal geometry is concerned, the concepts we are operating with are to be taken to be purely visual concepts, and if the physical techniques we use fail to produce the appropriate visual effects, so much the worse for those techniques or for our handling of them. The *standard* for whether the actual physical operations are the right ones or are satisfactorily conducted is set by the visual effects they produce, as we go through each step of the operation. But still, it might be objected, it is not simply the visual effect represented by the completed figure that satisfies us of the correctness of the solution. It is the fact that the figure can be produced, step by step, in a certain way. This is correct; but it shows only that we must not think of the visual concepts we are concerned with in too static a fashion. The point is already covered by the remark that the standard for whether the actual physical operations performed are the right ones or are satisfactorily conducted is set by the visual effects they produce *as we go through* each step of the operation. It is covered by Kant in his own jargon when he writes in a footnote:

Motion *of an object in space*, i.e. of a physical object, does not belong to a pure science and consequently not to geometry. Motion, however, *considered as the describing of a space*, is a pure act of the successive synthesis of the manifold in outer intuition in general by means of the productive imagination, and belongs not only to geometry, but even to transcendental philosophy.[1]

It might be helpful to think of geometrical constructions being produced before us, accompanied by the appropriate commentary, on a cinema screen. We may be wholly ignorant of the physical means by which this is actually being done. But we can be quite clear that, e.g., straight lines are being produced (in the geometrical sense, i.e. extended), circles being described, etc.

If we now turn back to the objections to the terminology of looks, phenomenal figures, etc., I think it should be obvious that this terminology is really harmless. To use it is only to say that in pure visual geometry we really are not concerned with the physical objects we set before ourselves in any aspect except one – the aspect in which they represent for us the visual concepts we *are* concerned with. Those physical objects may have all sorts of other characteristics; but what those characteristics are, and by what physical means the objects actually come to exhibit or suggest to us the characteristics we are concerned with, are questions equally irrelevant. To say that the objects of phenomenal geometry are not these physical objects at all but the phenomenal figures they present is simply to say that it is only in so far as those

[1] B 155.

objects do exhibit or suggest to us the visual characteristics in question that they have any relevance to phenomenal geometry.

Next we must consider a different class of objections, objections which express scepticism from the side of geometry itself. Is the notion of a phenomenal, an intuitive visual geometry really adequate to what we actually find in Euclidean geometry? For instance, even if the claim that it was adequate seemed plausible in the case of the plane geometry of two-dimensional figures, it seems a good deal less plausible for the geometry of three-dimensional figures. Again, is it really clear that the deliverances of our visual intuition, even in the case of plane geometry, actually do correspond to the propositions of Euclidean geometry? Consider a variant formulation of an axiom we have already had before us: "Two straight lines cannot enclose a space." If we stood in the middle of a long straight railway track and looked along it first in one direction and then in the other, should we not have the visual impression of two straight lines converging, and even meeting, in each direction, and hence of two lines satisfying our intuitive visual requirements for being straight and at the same time satisfying our intuitive visual requirements for enclosing a space? Or consider again: "Between any two points on a straight line there is a further point." How can we even decide whether this accords with our visual intuition or not? What picture is relevant? Does it help just to look at a straight line? Any way we might think of for testing it against our visual intuition, or our visual intuition against it, rather suggests that it is counter-intuitive. For example, we might draw, or imagine a straight line and then make or imagine a gap in it and think of the two ends of the gap as being two points on the original line. We might then be tempted to represent our proposition in visual terms by the thought that however narrow we make the gap, it would always be possible to make it narrower without making it disappear. But this appears actually to run counter to our visual intuition.

These objections are more serious. They call, not for a total abandonment of the account given, but rather for a fairly drastic modification of it. Not all the points have equal weight. Thus the example of the railway track can be dismissed as not being what it claims to be, viz. an example of a visually apprehended figure of two straight lines enclosing a space. The subject has one picture of straight lines converging, even meeting; then, when he turns round, another such picture. He has no single picture which he could properly describe in terms of seeing two lines both as straight and as enclosing a space. But we cannot in this way dismiss the objection based on the proposition that between any two points on a straight line there lies a point. We have here to admit an element of conceptual idealization in geometry, an element, that is to say, to which we can find nothing exactly corresponding in terms of visually instantiable concepts. It is a relief to be forced so plainly and unmistakably to admit it here. For it seems, though less plainly, to be present in the notion of the infinite extent of Euclidean space, as in that of its infinite divisibility. The only relevant pictures we can give ourselves – in terms of producing straight lines – seem to demand the notion of infinitude; yet *that* is not something of which we can give ourselves a picture.

Neither this admission, nor others forced upon us by the actual content of Euclidean geometry, require a total abandonment of the account. Thus we can admit that the pictures we give ourselves are not in all respects adequate to the idealized concepts or meanings pictured without giving up the idea that the picturing of meanings plays an essential role in one interpretation of Euclidean geometry. It would be preferable to call it, not simply "the phenomenal interpretation", but "the idealized phenomenal interpretation"; idealized, one should add, in certain quite compelling and quite specifiable ways. This modification, indeed, might be said to bring us, in one respect, still closer to Kant; for the idea that the concepts dealt with were quite straightforwardly visual concepts would have seemed to him to make them too grossly sensible. The idealization of the concepts which we are forced to make, and to admit, provides extra justification for the qualification "pure" in such phrases as "power of pure outer intuition", "construction in pure intuition", etc.

Yet such objections, and the course of the whole discussion, do force us to recognize the modesty of the claim that can finally be made. It is certainly impossible to give, in Kantian terms alone, a comprehensive and accurate account of Euclidean geometry in all aspects of its mathematical structure and its applications. It *is* possible, on the other hand, to draw attention to one aspect of that complex intellectual phenomenon, in the light of which we

INDEX